"The canon of modern Irish able as Ireland itself has been surprising re-thinking of the repertoire cracks open the hard shell of assumptions to reveal the rich variousness of a dynamic and contrary tradition."

Fintan O'Toole, *The Irish Times*, Ireland

FIFTY KEY IRISH PLAYS

Fifty Key Irish Plays charts the progression of modern Irish drama from Dion Boucicault's entry on to the global stage of the Irish diaspora to the contemporary dramas created by the experiences of the New Irish.

Each chapter provides a brief plot outline along with informed analysis and, alert to the cultural and critical context of each play, an account of the key roles that they played in the developing story of Irish drama. While the core of the collection is based on the critical canon, including work by J. M. Synge, Lady Gregory, Teresa Deevy, and Brian Friel, plays such as Tom Mac Intyre's *The Great Hunger* and ANU Productions' *Laundry*, which illuminate routes away from the mainstream, are also included. With a focus on the development of form as well as theme, the collection guides the reader to an informed overview of Irish theatre via succinct and insightful essays by an international team of academics.

This invaluable collection will be of particular interest to undergraduate students of theatre and performance studies and to lay readers looking to expand their appreciation of Irish drama.

Shaun Richards is Emeritus Professor of Irish Studies at Staffordshire University. Publications include *Mapping Irish Theatre: Theories of Space and Place* (Cambridge University Press, 2013), co-authored with Chris Morash, and *Contemporary Irish Documentary Theatre* (Bloomsbury, 2020), co-edited with Beatriz Kopschitz Bastos.

ROUTLEDGE KEY GUIDES

Fifty Key Theatre Directors
Shomit Mitter and Maria Shevtsova

Fifty Key Contemporary Thinkers
John Lechte

Art History
The Key Concepts
Jonathan Harris

Fifty Contemporary Choreographers
Jo Butterworth and Lorna Sanders

Fifty Key Figures in Latinx and Latin American Theatre
Paola S. Hernández and Analola Santana

Fifty Key Stage Musicals
Edited by Robert W. Schneider and Shannon Agnew

Fifty Key Irish Plays
Edited by Shaun Richards

Fifty Key Figures in Queer US Theatre
Edited by Jimmy A. Noriega and Jordan Schildcrout

For a full list of titles in this series, please visit: https://www.routledge.com/Routledge-Key-Guides/book-series/RKG

FIFTY KEY IRISH PLAYS

Edited by
Shaun Richards

LONDON AND NEW YORK

Cover image: Courtesy of the Abbey Theatre Archive. Set design by Dorothy Travers Smith of Lear's Palace for the Abbey Theatre's first production of *King Lear* by William Shakespeare, Abbey Theatre, 1928. The scorched corner of the image is witness to the fire that destroyed the Abbey in 1951.

First published 2023
by Routledge
4 Park Square, Milton Park, Abingdon, Oxon OX14 4RN

and by Routledge
605 Third Avenue, New York, NY 10158

Routledge is an imprint of the Taylor & Francis Group, an informa business

British Library Cataloguing-in-Publication Data
A catalogue record for this book is available from the British Library

Library of Congress Cataloging-in-Publication Data
Names: Richards, Shaun, 1947– editor.
Title: Fifty key Irish plays / edited by Shaun Richards.
Description: Abingdon, Oxon ; New York, NY : Routledge, 2023. |
Includes bibliographical references and index.
Identifiers: LCCN 2022005922 (print) | LCCN 2022005923 (ebook) |
ISBN 9781032066509 (hardback) | ISBN 9781032066493 (paperback) |
ISBN 9781003203216 (ebook)
Subjects: LCSH: English drama–Irish authors–History and criticism. |
Theater–Ireland–History. | Ireland–In literature.
Classification: LCC PR8783 .F54 2023 (print) |
LCC PR8783 (ebook) | DDC 822.009/9415–dc23/eng/20220425
LC record available at https://lccn.loc.gov/2022005922
LC ebook record available at https://lccn.loc.gov/2022005923

ISBN: 9781032066509 (hbk)
ISBN: 9781032066493 (pbk)
ISBN: 9781003203216 (ebk)

DOI: 10.4324/9781003203216

Typeset in Times New Roman
by Newgen Publishing UK

For Lucette – always.

CONTENTS

ALPHABETICAL LIST
OF CONTENTS

NOTES ON CONTRIBUTORS

Csilla Bertha is Associate Professor at the University of Debrecen, Hungary. She is a member of the International Advisory Board of *Irish University Review*, the Editorial Board of *Hungarian Journal of English and American Studies*, the honorary chair of the Hungarian Yeats Society, and has published widely (in English and Hungarian) on Irish drama and theatre, interart relations, memory, sites of memory, and parallels between Irish and Hungarian literature. Her *A drámaíró Yeats* [*Yeats the Playwright*, 1988], was the first book on Yeats's drama in Hungary. She co-authored and co-edited volumes, such as *More Real than Reality* (ABC-CLIO, 1991), *The Celebration of the Fantastic* (ABC-CLIO, 1992), *A Small Nation's Contribution to the World* (Colin Smythe, 1994), *Worlds Visible and Invisible* (Lajos Kossuth University, 1994), *Brian Friel's Dramatic Artistry* (Carysfort Press, 2006), and several special journal issues.

Scott Boltwood has taught at Ulster University, Coleraine, and the Queen's University of Belfast; he is currently Chair of English at Emory & Henry College in Virginia. He has written *Brian Friel, Ireland and the North* (Cambridge University Press, 2009) and *Brian Friel* (a Readers' Guide to Essential Criticism, Palgrave Macmillan, 2018), and edited *Renegotiating and Resisting Nationalism in 20th-Century Irish Drama* (Colin Smythe, 2009). He has written on Dion Boucicault, Augusta Gregory, Stuart Love, and Brian Friel, and he is currently working on the Ulster Group Theatre.

David Clare is Lecturer in Drama and Theatre Studies at Mary Immaculate College, University of Limerick. His books include the monographs *Bernard Shaw's Irish Outlook* (Palgrave Macmillan, 2016) and *Irish Anglican Literature and Drama: Hybridity and Discord* (Palgrave Macmillan, 2021) and the edited collections *The*

Gate Theatre, Dublin: Inspiration and Craft (Carysfort/Peter Lang, 2018) and *The Golden Thread: Irish Women Playwrights, 1716–2016* (2 vols, Liverpool University Press, 2021). Dr Clare is also curator of the Irish Research Council-funded database. See www.classicirishpl ays.com.

Lisa Coen is co-founding publisher at Tramp Press. Named for Synge, Tramp aims to publish exceptional, daring new writing. Their award-winning titles include *A Ghost in the Throat* by Doireann Ní Ghríofa, *handiwork* by Sara Baume, *Notes to Self* by Emilie Pine, and *Solar Bones* by Mike McCormack.

David Cregan is an Associate Professor of Theatre at Villanova University. He studied at Trinity College in Dublin and is dedicated to prison teaching, equity, and inclusion. He is the author of *Frank McGuinness's Dramaturgy of Difference and Irish Theatre* (Peter Lang, 2011) and editor of *Deviant Acts: Essays on Queer Performance* (Carysfort Press, 2009).

Joan Fitzpatrick Dean's publications include the Irish Film Institute/ Cork University Press monograph *Dancing at Lughnasa* (2003), *All Dressed Up: Modern Historical Irish Pageants* (Syracuse University Press, 2014), and *Pageant* (Bloomsbury, 2021).

Lisa Fitzpatrick is the author of *Rape on the Contemporary Stage* (Palgrave Macmillan, 2018) and has published widely on Irish women's writing and post-conflict theatre. She is Senior Lecturer in Drama at the University of Ulster in Derry, and is associate editor of *Theatre Research International*. She co-convenes the Feminist working group of the IFTR, and is a founding member of the Irish Society for Theatre Research.

J. Paul Halferty is Assistant Professor in Drama Studies at University College Dublin, where he also serves as Director of the Centre for Canadian Studies. His work has been published in *Theatre Research in Canada*, *Canadian Theatre Review*, and in the anthology *Queer Theatre in Canada*. With Cathy Leeney, he is co-editor of the anthology, *Analysing Gender in Performance* (Palgrave, 2022).

Miriam Haughton is Director of Postgraduate Studies in Drama, Theatre and Performance at NUI Galway and Vice-President of the Irish Society for Theatre Research. Miriam is author of *Staging*

Trauma (Palgrave Macmillan, 2018), and co-editor of *Theatre, Performance and Commemoration* (Methuen, 2022), *Legacies of the Magdalen Laundries* (Manchester University Press, 2021), and *Radical Contemporary Theatre Practices by Women in Ireland* (Carysfort Press, 2015). Miriam has published in *Modern Drama*, *Contemporary Theatre Review*, *Performance Paradigm*, *New Theatre Quarterly*, *Irish Studies Review*, and *Mortality* in addition to multiple edited collections.

Charlotte Headrick is Professor Emerita of Theatre Arts at Oregon State University. She has directed numerous premieres and productions of Irish plays all over the United States, particularly those written by women. She is co-editor with Eileen Kearney of *Irish Women Dramatists 1908–2001* (Syracuse University Press, 2014) and is widely published in the field of Irish drama. She is the recipient of the Kennedy Center/American College Theater Festival Medallion for service to that organisation. In February 2021, she presented a paper (virtually) in Waterford, Ireland on directing the American Premiere of Teresa Deevy's *The King of Spain's Daughter* which was produced with American Sign Language Interpreters shadowing the speaking actors.

Eamonn Jordan is Professor in Drama Studies at the School of English, Drama and Film, University College Dublin. His books include: *The Feast of Famine: The Plays of Frank McGuinness* (Peter Lang, 1997), *Dissident Dramaturgies: Contemporary Irish Theatre* (Irish Academic Press, 2010), *From Leenane to LA: The Theatre and Cinema of Martin McDonagh* (Irish Academic Press, 2014), *The Theatre and Films of Conor McPherson: Conspicuous Communities* (Methuen, 2019), and *Justice in the Plays and Films of Martin McDonagh* (Palgrave Pivot, 2019).

Marie Kelly is Lecturer in the Department of Theatre (School of Film, Music and Theatre), University College Cork. Marie began her career at the Abbey Theatre working both as Assistant to the Artistic Director and as Head of Casting. Marie has an MA in Modern Drama and Performance (2005) and a PhD in Drama Studies (2011), both from the School of English, Drama and Film at University College Dublin. She is a member of the Board of Everyman Theatre (Cork) and Co-President of the Irish Society for Theatre Research. She has published on the plays of Tom Mac Intyre, Mark O'Rowe, and on the work of British theatre director, Katie Mitchell.

Mária Kurdi is Professor Emerita in the Institute of English Studies at the University of Pécs, Hungary. Her research focuses on modern Irish drama and theatre. Among her books are: *Representations of Gender and Female Subjectivity in Contemporary Irish Drama by Women* (Mellen, 2010), *Approaches to Irish Theatre through a Hungarian's Lens* (University of Pécs, 2018) and a monograph on J. M. Synge in Hungarian (Kronosz, 2021). Her edited volumes include *Radical Contemporary Theatre Practices by Women in Ireland* (co-edited with Miriam Haughton, Carysfort Press, 2015). In 2021 Peter Lang published *The Theatre of Deirdre Kinahan*, co-edited by Kurdi with Lisa Fitzpatrick. Currently she is editing one of the *HJEAS* Books, New Series, on age and ageing in contemporary literature, forthcoming in 2022.

Luke Lamont is a Dublin-based researcher who works in University College Dublin (UCD) and the Abbey Theatre. In 2020, Luke received his PhD from UCD; this examined the emergence of documentary theatre in Ireland, and was funded by the Irish Research Council. Luke has particular interest in documentary, verbatim theatre – and hybrid adaptions thereof – as well as site-specific theatre and auto-performance. Luke holds a BA in English and Philosophy from UCD, and an MPhil in Irish Writing from Trinity College Dublin.

José Lanters is Emerita Professor of English at the University of Wisconsin-Milwaukee. She has published extensively on Irish drama and fiction. Her books include *The "Tinkers" in Irish Literature* (Irish Academic Press, 2008); *Beyond Realism: Experimental and Unconventional Irish Drama since the Revival*, co-edited with Joan FitzPatrick Dean (Rodopi/Brill, 2015); and *The Theatre of Thomas Kilroy: No Absolutes* (Cork University Press, 2018).

Hélène Lecossois is Professor of Irish Literary Studies at the University of Lille (France). The primary focus of her research is the relation of theatre to history. Her other research interests include modernism, twentieth-century Irish drama, postcolonial and performance studies. Her recent publications include *Performance, Modernity and the Plays of J. M. Synge* (Cambridge University Press, 2020).

Ben Levitas is Reader in Theatre History at Goldsmiths, University of London. His publications include *The Theatre of Nation: Irish Drama and Cultural Nationalism 1890–1916* (Clarendon Press, 2002), *W. B. Yeats in Context* (Cambridge University Press, 2009, co-edited with David Holdeman), and *Irish Theatre in England* (Carysfort Press, 2007, co-edited with Richard Cave).

James Little is a postdoctoral researcher at Masaryk University, Brno and Charles University, Prague. He is the author of *Samuel Beckett in Confinement: The Politics of Closed Space* (Bloomsbury Academic, 2020) and *The Making of Samuel Beckett's Not I / Pas moi, That Time / Cette fois and Footfalls / Pas* (Bloomsbury and University Press Antwerp, 2021). His recent work can be found in the *Contemporary Theatre Review*, *Text and Performance Quarterly*, and the *Irish University Review*.

Patrick Lonergan is Professor of Drama and Theatre Studies at National University of Ireland, Galway and is a member of the Royal Irish Academy. He has edited or written eleven books on Irish drama and theatre, including *Theatre and Globalization* (winner of the 2008 Theatre Book Prize), *The Theatre and Films of Martin McDonagh* (Methuen Drama, 2012), *Theatre and Social Media* (Methuen Drama, 2015), and *Irish Drama and Theatre Since 1950* (Bloomsbury, 2019). He is on the board of directors of the Galway International Arts Festival, a member of Future Earth Ireland, and is an Editorial Associate of *Contemporary Theatre Review*. He has lectured widely on Irish drama internationally, including recently in Princeton, Florence, Florianapolis (Brazil), Wroclaw, and Tokyo. He was the 2019 Burns Visiting Fellow for Irish Studies at Boston College.

Michael McAteer is Associate Professor (habil.) at the Institute of English and American Studies, Pázmány Péter Catholic University, Budapest. His books include *Yeats and European Drama* (Cambridge University Press, 2010), the edited volume *Silence in Modern Irish Literature* (Brill, 2017), and, most recently, *Excess in Modern Irish Writing: Spirit and Surplus* (Palgrave, 2020). Recent publications also include a book chapter on Yeats and Flann O'Brien in the edited volume *Gallows Humour: Flann O'Brien* (Cork University Press, 2020) and a journal article on Yeats and Alfred Jarry in *Modern Drama* (2022).

Deirdre McFeely is a former Adjunct Lecturer at Trinity College Dublin. She is the author of *Dion Boucicault: Irish Identity on Stage* (Cambridge University Press, 2012), a contributor on the plays of Maura Laverty to *A Stage of Emancipation: Change and Progress* *at the Dublin Gate Theatre* (Liverpool University Press, 2021), and (with Cathy Leeney) to *The Golden Thread: Irish Women Playwrights, 1716–2016* (Liverpool University Press, 2021). She is the co-editor (with Cathy Leeney) of *The Plays of Maura Laverty: Liffey Lane; Tolka Row; A Tree in the Crescent* (Liverpool University Press, 2022).

Charlotte McIvor is a Lecturer in Drama and Theatre Studies and Deputy Head of the School of English and Creative Arts at the National University of Ireland, Galway. She is the author of *Migration and Performance in Contemporary Ireland: Towards A New Interculturalism* (Palgrave Macmillan, 2016) and the co-editor of *The Methuen Companion to Interculturalism and Performance* (with Daphne P. Lei, Methuen, 2020), *Interculturalism and Performance Now: New Directions?* (with Jason King, Palgrave Macmillan, 2019), *Devised Performance in Irish Theatre: Histories and Contemporary Practice* (with Siobhán O'Gorman, Carysfort Press, 2015) and *Staging Intercultural Ireland: Plays and Practitioner Perspectives* (with Matthew Spangler, Cork University Press, 2014). Her work has also appeared in *Theatre Research International, Theatre Topics, Modern Drama, Irish University Review, Irish Studies Review* and multiple edited collections. In addition, she is a theatre and creative arts practitioner, and a co-lead with responsibility for Creative Arts and Communications in NUI Galway's Active* Consent Programme, a national-level initiative which supports young people and those that are important to them (teachers, parents, college staff and policy makers) in building their knowledge of consent as a key component of positive sexual health and well-being.

Christina Hunt Mahony is a Research Fellow in the School of English at Trinity College, Dublin and former director of graduate Irish Studies at The Catholic University of America. She is the author of *Contemporary Irish Literature: Transforming Tradition* (Palgrave, 1999) and editor of *Out of History: Essays on the Writings of Sebastian Barry* (Carysfort Press, 2006). She has contributed chapters to *The Oxford Handbook of Modern Irish Theatre* (Oxford University Press, 2016) and *A History of Irish Autobiography* (Cambridge University Press, 2018).

Kelly Matthews is Professor of English at Framingham State University in Massachusetts. Her monograph, *The Bell Magazine and the Representation of Irish Identity*, was published by Four Courts Press in 2012, and she co-edited *The Country of the Young: Interpretations* *of Youth and Childhood in Irish Culture*, published by Four Courts in 2013. Her current research project focuses on the first decade of Brian Friel's career (1956–1966), drawing upon new archival material from *The New Yorker* and the BBC.

Victor Merriman is Professor of Critical Studies in Drama at Edge Hill University. He is author of *Because We Are Poor: Irish Theatre in the 1990s* (Carysfort Press, 2011), and *Austerity and the Public Role of Drama: Performing Lives-in-Common* (Palgrave Macmillan, 2019). He has published and lectured internationally on Irish theatre, postcoloniality, drama pedagogy, and public policy.

Hiroko Mikami is Professor of Irish Studies at Waseda University, Tokyo, where she also serves as director of the Institute for Irish Studies. She authored *Frank McGuinness and his Theatre of Paradox* (Colin Smythe, 2002) and co-edited/authored *Ireland on Stage: Beckett and After* (Carysfort, 2007) and *Irish Theatre and Its Soundscapes* (Glasnevin, 2015). She has translated many contemporary Irish plays into Japanese, including Tom Murphy's *Bailegangaire* and *A Thief of a Christmas*.

James Moran is Professor of Modern English Literature and Drama at the University of Nottingham, UK. He is the author of *Staging the Easter Rising: 1916 as Theatre* (Cork University Press, 2005), *Irish Birmingham: A History* (Liverpool University Press, 2010), *The Theatre of Seán O'Casey* (Bloomsbury, 2013) and editor of *Four Irish Rebel Plays* (Irish Academic Press, 2007). His recent books include an edited collection of Bernard Shaw's *Playlets* (Oxford University Press, 2021), and the monograph *Modernists and the Theatre* (Bloomsbury, 2022).

Chris Morash is the Seamus Heaney Professor of Irish Writing in Trinity College, Dublin. His publications include *Yeats on Theatre* (Cambridge University Press, 2021), *The Oxford Handbook of Modern Irish Theatre* (co-edited with Nicholas Grene; Oxford University Press, 2016), *Mapping Irish Theatre* (with Shaun Richards; Cambridge University Press, 2013) and *A History of Irish Theatre: 1601–2000* (Cambridge University Press, 2001). In 2021, he curated the *Unseen Plays* series for the Abbey Theatre. He is a Member of the Royal Irish Academy.

Catherine Morris is Senior Lecturer in Creative Writing at Liverpool Hope University. She is the author of *Alice Milligan and the Irish Cultural Revival* (Four Courts Press, 2012). She was guest curator on the *El Lizzitzsy: The Artist and the State* exhibition at the Irish Museum of Modern Art in which Milligan's theatre practice was explored in a new theatre work called Gag by artist Sarah Pierce. She is the co-founder of the Centre for Creative Arts Research at NUI Galway, board member of the University Network of European Capitals of Culture, and co-editor of *James Connolly Special Issue of Interventions: International Post Colonial Journal* (2008), *The Art of Reimagining: European Capitals of Culture* (Moore Institute, 2021), and *Performing in Digital: Special Issue of Research in Drama Education* (Summer 2022). She is currently completing an experimental performance work, *Intimate Power: Autobiography of a City*, that is set in Liverpool.

Christopher Murray taught for many years in the School of English, Drama and Film at University College Dublin. Among his books are *Robert William Elliston, Theatrical Manager: A Theatrical Biography* (Society For Theatre Research, 1976), *Twentieth-Century Irish Theatre: Mirror up to Nation* (Manchester University Press, 1997), *Seán O'Casey, Writer at Work: A Biography* (Gill & MacMillan, 2004), and *The Theatre of Brian Friel: Tradition and Modernity* (Methuen, 2014). He has also published over 100 articles and chapters in edited books on Irish drama. He is a former editor of *Irish University Review*.

Michael Parker's research explores modern and contemporary Irish, British, and postcolonial literature. He has published six books to date on poetry, fiction, and drama from the Republic and Northern Ireland, and their historical contexts. His current project, *Seamus Heaney: Legacies, Afterlives*, focuses on the poet's middle and late career. He teaches in the Department of Continuing Education, University of Oxford.

Michael Pierse is Senior Lecturer in Irish Literature at Queen's University Belfast. His research mainly explores the fiction, theatre, and culture of Irish working-class life. Over recent years, this work has expanded into new multi-disciplinary contexts, including the study of festivals and conflict, and the intersections of race and class on the Irish stage. He is author of *Writing Ireland's Working-Class: Dublin After O'Casey* (Palgrave Macmillan, 2011) and editor of the collections, *A History of Irish Working-Class Writing* (Cambridge University Press, 2017), *Rethinking the Irish Diaspora: After The Gathering* (Palgrave Macmillan, 2018; co-edited with Devlin Trew), and *Creativity and*

Resistance in a Hostile World (Manchester University Press, 2020; co-edited with Mahn, Malik, and Rogaly).

Ondřej Pilný is a Professor of English and American Literature and the Director of the Centre for Irish Studies at Charles University, Prague. He is the author of two books, *The Grotesque in Contemporary Anglophone Drama* (Palgrave, 2016) and *Irony and Identity in Modern Irish Drama* (Litteraria Pragensia, 2006), and editor of multiple essay collections and journal issues, most recently *Cultural Convergence: The Dublin Gate Theatre, 1928–1960* with Ruud van den Beuken and Ian R. Walsh (Palgrave, 2021). His translations into Czech include works by J. M. Synge, Flann O'Brien, Samuel Beckett, Brian Friel, Martin McDonagh, Enda Walsh, and Mark O'Rowe.

Eglantina Remport is Senior Lecturer in Modern British and Irish Literature at Eötvös Loránd University, Budapest. Her research explores relations between painting, drama, and politics in the work of early twentieth-century Irish authors, particularly Lady Gregory, W. B. Yeats, J. M. Synge, and G. B. Shaw. She has published articles in the *Irish Studies Review*, *Irish University Review*, *Acta Universitatis Sapientiae: Philologica*, and a book chapter in *Utopian Horizons: Ideology, Politics, Literature* (Central European University Press, 2017). She is author of *Lady Gregory and Irish National Theatre: Art, Drama, Politics* (Palgrave Macmillan, 2018).

Paige Reynolds, Professor of English at College of the Holy Cross, Worcester, MA, has published on the subjects of modernism, drama and performance, and modern and contemporary Irish literature. She is the author of *Modernism, Drama, and the Audience for Irish Spectacle* (Cambridge University Press, 2007) and editor of *Modernist Afterlives in Irish Literature and Culture* (Anthem Press, 2016), as well as editor of *The New Irish Studies* and *Irish Literature in Transition, Volume 6, 1980–2020* (with Eric Falci), both published in 2020 for Cambridge University Press.

Shaun Richards is Emeritus Professor of Irish Studies at Staffordshire University, UK. He has published on Irish drama in major journals and edited collections, including *Irish Studies Review*, *Irish University Review*, *Modern Drama*, Cambridge University Press's *Irish Literature in Transition* series, *The Palgrave Handbook of Irish Theatre and Performance*, and *The Oxford Handbook of Modern Irish Theatre*. He is the co-author, with Chris Morash, of *Mapping*

Irish Theatre: Theories of Space and Place (Cambridge University Press, 2013) and co-editor, with Beatriz Kopschitz Bastos, of *Contemporary Irish Documentary Theatre* (Bloomsbury, 2020).

Marilynn Richtarik is a Professor of English at Georgia State University in Atlanta and the author of *Acting Between the Lines: The Field Day Theatre Company and Irish Cultural Politics 1980–1984* (Oxford University Press, 1994) and *Stewart Parker: A Life* (Oxford University Press, 2012). In 2017, she taught and conducted research at Queen's University Belfast as a US Fulbright Scholar and published an edition of Stewart Parker's autobiographical novel *Hopdance* (The Lilliput Press, 2017). She is currently writing a book about literary reactions and contributions to the peace process in Northern Ireland that culminated in the 1998 Belfast (Good Friday) Agreement.

Melissa Sihra is Associate Professor of Drama and Theatre at Trinity College Dublin. She is author of *Marina Carr: Pastures of the Unknown* (Palgrave Macmillan, 2018) and editor of *Women in Irish Drama: A Century of Authorship and Representation* (Palgrave Macmillan, 2007). She is co-editor, with Elaine Aston, of the Cambridge University Press Elements Monograph Series *Women Theatre Makers*.

Ruud van den Beuken is an Assistant Professor at Radboud University Nijmegen (The Netherlands). He is the Assistant Director of the NWO-funded Gate Theatre Research Network. He has published articles in *Irish Studies Review* and *Études irlandaises*, and contributed chapters to *The Gate Theatre, Dublin: Inspiration and Craft* (Carysfort/Peter Lang, 2018) and *Navigating Ireland's Theatre Archive: Theory, Practice, Performance* (Peter Lang, 2019). He has also co-edited various volumes, including *Cultural Convergence: The Dublin Gate Theatre, 1928–1960* (Palgrave Macmillan, 2021) and *A Stage of Emancipation: Change and Progress at the Dublin Gate Theatre* (Liverpool University Press, 2021). His monograph *Avant-Garde Nationalism at the Dublin Gate Theatre, 1928–1940* was published by Syracuse University Press in 2021.

Clare Wallace is Associate Professor at the Department of Anglophone Literatures and Cultures, Charles University in Prague. She is has written widely on Irish and British theatre. Among her recent publications are a chapter on Stella Feehily in *The Golden Thread: Irish Women Playwrights, 1716–2016* (Liverpool University Press, 2021),

"Ambivalent Attachments, Catharsis and Commemoration: David Ireland's Cyprus Avenue at the Abbey Theatre in 2016," *Scene* 8.1&2 (2020), and "Marina Carr's *Hecuba*: Agency, Anger and Correcting Euripides," *Irish Studies Review* 27.4 (2019). Her latest project is a volume of co-edited essays titled *Crisis, Representation and Resilience: Perspectives on Contemporary British Theatre* (Bloomsbury, 2022).

Ian R. Walsh is Lecturer in Drama and Theatre Studies at NUI Galway. He was awarded a PhD from University College Dublin in 2010 and has worked as a freelance director of both theatre and opera. He has published widely on Irish theatre in peer-reviewed journals and edited collections, most recently co-editing with Siobhán O'Gorman and Elaine Sisson *Staging Europe at the Gate*, a special issue of *Review of Irish Studies in Europe*, 4.1 (2021). His books include *Experimental Irish Theatre: After W.B. Yeats* (Palgrave, 2012); *The Theatre of Enda Walsh* (Carysfort, 2015/Peter Lang, 2019) co-edited with Mary Caulfield; *Cultural Convergence: The Dublin Gate Theatre, 1928–1960* (Palgrave, 2020) co-edited with Ondřej Pilný and Ruud van den Beuken; and *Contemporary Irish Theatre: Histories and Theories* (Palgrave, 2022) co-written with Charlotte McIvor.

INTRODUCTION

When, in 2000, Declan Hughes declared "I could live a long and happy life without seeing another play set in a Connemara kitchen, or a country pub,"[1] he was echoing the decision of Tom Murphy and his friend Noel Donoghue some forty years earlier, that whatever they wrote a play about "one thing is fucking sure, it's not going to be set in a kitchen."[2] Assumptions about the characteristics of the typical Irish play are often based on the form rejected by Hughes and Murphy, namely the rural, realist set rendered with an almost anthropological accuracy; a form which dated from the beginnings of a self-consciously Irish theatre in the early twentieth century. As Frank Fay, one of the first directors of the Abbey Theatre, observed:

> Most of the plays in the company's repertoire are peasant plays, that is plays dealing with peasant life. They are dressed exactly as in real life, the dresses being specifically made by the tailors employed by the peasantry, and the properties are absolutely correct.[3]

These dominated the repertoire of the Abbey and its antecedents with twice as many peasant plays as poetic plays staged between 1902 and 1908. But the presence of non-realist plays whose form was more indebted to symbolist theatre is itself striking. In many ways the tension between these two forms marks the development of Irish theatre throughout the twentieth century with protests against the dominance of realism being matched by claims that its reign was over, and a new era of experimental drama ushered in. The plays included in this collection explore these contrasting forms of Irish theatre, capturing a drama which is more varied than often assumed with innovative plays appearing even in periods judged to be "stuck in the pit of naturalism."[4]

DOI: 10.4324/9781003203216-1

However, the question as to where to begin such a study is a vexed one. From Brian Friel's perspective in 1972, Boucicault, Shaw, and Wilde should be "dropped from the calendar of Irish dramatic saints" as they "wrote within the English tradition." Irish theatre, he argued, began with the Irish Literary Theatre's production of W. B. Yeats's *The Countess Cathleen* (1899), which ushered in a drama of "high seriousness."[5] This exclusion from the canon of Irish drama of work such *The Shaughraun* (1874), *The Importance of Being Earnest* (1895), and *John Bull's Other Ireland* (1904) followed the views of W. B. Yeats, Lady Gregory, and J. M. Synge who founded the Abbey Theatre in 1904. In Yeats's view, playwrights such as Wilde and Shaw had strayed away from Irish themes and Irish feelings. While Synge judged that the *The Shaughraun* contained too much of "the careless Irish humour of which everyone has had too much."[6] The Abbey aspired to the status of a modern European art theatre and so rejected any association with a theatre of commerce and popular taste. Contemporary criticism, however, is informed by Declan Kiberd's judgement that it is "possible to see Wilde and Shaw as cultural godfathers of the Irish Renaissance,"[7] while if Boucicault is not included in considerations of Irish drama "you begin to seriously distort the nature of what the theatrical canon might be."[8]

Developed definitions of Irish theatre, however, do date from Friel's drama of "high seriousness" when Yeats and Lady Gregory declared that Irish audiences were weary of misrepresentations of Ireland as a place of "buffoonery and easy sentiment" and asserted that theatre should show the country as the home of an "ancient idealism."[9] This, in Loren Kruger's terms, is the start of the project of "theatrical nationhood" in which the theatre sought to define a nation and establish a national audience.[10] Maude Gonne MacBride's "A National Theatre" (1903) articulated the dominant position, that as the peasants of the rural west embodied an authentic Irishness then the national theatre must "draw its vitality from that hidden spring."[11] As the riots which surrounded J. M. Synge's *The Playboy of the Western World* (1907) revealed, however, claims as to authentic representations were open to often violent dispute. Typical of the many letters received by the Dublin press is that from a self-styled "Western Girl" who claimed that as she was "well acquainted with the conditions of life in the West" she could authoritatively state that "this play does not truly represent these conditions."[12] Similar disputes about representation are found again in critical responses to plays from Lennox Robinson's *Harvest* (1910) and Sean O'Casey's *The Plough and the Stars* (1926) to Martin McDonagh's *The Beauty Queen of Leenane* (1996).

Alongside questions of accuracy of content in nominally realistic plays, the early Irish theatre was also divided over the issue of the appropriateness of form. While Yeats, along with Lady Gregory and Synge, had established the Abbey in 1904, by 1919 he felt that its success was for him "a discouragement and a defeat" since as it was founded on the prosaic form of realism it lacked the "mysterious art" that he desired.[13] Theatre, he believed, should be capable of transcending mortality and the mundane, a radical objective to be achieved by ritual, stylisation, music, and dance. The seeds of *Waiting for Godot* (1953) can be found in Yeats's *Purgatory* (1938) but the drama to which he aspired, based on his understanding of Japanese Noh theatre, was only to be achieved intermittently and never fully successfully. However the impulse to explore Irish experience through forms other than realism remained constant, running from Yeats's *At the Hawk's Well* (1916), through Denis Johnston's *The Old Lady Says "No!"* (1929) and on to Tom Mac Intyre's *The Great Hunger* (1983), Dermot Bolger's *The Lament for Arthur Cleary* (1989), and the hallucinatory world evoked in Mark O'Rowe's *Terminus* (2007). Moreover the search for the means to stage social traumas has seen innovations such as Tom Murphy's Brechtian-inflected *Famine* (1968), a dramatization of the Great Hunger that scarred the Irish consciousness for generations, and Mary Raftery's *No Escape* (2010), the first Irish documentary drama, whose verbatim staging of the Ryan Report gave a voice to those who suffered across decades of institutional child abuse; neither play subscribing to the form of realism pioneered by the Abbey.

While the Abbey became the National Theatre of Ireland in 1925, the first state-sponsored theatre in the anglophone world, there were other theatres committed to other forms – and the drama of other nations. The Dublin Drama League was founded in 1918 by Yeats, Lennox Robinson, and others to stage work by playwrights such as Pirandello, Toller, O'Neill, and Strindberg, giving audiences and actors relief from "the treadmill of peasant parts."[14] This was succeeded by the Gate Theatre, founded in 1928 by Hilton Edwards and Micheál mac Liammóir, after the model of "certain *avant-garde* experimental theatres of the Continent."[15] In the Introduction to his edited collection of Gate plays published in 1936, the American critic Curtis Canfield claimed there was no longer a place for "the usual naturalistic form" in a modernising Ireland whose theatre was "in an interesting state of transition from Realism to Experimentation and Expressionism."[16] Against Canfield's claims, however, the fact that the same promptbook, props – and even actors – were used in the

3

Abbey's thirty-plus productions of *The Plough and the Stars* across some twenty-five years following its premiere in 1926 shows that cultural conservatism, as much as a shortage of cash, was a determining factor on the production style of the Irish stage. As argued by Fintan O'Toole, in the 1930s Irish theatre entered "a long period of decline and decadence."[17]

That there was resistance to this sense of cultural entropy across the 1930s and 1940s is undeniable. Mary Manning, editor of the Gate's house journal *Motley*, declared that the Gate was part of the modern progressive element in the country which, along with the rapid urbanisation of society, meant that "We can never again be described as an Abbey kitchen interior, entirely surrounded by the bog!"[18] Manning's *Youth's the Season–?* (1936) presented this new Ireland of Dublin's brittle bright-young-things, an antidote to any vestiges of "Peasant Quality," the standard by which Abbey plays were judged. But innovative as the Gate was, in 1950 mac Liammóir could still signal dissatisfaction as they continued to search for "those authors who will deliver it from the cumbersome drawingroom and library set ... from the limitations of those literal and representative surroundings."[19]

Powerful plays such as *Home is the Hero* (1952) and *The Wood of the Whispering* (1953) were produced under the broad remit of realism but in 1955 Gabriel Fallon could complain of "the mediocrity which affects the theatre,"[20] a state linked, in his view, to the rejection by Yeats and Lady Gregory, decades earlier, of experimental works by Sean O'Casey and Denis Johnston. As summarised by Tom Kilroy in 1959, "[during] the last twenty years few Irish dramatists have been in any way exciting technically."[21] But if modernisation, as prematurely anticipated by Canfield in 1936, was the driver of theatrical innovation this was about to receive governmental imprimatur in the form of T. K. Whitaker's *Programme for Economic Expansion* (1958) with its encouragement of foreign investment and conclusion that it was "time to shut the door on the past."[22] The Dublin Theatre Festival, which was initiated in 1957 with a visit from Jean Vilar's Théâtre National Populaire, signalled a commitment to cultural as well as economic modernisation. It was under the auspices of the Festival that Brian Friel's *Philadelphia, Here I Come!* was produced in 1964, a play regarded by Richard Pine as a "liminal, transformative moment in Irish theatre" because of its innovative staging.[23] Already, two years earlier, Hugh Leonard's *Stephen D.* (1962), like Friel's a Gate production for the Theatre Festival, had shown a new awareness of non-naturalistic staging with an opening in which "the dialogue between Stephen and the President was delivered as they walked down into the auditorium and completed a circuit of the stalls, during which time the house lights were switched on."[24]

Paradoxically, it was in the 1980s when the drive to modernisation was fully underway, with factories of Microsoft and Intel being established in the country, that two of the most powerful plays of peasant life were staged: Brian Friel's *Translations* (1980) and Tom Murphy's *Bailegangaire* (1985). But they were, argued Tom Kilroy, "theatrical elegies" with a clear sense that the form they have inherited is "at the end of its tether." As Ireland moved from a rural world of thatched cottages to one of high-rises and Ryanair, "the most durable of all Irish theatrical genres, the Irish peasant play" was no longer relevant to a modern generation who simply "find it a bore."[25]

Indeed, said Declan Hughes, the rural world was no longer the objective corelative for Ireland, "culturally it's played out. It no longer signifies. Mythologically, it doesn't resonate any more."[26] Accordingly the protagonist of his *Digging for Fire* (1991) argues, to a soundtrack provided by The Pixies, Tom Waits, and New Order, that the culture of globalised Dublin is indistinguishable from that of New York. While the critical and commercial success of Conor McPherson's *The Weir* (1997), with its setting in a rural pub, seemed to refute Hughes's argument and cast into doubt the suggestion that naturalism was now "virtually impossible,"[27] the 1990s saw new directions taken by plays such as Martin McDonagh's *The Beauty Queen of Leenane* (1996) and Marina Carr's *By the Bog of Cats* (1998) whose sets, while suggesting realism, evoked the style in ways which undermined its fundamental premise of giving a window on an easily identifiable Irish world. Indeed Fintan O'Toole suggests that "It is easy to be fooled by the apparently traditional, naturalistic form"[28] of McDonagh's plays, while for Eamonn Jordan, while the superficial impression of Carr's work was of realism, "the disparate elements do not coalesce into meaningful mimetic structures."[29] Even though one of the most successful play of the decade was *Dancing at Lughnasa* (1990) with its setting in a cottage of the 1930s, what is staged is a memory, an evocation of a lost world idealised in Joe Vanek's set of a golden wheat field which came to be the defining image of the play.

The sense of an Ireland which was changing as old certainties were eroded was the focus of *The Field* (1965) with even *A Handful of Stars* (1988), which carried realism into the 1980s, marked by an elegiac sense of a world which was waning. Evocations of a lost world of certainty also distinguished *The Steward of Christendom* (1995). Indeed, if modernity impacted on Irish authenticity, smoothing away, as Canfield posited in 1936, those "salient features which once made

Dublin different from London or New York"[30] it also brought to the fore lives lived outside the provenance of an Ireland which, since the creation of the Free State in 1922, had preferred images of a nation unmarked by internal differences. The self-destructive violence consequent on embracing the exclusionary ideas of nationalist purity are staged in Tom Kilroy's *Double Cross* (1986) while the counter value of giving expression to the realities of others is captured nowhere more strikingly than in *Observe the Sons of Ulster Marching Towards the Somme* (1985), Frank McGuinness's empathetic engagement with the losses of the Ulster Division in the First World War which engages with one of the foundations of Unionist beliefs which, since the outbreak of the "Troubles" in 1968, had become part of the complexities with which Irish drama also had to grapple.

The subject of sectarian differences and conflict had informed drama since at least St John Ervine's *Mixed Marriage* (1911), and in the character of Bessie Burgess it shadowed *The Plough and the Stars* (1926) just as it provided the dynamic of *The Hostage* (1958), but its modern manifestation was Sam Thompson's *Over the Bridge* (1960) whose exploration of the violence in a Belfast shipyard pointed prophetically towards a subject which informed drama as varied as Friel's *The Freedom of the City* (1973), Stewart Parker's *Northern Star* (1984), and Owen McCafferty's *Quietly* (2012). But Christina Reid's *Tea in a China Cup* (1983) and Anne Devlin's *Ourselves Alone* (1985), two nominally "Troubles" plays, also exposed the situation of women in a patriarchal society whose oppressive power predated the conflict and was not bounded by borders. But although theatre sometimes gave voice to women playwrights it was never without opposition and struggle.

Yeats's retrospective designation of *Kathleen ni Houlihan* (1902) as "that play of mine" excised Lady Gregory's part in its composition and established a century-long pattern of female marginalisation.[31] Alice Milligan's *The Last Feast of the Fianna* (1900) was staged by the Irish Literary Theatre, the company which gave birth to the Abbey, but her innovative theatre has barely been acknowledged. Although Lady Gregory's position as a director of the Abbey meant that her plays, such as *The Gaol Gate* (1904), were certain of a production the general situation of women playwrights, like that of the protagonist of Teresa Deevy's *Katie Roche* (1936), was one in which their prospects were always prescribed by male preferences. The dominance of the realist set of the cottage kitchen came to compound a conflation of family and nation in which woman were celebrated as mothers while silenced in society as stage worlds reflected images of the prevailing orthodoxy. That some plays such as Elizabeth Connor's comedy of gender role reversals, *An Apple a Day* (1942), and Maura Laverty's unsentimental domestic drama *Tolka Row* (1951) could break through the barriers only highlighted the relative absence of such work from the Abbey and the Gate respectively. More recently *Eclipsed* (1992), Patricia Burke Brogan's drama of the pernicious Magdalen laundries, was produced by Punchbag, one of a new wave of companies which sprang up across Ireland and, especially in the case of Druid Theatre, Galway, established a counter to Dublin's dominance in defining the nation's theatre. When the Abbey's choice of plays to commemorate the centenary of the Easter Rising of 1916 included only one work by a woman playwright, *Me, Mollser* by Ali White, intended for a theatre in education programme rather than either of the theatre's stages, the response of #WakingTheFeminists to the Abbey's "Waking the Nation" programme exposed the predominant narrow conception of Ireland's theatrical culture.[32]

Despite such debates about inclusion and representation, the picture of Irish drama in the twenty-first century is one in which a multiplicity of companies produce work in theatres in and beyond Ireland. Sebastian Barry's view that "The new Irish theatre is a moveable feast that moves quite naturally and lightly between Dublin, Belfast, London, New York"[33] acknowledges a global reach to Irish theatre not seen since the nineteenth-century hey-day of Boucicault. It is also varied in terms of forms, themes, and venues: *A Walworth Farce* (2006) undermines traditional views of the sanctity of the Irish family in a farce performed in the style of the Three Stooges; *I ♥ Alice ♥ I* (2010) explores the relationship between two middle-aged lesbians in a form which masquerades as documentary; *Laundry* (2011) gives audiences an immersive experience of the Magdalen laundries in a site-specific work; *Spinning* (2014) examines social issues through overlapping storylines which fragment a conventional realist narrative. And all four plays were produced outside of the one-time hegemony of the Abbey and the Gate, being staged by Druid, HotForTheatre, ANU, and Fishamble respectively.

A changing theatre in a changing Ireland had been Curtis Canfield's view in 1936 but that seems even more apposite in the contemporary moment as Synge's Christy Mahon is transformed into Nigerian immigrant Christopher Malomo in Bisi Adigun and Roddy Doyle's adaptation of *The Playboy of the Western World* (2007) at the Abbey, and Mirjana Rendulic's *Broken Promise Land* (2013), a monologue recounting a Croatian woman's journey from war-torn Zagreb to find refuge in Ireland, plays in The Theatre Upstairs in Lanigan's pub on

Dublin's Eden Quay. Irish theatre is still "serious" to return to the term with which Brian Friel dismissed Boucicault but now enjoys a condition in which seriousness can embrace differences – those of life-styles, experiences, and cultures as well as those of forms, themes, and theatres.

Shaun Richards

Notes

1 Declan Hughes, "Who the Hell Do We Think We Still Are?" in *Theatre Stuff: Essays on Contemporary Irish Theatre*, ed. Eamonn Jordan (Dublin: Carysfort Press, 2000), 13.
2 Quoted in Tom Kilroy, "A Generation of Playwrights," *Theatre Stuff*, 5.
3 Frank Fay, "Some Account of the Early Days of the INTS," in *The Abbey Theatre: Interviews and Recollections*, ed. E. H. Mikhail (London: Macmillan, 1988), 76.
4 Gabriel Fallon, "The Future of the Irish Theatre," *Studies* Vol. 44, no. 173 (1955): 99.
5 Brian Friel, "Plays Peasant and Unpeasant," in *Brian Friel, Essays, Diaries, Interviews: 1964–1999*, ed. Christopher Murray (London: Faber & Faber, 1999), 51.
6 J. M. Synge, "A Note on Boucicault and Irish Drama," in *Collected Works, Vol. 2, Prose*, ed. Alan Price (London: Oxford University Press, 1966), 398.
7 Declan Kiberd, "The London Exiles: Wilde and Shaw," in *The Field Day Anthology of Irish Writing Vol. II*, ed. Seamus Deane (Derry: Field Day Publications, 1991), 372.
8 Fintan O'Toole, *Critical Moments: Fintan O'Toole on Modern Irish Theatre*, ed. Julia Furay and Redmond O'Hanlon (Dublin: Carysfort Press, 2003), 294.
9 Lady Gregory, *Our Irish Theatre* (London: Putnam, 1913), 8.
10 Loren Kruger, *The National Stage: Theatre and Cultural Legitimisation in England, France, and America* (Chicago: University of Chicago Press, 1992), 3.
11 Maude Gonne MacBride, "A National Theatre," *The United Irishman*, No. 243, 24 October 1903, 2.
12 Quoted in James Kilroy, ed., *The "Playboy" Riots* (Dublin: Dolmen Press, 1971), 9.
13 W. B. Yeats, *The Collected Works, Vol. VIII*, ed. Mary Fitzgerald and Richard J. Finneran (New York: Scribner, 2003), 128.
14 Gabriel Fallon, "Thanks to the Dublin Drama League," *The Irish Monthly* Vol. 68, no. 806 (1940): 446.
15 Hilton Edwards, "Production," in *The Gate Theatre*, ed. Bulmer Hobson (Dublin: Gate Theatre, 1934), 21.
16 Curtis Canfield, "Preface," *Plays of Changing Ireland* (New York: Macmillan, 1936), xii.

17 Fintan O'Toole, "Irish Theatre: The State of the Art," *Theatre Stuff,* 48.

18 Mary Manning, "Dublin Has Also Its Gate Theater," *Boston Evening Transcript,* 17 January 1935.

19 Micheál mac Liammóir, *Theatre in Ireland* (Dublin: Cultural Relations Committee, 1950), 42.

20 Fallon, "The Future of the Irish Theatre," 100.

21 Thomas Kilroy, "Groundwork for an Irish Theatre," *Studies* Vol. 48, no. 190 (1959): 195.

22 T.K. Whitaker, *Programme for Economic Expansion* (Dublin: Government Papers, 1958), 99.

23 Richard Pine, *The Diviner: The Art of Brian Friel* (Dublin: University College Dublin Press, 1999), 41.

24 Hugh Leonard, "Production Note," *Stephen D* (London: Faber & Faber, 1996), 7.

25 Kilroy, "A Generation of Playwrights," *Theatre Stuff,* 2.

26 Hughes, 12.

27 O'Toole, "Irish Theatre: The State of the Art," 51.

28 Fintan O'Toole, "Introduction," *Martin McDonagh: Plays:1* (London: Methuen, 1999), xi–xii.

29 Eamonn Jordan, *Dissident Dramaturgies: Contemporary Irish Theatre* (Dublin: Irish Academic Press, 2010), 7.

30 Canfield, xi–xii.

31 W. B. Yeats, "The Man and the Echo" (1938), in Norman A. Jeffares, *Yeats's Poems* (London: Macmillan, 1989), 469.

32 See www.wakingthefeminists.org/

33 Sebastian Barry, "Foreword," in *Far from the Land: Contemporary Irish Plays,* ed. John Fairleigh (London: Methuen, 1998), xi.

Further Reading

Lonergan, Patrick. *Irish Drama and Theatre Since 1950.* London: Bloomsbury, 2019.

Roche, Anthony. *The Irish Dramatic Revival 1899–1939.* London: Bloomsbury, 2015.

FIFTY KEY IRISH PLAYS

THE SHAUGHRAUN (1874) BY DION BOUCICAULT

The Shaughraun was not Dion Boucicault's first play that prominently featured an Irish character; *The Irish Heiress* (1842) was the first of nine such plays that predate it. Nor was it considered his first "Irish" play, one that presented the action sympathetic to its Irish characters. *The Colleen Bawn*, with the sentimental rogue Myles-na-Coppaleen and innocent heroine Eily O'Connor, was the first in what became known during Boucicault's life as his Irish trilogy (*The Colleen Bawn* [1860], *Arrah-na-Pogue* [1864], *The Shaughraun* [1874]). Indeed, it was not even his first play to sympathetically portray Irish nationalism; he accomplished that in *Arrah-na-Pogue,* a decade before. But more than any other play *The Shaughraun* balances a sentimental view of Irishness with a robust endorsement of Irish nationalism in a manner not seen in the Victorian theatre, and he did so in a way that made Irish heroism synonymous with its English counterpart. Moreover, Boucicault combined this with a public showmanship that kept the cause of Fenian prisoners, *The Shaughraun*, and his own name in the papers from its premiere at Wallack's Theatre in New York in November 1874 through its London production at Drury Lane from August 1875 through March 1876.

The play opens before a humble cottage in the shadow of Suil-a-more castle, where Claire Ffolliott, Robert's sister, and Arte O'Neal, his fiancée, bide their time while Robert is "working out his sentence in Australia," following his conviction for Fenian activities.[1] Reconnoitering the area, Captain Molineux discovers Robert's sister Claire alone churning butter, and assuming her to be a mere servant, he flirtatiously banters with her. Asking this assumed milk-maid to fetch her mistress, he steals a kiss from her before sending her on her way, jocundly commenting, "Don't hide your blushes. They become you." In these opening minutes of the play, Boucicault uses Molineux to give voice to an English lack of regard for Ireland, even complaining that "Irish names are so unpronounceable" when he finds that he has mispronounced "Shoolabeg" (174).

However, Molineux's casual belief in his imperialist superiority evaporates when Arte O'Neal returns to introduce herself and clarify that Claire is her cousin, Robert Ffolliott's sister, and thus a member of the local gentry. Molineux gives voice to his unexpected embarrassment, providing Claire the opportunity to invert the play's assumed colonial (and gender) hierarchy by assuring the flustered Englishman, "Don't hide your blushes, Captain, they become you" (174). Although Molineux attempts to restore his imperialist

DOI: 10.4324/9781003203216-2

equanimity by sympathizing with Arte for "the Irish extravagance of your ancestors" that he assumes has caused her current poverty, she coldly retorts, "the extravagance of their love for their country," again throwing Molineux off balance and causing him to admit that he feels "astray on an Irish bog" (175).

Although rooted in Boucicault's earlier romance between the Irish heiress Anne Chute and the Anglicised Irishman Kyrle Daly in *The Colleen Bawn*, Boucicault uses the romance between Claire and Molineux to explore the animosities between Victorian England and Ireland. It is also important to note that this cross-cultural romance informs such later examples as those between Broadbent and Nora in Shaw's *John Bull's Other Island* (1904) and Yolland and Maire in Friel's *Translations* (1980). However, unlike these future examples, Claire struggles against her growing affection for this endearing English soldier, lamenting in Act 2, "I hate his country and his people" (192), and even admitting to him, "every throb of your honest heart has been a knife in mine" (205).

It soon becomes clear that Molineux is in charge of the operation to arrest Claire's brother Robert, who has escaped from Australia and is rumoured to have returned. But before the audience can assume that Boucicault will position Molineux as the play's agent of English oppression, the scene is interrupted by Corry Kinchela, the local squireen and magistrate, Robert's guardian and trusted advisor. Upon Kinchela's entrance Molinuex remarks to the audience, "This fellow is awfully offensive to me" (176), and his disrespectful rebuff of the ingratiating squireen earns Molineux the praise of both Irish ladies. In the first two plays of his Irish trilogy, Boucicault facilitates the reconciliation of the English and Irish by shifting any cultural opprobrium to representatives of the Irish middle class, who are portrayed as gauche careerists seeking to rise above their station. Yet, rather than the "pettifogging attorney" seen in *Colleen Bawn*, Kinchela is a true villain: under his stewardship of Robert's finances, he has driven the estate into bankruptcy and sought to coerce Robert's fiancée to marry him, all under the guise of loyalty to him.

With Molineux's exit to return to his barracks, Claire and Arte welcome Father Dolan, the beloved priest, who has arrived for a private conversation with Kinchela. After the ladies have departed, Dolan enumerates the long history of Kinchela's crimes against Robert, which culminated in the youth's false conviction for treason: "'twas by your manes, and to serve this end, my darling boy [...] was denounced and convicted" (178). Dolan departs after declaring his intention to always aid Robert, and Kinchela's henchman Harvey Duff arrives with the news that Robert Ffolliott has secretly returned. Although Duff panics over the prospect that Robert and his supporters will seek revenge, Kinchela is confident that they can arrange Ffolliott's death before the government announces the Queen's pardon and the "release all Fenian prisoners under sentence" (179).

The remaining three scenes of Act 1 introduces the audience to Robert and Conn, but begin with Molineux wandering "the rocks [of] the sea coast" (180), having lost his way musing over Claire. He stumbles upon Robert, disguised as a common sailor, and they exchange views on the two women of the estate. Once they establish that Robert admires Arte as much as Molineux does Claire, they drink to them both from Robert's flask. However, Robert's cultured speech and American whiskey suggest his true identity. Recognizing an affinity that transcends their differences, the soldier departs, after transparently mentioning to Robert that he will return later in the evening with a detachment of soldiers to search for "a very dangerous person who will be or has been landed on this coast" (181). The remaining scenes of Act 1 serve to introduce Conn, the Shaughraun—originally played by Boucicault himself—to the audience, presenting him as an endearing rogue who spends his time drinking, poaching, and fiddling, though his devotion to Robert and the priest's maid Molly is never in doubt.

In the final moments of Act 1, having been led by Duff, Molineux arrives with soldiers to search Dolan's house for Robert, who is hiding in the kitchen. However, out of respect for the priest, Molineux agrees to depart if Dolan gives his word that Robert is not on the premises. The priest experiences "a passionate struggle with himself" in this effort to lie, until Robert emerges and surrenders to Molineux (189). The eight scenes of Act 2 centre on Robert's imprisonment and Kinchela's attempt to exploit Robert's continued trust to arrange his murder as part of a failed prison escape. However, believing Kinchela's plan to be authentic, Robert enlists Conn to aid him, and his sister is soon delegated by Conn to light a bonfire to signal the sailors ready to rescue him.

Boucicault's plays were known for the "sensation" scenes that punctuated many of his plays, from the burning tenements in *The Poor of New York* (1857) to a blazing river boat in *The Octoroon* (1859). Similarly, Act 2 of *The Shaughraun* culminates with Robert's escape to the ruins of St. Bridget's Abbey where he is shot attempting to scale its crumbling edifice. However, Kinchela and Duff despair when they realise that they have not killed Ffolliott, but only Conn in disguise. The first two scenes of Act 3 stage Conn's wake, which is noteworthy for the affecting keening scene of women around his body. But the scene's pathos quickly dissolves when Conn steals a glass of whiskey, winking to the audience, when the women are distracted. Conn's charade is disrupted altogether when Molineux arrives to announce that Robert has received amnesty but Kinchela and Duff have escaped having kidnapped Arte and Moya. Well ahead of the pursuing posse, Conn aids the women in foiling the villains' escape, and the main characters arrive with a vengeful crowd to arrest them. Arte and Robert are reunited, and her brother encourages Claire to marry Molineux: "He has earned you, Claire" (219). However, Father Dolan cannot quite agree to the union of Conn and Moya, so the rogue again turns to the audience, asking them to "hould out your hands once more to a poor Shaughraun" (219).

Scott Boltwood

Note

1 Dion Boucicault, *The Shaughraun*, in *Plays by Dion Boucicault* (Cambridge: Cambridge University Press, 1984), 175. Subsequent references are entered in parentheses.

Further Reading

Boltwood, Scott. "Dion Boucicault: From Stage Irishman to Staging Nationalism." In *A Companion to Irish Literature. Vol I*, edited by Julia Wright, 460–75. London: Blackwell Publishing, 2010.

McFeely, Deirdre. *Dion Boucicault: Irish Identity on Stage*. Cambridge: Cambridge University Press, 2012.

Richards, Shaun. "Dion Boucicault and a Globalised Irish Theatre." In *Irish Literature in Transition, Vol. 3, 1830–1880*, edited by Mathew Campbell, 280–98. Cambridge: Cambridge University Press, 2019.

Watt, Stephen. "The Inheritance of Melodrama." In *The Oxford Handbook of Modern Irish Theatre*, edited by Nicholas Grene and Chris Morash, 19–23. Cambridge: Cambridge University Press, 2016.

THE IMPORTANCE OF BEING EARNEST (1895)
BY OSCAR WILDE

"The very essence of romance is uncertainty," declares Algernon Moncrieff to his friend Ernest Worthing in the opening scene of Wilde's famous comedy. "If I ever get married, I'll certainly try to forget the fact."[1] Thus begins a play that elegantly examines the creative possibilities of fluid identity and the wilful manipulation of verifiable truth. Luxuriating in his *"artistically furnished"* London flat, Algernon's challenge to moral norms presents a heterodox foil to his guest, a companion pleasure seeker now determined on the romantic simplicities of marriage. No sooner has Ernest declared his sincere intention to propose to Algernon's cousin Gwendolen, than his host produces an inconvenient object, exposing Ernest's double life with the help of an engraved cigarette case dedicated from "little Cecily" to "Uncle Jack." This artifact is no mere plot device of traditional farce or theatrical dilemma. Algernon's intention is not to force a shaming confession that Ernest is a false identity, but to double down on Jack/Ernest's duality, embracing him as a fellow "Bunburyist" – Bunbury being a character Algernon has invented (with a comically chronic illness) as an excuse for pleasurable diversion. Intrusive fact is parlayed into a case for double lives, free from the inhibitions of "high moral tone" (259).

In part the exchange alludes to the secret world of gay men, but it also involves a formal escape from a marriage of convenience to theatrical convention. Revelation becomes an occasion for conceptual agility and verbal panache, acknowledging that the pleasure of this performance lies in brilliant departure from the chores of routine dialogue. What Algernon offers is not merely a disquisition on the virtues of adultery – "in marriage three is company, two is none" (260) – but a holiday from character, in both senses of the word. The relationship between Algernon and Jack is that between style and narrative, in which the former languidly mocks the social frame within which the latter is seeking sanctuary. Algernon rejects character in favour of attitude, reluctant to be dictated to by dramatic coherence, delivering *bon mots* as an early signal of a performance beyond the drama, the *deus ex machina* that is Wilde delivering of himself. Thus Algernon responds to Jack's expository account of his rural role as a responsible guardian with the enduring observation that, "[t]he truth is rarely pure and never simple!" (259). It is an observation borne out when Jack discovers that Gwendolen reciprocates his love because his false name denotes solidity (and is, after all, only nearly eponymous).

The first act offsets such Wildean pyrotechnics with his strongest character, Gwendolen's mother Lady Bracknell, who arrives just as Jack has successfully proposed. Bracknell's cross-examination gathers the most significant evidence where prospects of matrimony are concerned: social and financial status. Her declarative response to Jack's admission of his adoption, having been abandoned in Victoria railway station – "found!" and "handbag?" (268) – presents one of theatre's most celebrated examples of comic indignation. Lady

Bracknell's magnificent caricature presents the grotesque demands of late Victorian hierarchy, despotically establishing fact as a defence of social status, "the very essence of matronly modernity" as one contemporary critic described her.[2] Hers is the logic that underpins privilege and its renewal, and it is through her person that Wilde reaches for themes that draw reinvention into the sphere of the political. Through her, the popular farce that formed the basis of Wilde's dramatic satire is implicitly held up as a form that utilises plot to reinforce the status quo, while morality is energised as a set of axiomatic virtues used to enact shame and deploy modes of disgrace. If Victorian London gave itself to farce, it was because the perils of transgression were farcically severe.

Instead, Wilde affords his audience a licence to think subversively as a fantastic delinquency from material obligation. Seduced by the glamour of heterodoxy, the audience is invited to revel in alternative social contracts. For Bracknell, Jack/Ernest's holdall origins are redolent of "the worst excesses of the French revolution" (268). For Wilde, the countenance of violent upheaval was family baggage. To be true to his own parentage would be to consider a scandalous sex life and/or plot against the Imperialist order from his native Dublin. His father, Sir William Wilde, was a leading ophthalmic surgeon accused of seducing his patients; his mother, Jane Elgee (Speranza), a sometime radical nationalist poet and journalist who had backed the Young Ireland rebellion of 1848. Wilde may have considered it his tragedy not to be more like her, but his precocious success at Oxford, his semi-secretive life as a gay man, his celebrated aestheticism, also taught him the possibilities and pitfalls of self-fashioning. Wilde's instantly notorious novella *The Picture of Dorian Gray* (1890) had reimagined art as a Gothic act masking and marking sinful pleasure, while two seminal essays, "The Decay of Lying" and "The Soul of Man Under Socialism" (both 1891) proposed a post-decadent dialectic, synthesising aesthetic invention and utopian individualism. Similar themes of transgression found their way into the innovative symbolism of *Salome* (1893) and *Earnest*'s antecedents *Lady Windermere's Fan* (1892) and *An Ideal Husband* (1895). When on a cold Valentine's Day in 1895 *Earnest* premiered to a rapturous reception it may have seemed Oscar had conquered repressive stricture. Three months later, when he was sentenced to penal servitude for "gross indecency," reinvention was shown to be a more contingent accomplishment.

Perhaps because it wittily presents the flip side to catastrophe, *Earnest* endured into sustained success, a rejoinder to intersectional vulnerability. Act Two performs a series of divertissements on gender roles that remain dazzling. Relocated to Jack's country seat where the play finds completion, Wilde introduces young Cecily Cardew and her governess Miss Prism. As Algernon enters, armed with the card of Ernest Worthing and presenting himself as Jack's errant brother, he appears every inch the suave predator. But Cecily is immediately his equal, noting his bona fides but warily disapproving of the "hypocrisy" of "pretending to be wicked and being really good all the time" (277). Algernon, *"taken aback"* by the object of his affections, finds he has been pre-empted by her subjective desires, reinforced by unilateral diary entries and the letters she has written on his behalf. Affection is reciprocated, but only along the narrative lines determined by language and its connotations, Cecily echoing Gwendolen in announcing that her true love requires the "absolute confidence" the name Ernest inspires (288). Although they are briefly at odds, believing themselves to be in competition for the same man, the two women are soon united in sisterhood. Farce is overwritten by a nascent feminist alliance that sets gender into a performative flux. As Cecily riffs, "once a man begins to neglect his domestic duties he becomes painfully effeminate, does he not? And I don't like that, it makes men so very attractive" (290).

Thus, the Wildean voice is also articulated by his women, a mobile persona reinforcing gender fluidity and playfully askance from theatrical form as from social convention. As Gwendolen puts it: "In matters of grave importance, style, not sincerity, is the vital thing" (301). By the third and final act, altering the facts appears merely a matter of restating reality via the act of Christening, by which Miss Prism's friend Canon Chausible offers to rename both Algernon and Jack. But fiction has other means; farce is given a final flourish in the revelation that Miss Prism had been responsible for Jack's abandonment, having confused his infant existence with the manuscript of her novel, the "revolting sentimentality" of which is hence his twin. It seems an easy mistake to make, as a happy resolution beckons. Jack's mother is revealed as Lady Bracknell's sister and his name naturally taken from his father General Moncrieff, showing him to be an Ernest all along. Yet Wilde's play subtly abjures sentiment by keeping snobbery in view.[3] Cecily is admitted to the family by dint of the fact of her funds: Lady Bracknell notes her £150,000 as a sign of "solid qualities [...] in an age of surfaces" (304), while Jack/Ernest finds that he is lost property in more ways than one, since as Algernon's restored elder brother, his is the inheritance. The absurdity of chance bringing love or justice is securely signed off in the coruscating celebration of unlikelihood. As character is absorbed into conceit, parentage is made contrivance. Newly minted Ernest Moncrieff is shown in no uncertain terms to be a Wilde child, born to show theatre as the only place the truth of falsity can be fully known.

Ben Levitas

Notes

1 Oscar Wilde, *Plays* (Penguin, 1954), 255. Subsequent references are entered in parentheses.
2 Joseph Donohue, "Reception and Performance History of The Importance of Being Earnest," in *Wilde in Context,* ed. Kerry Powell and Peter Raby (Cambridge, Cambridge University Press, 2013), 307–18.
3 Kerry Powell, *Acting Wilde: Victorian Sexuality, Theatre and Oscar Wilde* (Cambridge: Cambridge University Press, 2009), 101–22.

Further Reading

Donohue, Joseph with Ruth Berggren. *Oscar Wilde's The Importance of Being Earnest.* Gerrards Cross: Colin Smythe, 1995.
Ellman, Richard. *Oscar Wilde*. London: Penguin, 1987.
Price, Graham. *Oscar Wilde and Contemporary Irish Drama: Learning to be Oscar's Contemporary.* London: Palgrave Macmillan, 2018.

THE LAST FEAST OF THE FIANNA (1900) BY ALICE MILLIGAN

In 1975 Alice Milligan headed a document that listed women playwrights whose work had been staged by the Abbey, presumably because she was the first female playwright to stage a play with Ireland's National Theatre. *The Last Feast of the Fianna* was performed in the spring of 1900 at the Gaiety Theatre in Dublin during the second season of the Irish Literary Theatre, the precursor of the Abbey. Given that it took #WakingTheFeminists in 2016 to shine a light on the discrimination women face in trying to make careers in the National Theatre, it is obvious that the list drawn up four decades earlier was simply another way of burying "Women Playwrights" in the archive. However, the historic impact of Ireland's National Theatre meant those associated with its early formation were guaranteed even a small place in its celebrated founding story.

The Last Feast of the Fianna is a one-act play that is just the first part in Milligan's Ossianic trilogy that she actually staged as a single piece of theatre.[1] What was billed in 1900 as *The Last Feast of the Fianna* can therefore only be understood as a montage of performance practices unique to Milligan's cultural work. Introducing the trilogy as an example of National Theatre that drew on Ireland's bardic traditions and mythology, Milligan explained: "I wrote it as far as possible in the style of the dialogues [between Oisín and St Patrick] so as to represent what a Gaelic drama would have been like if it had been developed further."[2] In the staged version of *The Last Feast of the Fianna* then Oisín recalls: feasting with the Fianna warriors (part one of the published trilogy play script), leaving to live out his life in the land of eternal youth and forgetfulness, his emotional return journey to an Ireland that has changed beyond recognition. These memories were performed through a mixed media of scripted dialogue, costumed tableaux, off-stage bi-lingual storytelling and magic lantern projections of photographs on glass-slides onto gauze stage partitions. Milligan attempted to write this part of her trilogy in stanzas through which stylised non-naturalistic language is heightened. An example of this is when Oisín describes the arrival of Niamh who will take him to Tír na nÓg (the land of eternal youth): "Look! On the golden, curving stand I see a wave burst in foam. It is not a wave but a white horse, and a graceful woman is the rider."[3] The Oisín and Patrick debate that Milligan staged is also a debate about the difference between oral and written culture; the unofficial and the official at the centre of the Irish/English colonial encounter. Her symbolic division of the stage establishes two opposed imaginings of Ireland: while the conflictual dialogues of Oisín and Patrick occupy the outer borders, the core affirms the glories of a heroic and communitarian past. Through Milligan's theatrical work the tableaux mode conveys the inner realm, articulating an "unofficial" culture in which the national finds expression. In a letter to the press, Milligan gave some insight into the staging of not only this play but how the whole trilogy can be staged as a unified performance: "During the narration, Oisín, by magic art, is to summon up for the benefit of the astonished clerics visions of the chief scenes in his heroic youth. These in a series of beautiful tableaux, appearing behind a gauze curtain in an inner stage, will form the chief feature of the entertainment."[4]

Newly trained actors of the Irish Literary Theatre were cast by Milligan alongside members of the Gaelic League and veteran Fenian activists and former political prisoners led by John O'Leary. Engaging public figures and members of the public to perform their own versions of her plays was characteristic of Milligan's theatre practice: local people's visibility as agents of change on- and off-stage offered an additional emotional texture to the communitarian and educational impetus of her work. Audience members were transformed from passive theatre-goers into a collective who projected alternative cultural and political lives in costumes they made, scripts they co-wrote that were performed on stages they most often had built. While the most famous production of a Milligan play took place inside a traditional theatre setting, most of her theatre work was staged outdoors in fields loaned by the Gaelic League or co-operative societies. Music and gesture were especially important, not only for the inclusion of people at different stages of learning Irish, but also so that the narrative could be easily understood at a distance. When Milligan reviewed a tableaux performance of her plays that took place at an Anti-Partition meeting in a field in Antrim in 1938, she stated that the nationalist community at the back of the field understand the political symbolism of their code: "everyone knows" what the pictures mean, she declared.[5]

The staged trilogy always included live music: in the Irish Literary Theatre production Milligan's sisters Charlotte Milligan Fox and Edith Wheeler wrote a musical score for the play that they performed from the wings of the theatre. By yoking together these opposed representational modes, Milligan created what was considered by many in 1900 as an "impure" theatrical form that knots together enactment and stasis, speech and spectacle, polemic and pictorialism. Reviewing the play, Patrick Pearse completely dismissed Milligan's radically innovative dramaturgy: "At this stage of the day few intelligent people will be found to hold that works written in the English language are Irish literature."[6] Lady Gregory found even the English language as spoken by the Irish on stage "intolerable."[7] However the *United Irishman* welcomed the Irish Literary Theatre's production as the first step towards an indigenous Irish language drama: "Miss Milligan's play is in itself with the breath of the Ossianic legends, as near perfection, from a Gaelic standpoint, as anything not written in Gaelic can come."[8]

In 1917, Frank Morrow, a key figure from the early days of the Ulster Literary Theatre, staged a revival of Milligan's Ossianic trilogy in Belfast. Oisín's mythical journey through an unrecognisable homeland in search of lost comrades carried a particular resonance in the context of war-torn Ireland and Europe. Many years later, in 1944, the seventy-eight-year-old Milligan recalled how Morrow's depiction of Oisín discovering his dead son Oscur evoked the buried potential of Ireland's Cultural Revival:

The ogham stone was carried in on the bier by the mourners ... and the procession moved along disclosing it to Oisín, who stood well to the front of the stage. On reading the name of his son on the stone, his memory is aroused, he cries aloud for vengeance declaring he will return to Eire. The visionary procession then passes away with the stone concealed in a mantle.[9]

Through its juxtaposition of enactment and tableaux, Milligan's theatrical work established a dialogue between the particularities of the dramatic process and the wider discourses of nation. The Irish Revival may have been united in its aim of regenerating a national drama, but the search for an appropriate language and subject matter wrought tremendous discord and confusion. As an Irish cultural nationalist who was both an English-speaker and a Protestant, Milligan combined within herself a multitude of conflictual identities and allegiances. Her plays deal with characters locked within struggles to consolidate their political and cultural affiliations; besides mirroring Milligan's own conflicts, they also connect with more general divisions besetting the Irish revivalist project. Milligan's interest in tableaux was not restricted to the dramatic contexts examined thus far. Instead, she worked with living pictures as a form in their own right – and so moved increasingly from the dominant tendencies of a cultural renaissance that prioritised literary rather than pictorial values. Milligan's commitment to living pictures was related to her concern with "voicelessness": articulate in its very muteness, the *tableau vivant* offered her a valuable space beyond the contested terrain of language.[10]

Catherine Morris

Notes

1 *The Last Feast of the Fianna* appeared in the September 1899 edition of the *Daily Express* as the first play in Milligan's Ossianic trilogy; it was followed by *Oisín in Tír na nOg* and *Oisín and Pádraic.*
2 National Library of Ireland, T. P. Gill papers, MS 13, 480 (9) Item 1.
3 Alice Milligan, *The Last Feast of the Fianna* (London: David Nutt, 1900), 15.
4 *Daily Express*, 21 January 1899.
5 Alice Milligan, "Historical pageant at Omagh field," *Derry Journal*, 12 May 1938.
6 *An Claidheamh Soluis*, 10 February 1900.
7 James Pethica, ed., *Lady Gregory's Diaries, 1892–1902* (Gerrards Cross: Colin Smythe, 1996), 227.

8 *United Irishman*, 24 February 1900.
9 Note attached to the 1944 bi-lingual publication of *Oisín in Tír na nÓg*, NLI IR 89162 (8 m 26).
10 Milligan's use of tableaux in theatre was explored as part of the "El Lissitzky: The Artist and State," Irish Museum of Modern Art, 2015. www. youtube.com/watch?v=Mp0-SOefClE. Accessed 10 December 2021.

Further Reading

Hill, Shonagh. *Women and Embodied Mythmaking in Irish Theatre*, 26–64. Cambridge: Cambridge University Press, 2019.
Morris, Catherine. "Alice Milligan: Republican Tableaux and the Revival." *Field Day Review* 6 (2010): 132–65.
Morris, Catherine. *Alice Milligan and the Irish Cultural Revival*. Dublin: Four Courts Press, 2012.

KATHLEEN NI HOULIHAN (1902) BY LADY AUGUSTA GREGORY AND W. B. YEATS

Kathleen (or *Cathleen*) *ni Houlihan* takes place in the small cottage of Peter and Bridget Gillane near Killala, Co. Mayo, on the west coast of Ireland, on the eve of Michael Gillane's wedding and the day of a landing of French troops in support of the United Irishmen rebellion of 1798. Peter and Bridget are seen preparing for their son's wedding to local woman Delia Cahel. Soon the family idyll is disturbed by the appearance of a strange old woman with "her cloak over her face" who appears to have been walking the roads of Ireland alone.[1] Against Michael's wishes, his mother invites the old woman into their home, offering her some food, drink and shelter. Upon request, the old woman shares her story of eviction, igniting sympathy in Michael but alarming his parents, who now consider her as an ominous presence. Peter and Bridget Gillane are right to be concerned: soon after hearing the old woman's story, Michael feels compelled to assist her in "getting [her] beautiful fields back again" and "putting the strangers out of [her] house" (308). Michael is determined to fight for her; even his bride, Delia Cahel, cannot draw him away from the lure of the strange, cloaked woman. After Michael and the old woman leave the house, he meets other Irishmen who are preparing to join forces with the newly arrived French soldiers to fight against British rule in Ireland. *Kathleen ni Houlihan* concludes with Patrick Gillane, Michael's younger brother, declaring to his family that outside the house he sees no ragged woman walking the roads but a young girl with "the walk of a queen" (311).

While still in the cottage, the old woman (or *Shan Van Vocht*) identifies herself as Kathleen ni Houlihan, the daughter of Houlihan. She is one of the female personifications of Ireland, a spirit who has called many Irishmen to fight for her freedom during Ireland's long history of invasions and conquest. Kathleen chants of the necessary self-sacrifice of Irishmen in times of old, as well as in times to come, promising them, as a reward, eternal existence in Irish cultural memory:

> They shall be remembered for ever,
> They shall be alive for ever,
> They shall be speaking for ever,
> The people shall hear them for ever.
>
> (311)

Songs of the Irish ballad tradition such as this and those of Thomas Moore, James Clarence Mangan and Thomas Davis have long been associated with the nationalist movement in Ireland. As the ending of the play makes clear, Michael's decision to follow Kathleen's balladry call to fight for her freedom transforms the spirit of Ireland from that of a haggard old wanderer into that of a beautiful young woman.

Authorship of *Kathleen ni Houlihan* was long contested between Lady Gregory and W. B. Yeats. She claimed much of the text as her own (or co-authored) in the manuscript version of the play, while he claimed it as his own invention in most of his public pronouncements and publications. Scholarship today considers the play to be a collaboration between the two playwrights, as was *The Pot of Broth* (1902) and *The Unicorn from the Stars* (1907). *Kathleen ni Houlihan* infuses peasant realism with political allegory in calling Irishmen to take arms against British rule in Ireland during the United Irishmen rebellion of 1798.[2] This revolutionary spirit was closer to Yeats's own feelings and political activism at the start of the twentieth century than to those of Lady Gregory. He had been flirting with Maud Gonne's nationalist circles in Ireland and France and had been President of a Centenary Association that organised events in Britain and France celebrating the United Irishmen rebellion of 1798. As poet and aspiring playwright, he had been experimenting with tonal speech and poetic dialogue, something he put to good use in *Kathleen ni Houlihan*. Kathleen's siren call to arms was to be uttered in elevated tonal speech, set apart from the Irish peasant dialogue of the Gillane family. Lady Gregory was responsible for the dialogue of the Gillanes, which she wrote in her special brand of Irish dialect that later became known as "Kiltartan." Joseph Holloway described the "intense pathos" of Maire nic Shiubhlaigh (Mary Walker), who played Kathleen on the opening night of the Abbey Theatre on 27 December 1904, when the play was billed with Yeats's *On Baile's Strand*, J. M. Synge's *In the Shadow of the Glen* and Lady Gregory's *Spreading the News*.[3]

Maire nic Shiubhlaigh was not the first to play Kathleen, this honour going to Yeats's long-time muse and love interest, Maud Gonne. *Kathleen ni Houlihan* premiered in St Teresa's Hall on 2 April 1902, produced by a radical women's nationalist association *Inghinidhe na hÉireann* (The Daughters of Erin) and directed by the Fay brothers, William and Frank. Gonne proved mesmerising in the role of Kathleen, rousing patriotic feeling among many young Irishmen and women on the night, as the play itself would do so for many years to come when the Abbey toured it in Ireland, Britain and the United States. On the night of the Dublin premiere of *Kathleen ni Houlihan*, Lady Gregory was away in Venice at a Renaissance palazzo on the Grand Canal, conversing with distinguished members of the British and European aristocracy. Yeats considered the play to be an important contribution to the Irish nationalist movement gathering force at the turn of the twentieth century and feared that it might have ultimately led to the Easter Rising of April 1916, the foundational moment of Ireland's move to political independence from Britain. Yeats was not entirely mistaken: both as playwrights and as leaders of the 1916 rebellion, Thomas McDonagh, Patrick Pearse and James Connolly were certainly influenced by *Kathleen ni Houlihan*. Furthermore, the play was scheduled to be performed on Easter Monday, 24 April 1916, the very day upon which the rebellion broke out in Dublin. Given the historical significance of this date, when Pearse read out the proclamation of an independent Irish Republic on the steps of the General Post Office, and the literary significance of *Kathleen ni Houlihan* for a whole generation of young Irish men and women, Yeats wonders with some justification in his 1938 poem "The Man and the Echo": "Did that play of mine send out/Certain men the English shot?"[4] After all, Irish politician Stephen Gwynn noted after the first performance of the play in 1902: "I went home asking myself if such plays should be produced unless one was prepared for people to go out to shoot and be shot."[5] Soon after the Irish War of Independence (1919–21) began, Lady Gregory herself played the role of Kathleen ni Houlihan at the Abbey Theatre in March 1919, with W. B. Yeats and Maud Gonne MacBride in attendance. At the time, the Irish Republican Army engaged in all-out assault on the Royal Irish Constabulary and

British army garrisons. Lady Gregory's performance was a poignant testimony to the tectonic shift in the Irish political landscape since the time of Maud Gonne's performance at the premiere of *Kathleen ni Houlihan* in 1902. The guerrilla war underway in 1919 was attributable, in some part at least, to the nationalist zeal that *Kathleen ni Houlihan* had aroused in Ireland during the early 1900s.

Eglantina Remport

Notes

1 Lady Gregory (and W. B. Yeats), *Kathleen ni Houlihan*, in *Lady Gregory: Selected Writings*, ed. Lucy McDiamid and Maureen Waters (Harmondsworth: Penguin, 1995), 304. Subsequent references are entered in parentheses.
2 Judith Hill, *Lady Gregory: An Irish Life* (Stroud: Sutton, 2005), 157.
3 Robert Hogan and Michael J. O'Neill, eds, *Joseph Holloway's Abbey Theatre: A Selection from His Unpublished Journal "Impressions of a Dublin Playgoer"* (Carbondale: Southern Illinois University Press, 2009), 51.
4 Norman A. Jeffares, *Yeats's Poems* (London: Macmillan, 1989), 469.
5 Stephen Gwynn, *Irish Literature and Drama in the English Language: A Short History* (London: Thomas Nelson, 1936), 158–9.

Further Reading

McAteer, Michael. *Yeats and European Drama*. Cambridge: Cambridge University Press, 2010.
Pethica, James. "'Our Kathleen': Yeats's Collaboration with Lady Gregory in the Writing of *Cathleen ni Houlihan*." *Yeats Annual* No. 6, 3–31. London: Palgrave Macmillan, 1988.
Pilkington, Lionel. *Theatre and the State in Twentieth-Century Ireland: Cultivating the People*. London: Routledge, 2001.

JOHN BULL'S OTHER ISLAND (1904)
BY BERNARD SHAW

Dublin-born, Nobel Prize-winning playwright Bernard Shaw moved to London at nineteen, hoping to become a successful writer. After a failed attempt to make it as a novelist, Shaw turned to playwriting, and, from 1892, he began producing scripts that placed him squarely in the long line of playwrights from Irish Protestant backgrounds who found success in London with plays aimed at English audiences. This tradition of the "Anglo-Irish comedy of manners"[1] began with Restoration playwrights George Farquhar and William Congreve and was carried on by later figures like Elizabeth Griffith, Oliver Goldsmith, R. B. Sheridan, and Shaw's contemporaries Oscar Wilde and Clotilde Graves.

In their scripts, these playwrights often slyly draw attention to their Irish backgrounds and transfer experiences from their Irish formative years to English contexts. They smuggle in gratuitous references to Ireland in otherwise "English" plays; they comment negatively upon the "English national character"; and they make subversive use of the Stage Irishman (a stock figure that English playwrights had used to mock the Irish but that these playwrights imbue with more intelligence and agency).

In Shaw's early plays, he utilises all of these tropes associated with the "Anglo-Irish comedy of manners." Indeed, while plays from throughout his career can be seen as fitting into this tradition – including the classic *Pygmalion* (1913) – Shaw actually underwent something akin to a conversion between the mid-1890s and early 1900s. Seeing the early plays of W. B. Yeats, Lady Gregory, and J. M. Synge convinced him that it was possible to create plays with wide reach that dealt directly with Ireland. And when they asked Shaw for a play for the opening of the theatre they were founding in Dublin, the Abbey, he composed his first thoroughly Irish play: *John Bull's Other Island*.

The play opens in the London office of two civil engineers, the Englishman Tom Broadbent and the Irishman Larry Doyle. Broadbent and his Cockney valet Hodson are preparing for a trip to Rosscullen in rural Ireland, where the firm is involved in a project. (They are part of a syndicate that is building a new golf resort and – all going well – a Hibernicised version of Ebenezer Howard's Garden City.) Even though Rosscullen is his native village, Doyle has not yet decided if he will be making the trip to Ireland, so Broadbent has decided to employ an Irish guide/assistant for the trip: Tim Haffigan, who is shown into the office by Hodson. Haffigan behaves in an over-the-top, Stage Irish way and is obviously more interested in getting money to buy drink than in being a helpful tour guide. When Doyle returns to the office, Tim gets unnerved and leaves relatively quickly but not before betraying his real Glasgow accent. Doyle proceeds to explain that he knows Haffigan's family back in Rosscullen and that Tim was actually raised in Scotland and was only putting on an "Irish" act to get money from Broadbent, a trick Irish people have long played on gullible English folks. Broadbent and Doyle then discuss Ireland at great length, with Doyle attempting to disabuse Broadbent of his ignorant and romantic notions regarding the "other island" belonging to "John Bull" (England). Eventually, Doyle agrees to accompany Broadbent to Rosscullen and to see his Irish family and friends for the first time in eighteen years.

Doyle's attempts to educate Broadbent in Act I were clearly wasted: the remaining three acts – all set in Rosscullen – demonstrate that Broadbent continues to view Ireland through the prism of unhelpful stereotypes brought over from England. However, Broadbent's bumbling charm results in him getting betrothed to Larry's former sweetheart (Nora), being nominated for the local parliamentary seat, and (with Doyle) effectively buying up the town in order to create the resort. Shaw uses speeches from a defrocked priest called Peter Keegan, a mystic who is widely respected by the locals, in order to decry the materialist values of Broadbent and Doyle. Keegan also sees that Broadbent's "duffer" act hypocritically hides secret, selfish motives and that Doyle's desecration of Rosscullen (and surrendering of Nora to Broadbent) is related to his Irish susceptibility to begrudgery, derision, and self-loathing. That said, Shaw does not spare Keegan: he suggests that Keegan is, like many Irish people, prone to disappearing into dreams/imagination. Keegan, for all of his prophetic vision, is not going to do anything to stop Broadbent and Keegan from turning Rosscullen into a soulless development controlled by a multi-national corporation.

Shaw's play was ahead of its time. He incisively analyses negative aspects of the "Irish national character" (including the tendency to seek refuge in begrudgery or dreams) that he feels were exacerbated by centuries of colonialism. This anticipates much Postcolonial Theory – and, in fact, many connections are made between Ireland and other British colonies in the play and its preface.

Additionally, Shaw perceptively predicts that multinational corporations will buy up beauty spots in Ireland to build golf courses and faux-Irish holiday villages – decades before resorts such as Trump's International Golf Club at Doonbeg became a reality. And Shaw anticipates exactly how banks and "vulture funds" with transnational connections will come to own much Irish property (effectively becoming Ireland's new absentee landlords). Broadbent and Doyle explain to Keegan that they have provided mortgages to local people that are worth more than the homeowners can repay, and that when they foreclose on those mortgages, their syndicate will effectively own Rosscullen – forcing local people into homelessness or emigration.

Another key aspect of the play is Shaw's overturning or complicating of old stereotypes of the English and the Irish. Previous Irish writers depicted the English as either "racist, officious hypocrites" or "sentimental, romantic duffers," whereas Shaw's Broadbent is an ingenious combination of the two; and Shaw's portrait of Broadbent influenced later "Stage English" figures created by James Joyce, Elizabeth Bowen, Sean O'Casey, and Brendan Behan.[2] Shaw's dismissal of crude Stage Irish stereotypes is symbolised by Tim Haffigan being effectively "bum-rushed" from the stage in Act I and the inclusion of a round tower – imported from Dion Boucicault's 1864 "Oirish" melodrama *Arrah-Na-Pogue* – in the Rosscullen landscape, while featuring a much grittier Irish reality than one finds in Boucicault's plays.

Ultimately, so much reality proved to be too much for the Abbey. Yeats told Shaw that he "said things in this play which are entirely true about Ireland, which nobody has ever said before," but explained that the Abbey had to reject it because it was "beyond the [theatre's] resources."[3] In reality, Yeats disliked the play's sprawling form and (presumably) the fact that it was "uncongenial to the whole spirit of the neo-Gaelic movement."[4] That is, it did not demonstrate the "ancient idealism" regarding Ireland's past and its potential future that Gregory and Yeats wanted to see embodied in the theatre's work.[5] Shaw's play premiered at London's Royal Court on 1 November 1904, and it was his first mainstream hit. The Prime Minister, Arthur Balfour, attended the play five times during its initial run, and King Edward VII laughed so hard during a performance that he broke his chair.

The play did have an Irish afterlife. Its Irish debut at Dublin's Theatre Royal was well-received in 1908. The Abbey first produced it in 1916, and they – together with Dublin's Gate Theatre and Belfast's Lyric Theatre – would produce several hit revivals over subsequent decades. Although the Abbey also demurred from premiering Shaw's *next* Irish-set play – *O'Flaherty, V.C.*, which he wrote for the theatre in 1915 – Shaw was actually more involved in the Revivalist project at the Abbey than many realise. The Abbey mounted the world premiere of Shaw's controversial *The Shewing-Up of Blanco Posnet* in 1909, and produced numerous Shaw plays from 1916 onwards (including *O'Flaherty, V.C.*, on tour in 1920). What's more, Shaw spoke at several Abbey fundraisers between 1904 and 1921, and he was even offered a chance to be the third director of the theatre after Synge's death. (He politely declined.) The Irish debuts of Shaw's final Irish-set play, *Tragedy of an Elderly Gentleman* (Part IV of 1921's *Back* to *Methuselah* cycle) and his classic, Irish-influenced, French play *Saint Joan* (1923) took place at Dublin's Gate and Gaiety, respectively.[6] However, Shaw's decision to engage in fully Irish work was first inspired by the Abbey's co-founders and begins with the seminal and prophetic play that he first wrote at their invitation, *John Bull's Other Island*.

David Clare

Notes

1 Vivian Mercier, "Shaw and the Anglo-Irish Comedy of Manners," *New Edinburgh Review* 28 (1975): 22–4.
2 David Clare, *Bernard Shaw's Irish Outlook* (New York: Palgrave Macmillan, 2016), Chapter 4.
3 Quoted in Michael Holroyd, *Bernard Shaw* (London: Vintage, 1998), 306. The quotes are from Yeats and Shaw, respectively.
4 Bernard Shaw, Preface to *John Bull's Other Island* (London: Penguin, 1984), 7.
5 Lady Gregory, *Our Irish Theatre* (London: Putnam, 1913), 8.
6 For the "Irish" aspects of *Saint Joan*, see Clare, 42–54.

Further Reading

Clare, David. *Bernard Shaw's Irish Outlook*, 77–94. New York: Palgrave Macmillan, 2016.
Bohman-Kalaja, Kimberly. "Undoing Identities in Two Irish Shaw Plays: *John Bull's Other Island* and *Pygmalion*." *Shaw* Vol. 30 (2010): 108–32.
Kent, Brad. "Shaw's Everyday Emergency: Commodification in and of 'John Bull's Other Island'." *Shaw* Vol. 26 (2006): 162–79.

THE GAOL GATE (1906) BY LADY AUGUSTA GREGORY

The Gaol Gate concerns two distraught Irishwomen, Mary Cahel and her daughter-in-law Mary Cushin, who have a heartfelt conversation at the gate of Galway Gaol while waiting to see Denis Cahel, Mary Cahel's son and Mary Cushin's husband. As dawn breaks, the gatekeeper of the prison comes to check on them, saying that it is "no place to be spending the night time."[1] The women nervously confess that they have a letter which they could not read because of their lack of education and their fear of local gossip around their locality of Daire-caol. They hope that this letter carries news of Denis's imminent release from prison. The gatekeeper informs them that the letter had been sent to summon them for a final conversation with Denis before his execution, which, it transpires, had already taken place on the previous day. He further informs them that while Denis was not the sole suspect of the case, he was the only one to be found guilty on the grounds that there was no evidence against his friends and neighbours. As a consequence, the two young men also imprisoned in relation to the case, Terry Fury and Pat Ruane, were acquitted of all charges and were released from prison the day before. Upon hearing this, Mary Cahel starts keening her son, not just out of grief at her loss, but also out of relief that he was never an informer after all, despite local gossip of him telling on his friends to save his own skin. *The Gaol Gate* thus ends in Mary Cahel's *caoineadh* (keen), praising her son as an Irish martyr who had taken on the sins of others to protect his fellow Irishmen and remaining defiant in the face of British colonial rule.

The play was first performed on 20 October 1906, billed with Lady Gregory's *Spreading the News* and William Boyle's *The Mineral Workers* at the Abbey Theatre. Since then, the short tragedy has been linked many times to the nationalist movement in Ireland, given the portrayal of an Irish felon unjustly sentenced to death by the partial and prejudiced British colonial judicial system. Contemporary nationalist newspaper reviews brought it to the attention of their readership, *The Freeman's Journal* remarking that *The Gaol Gate* displayed "an infinity of the deepest pathos."[2] More recent criticism also identifies the play with Irish nationalism of the 1900s.[3] While in its setting and its theme, the play undoubtedly carries nationalist sympathies, it is another example of how the politics of Lady Gregory's plays are more ambivalent and intricate that they might at first appear. For one thing, the actual crime for which Denis is imprisoned is never specified; nor is it ever confirmed whether or not Denis had indeed partaken in the crime for which he is hanged. For another, the narrators of this unspecified crime – Mary Cahel, Mary Cushin, the gatekeeper – were not witnesses to it, nor were they present in the court house during Denis's trial. The incident remains shrouded in mystery, with the audience left to *assume* that something very serious had occurred, possibly a murder.

This short tragedy certainly addresses injustices within the British judicial system in the Ireland of the 1900s: the gatekeeper discloses that the only evidence against Denis was a footprint that was found near the house where the incident took place. Lady Gregory, however, also raises for consideration the powerful influence of gossip in Irish rural society, as she had done in a humorous fashion in her famous comedies *Spreading the News* (1904) and *Hyacinth Halvey* (1906). While these plays depict village gossip comically, Lady

Gregory treats gossip in *The Gaol Gate* as a destructive influence, within which reputations of innocent people and their families can be blackened. At the beginning of the play, Denis's family members are distraught because they believe their loved one to be an informer. Denis's wife Mary Cushin declares that Terry Fury's mother, Pat Ruane's mother and Pat Ruane's wife all said that the local sergeant in Daire-caol had boasted about getting information from Denis by plying him with alcohol in prison. Again, it is never revealed whether the sergeant had actually done so or whether the women had made this claim in a moment of frenzy as the two young men were being arrested.

One thing is clear to the audience: Mary Cahel and Mary Cushin believe that Denis may have indeed given information to the police about what had happened. Mary Cushin laments at great length the difficulties that her family will face as a result when they return home to their local village from Galway Gaol. As social outcasts, the family will have no future and feel that their only option is to emigrate to America. Once the gatekeeper tells them that Denis did not give evidence against anyone Denis becomes a Christ-like figure for his mother – a sacrificial lamb – who gives up his own life for the sake of others: "Denis would not speak," she says, "he shut his mouth, he would never be an informer. [...] Come hither, Mary Cushin, till we'll shout it through the roads, Denis Cahel died for his neighbour!" (363). This situation is rather interesting when Denis's sacrifice is set against the unfathomable cowardice of his friends and neighbours: Mary Cahel hints that the whole village seems to know (from hearsay, of course) that Terry Fury had fired the gunshots (of the unspecified crime) as an act of vengeance (for another unspecified crime). Again, what is significant here is the female tragedy at the heart of the play: the mother's *caoineadh* at the end is in defiance of both British judicial rule in Ireland but also of her local Irish community. Contemporary criticism argues that Mary Cahel is the real hero of the play rather than Denis, and Lady Gregory herself would have agreed that the mother's psychological journey was central to the play.[4]

One theatre-goer, Joseph Holloway, wrote of the 20 October 1906 production, that the lighting of the characters and their grouping on stage was "worthy of a great artist's brush" and that it "added to the pathetic grandeur of the tragedy of human life."[5] He identifies here Lady Gregory's awareness of the centuries-old theatrical tradition of the *tableaux vivants*, according to which stage scenes were created to appear as if they were paintings. Lady Gregory herself had become well acquainted with the masterworks of European painting through her husband Sir William, and brought some of the techniques behind great artworks to the staging of her plays at the Abbey Theatre. This is evident in *The Gaol Gate* in the relation between foreground and background as Lady Gregory would have known it from major narrative paintings of the Spanish masters and the Pre-Raphaelites.[6] On stage, the foreground image of the two Marys appears as a realist genre painting; the story of Denis's trial reveals itself as the background to this image of the two keening women. As the background story reveals Denis as a Christ-like figure who sacrifices his life for others, the two Marys at the gate of Galway Gaol become allegories of Mary, mother of Jesus, and Mary Magdalene at the tomb of Jesus, with the gatekeeper as the angel who appears to them in Gospel accounts. Ultimately, *The Gaol Gate* blends together the Irish *caoineadh* tradition with the nineteenth-century tradition of the *tableaux vivants* to create a hauntingly beautiful modern image of the *Visitatio Sepulchri* (the Visitation of the Tomb) dating back to medieval Europe.[7] Lady Gregory blended these three traditions to emphasise the biblical allegory behind the story of the two distraught Irishwomen from Dairecaol, a small townland near her own home in Coole Park, Co. Galway.

Eglantina Remport

Notes

1   Lady Gregory, *The Goal Gate*, in *Lady Gregory: Selected Writings*, ed. Lucy McDiamid and Maureen Waters (Harmondsworth: Penguin, 1995), 359. Subsequent references are entered in parentheses.

2   *The Freeman's Journal*, "The Abbey Theatre: Two New Irish Plays," 23 October 1906, 10.

3   Cathy Leeney, *Irish Women Playwrights, 1900–1939: Gender and Violence on Stage* (New York/Bern: Peter Lang, 2010), 26–7; Lucy McDiarmid, *Poets and the Peacock Dinner: The Literary History of a Meal* (Oxford: Oxford University Press, 2014), 80–92.

4   Dawn Duncan, "Lady Gregory and the Feminine Journey: *The Gaol Gate, Grania*, and *The Story Brought by Brigit*," *Irish University Review* (Lady Gregory Special Issue) Vol. 34, no. 1 (Spring/Summer 2004): 138.

5   Robert Hogan and Michael J. O'Neill, eds, *Joseph Holloway's Abbey Theatre: A Selection from His Unpublished Journal "Impressions of a Dublin Playgoer"* (Carbondale: Southern Illinois University Press, 2009), 73.

6   Eglantina Remport, *Lady Gregory and Irish National Theatre: Art, Drama, Politics* (Basingstoke: Palgrave Macmillan, 2018), 121–56.

7   For further elaboration on the medieval tradition of the *Visitatio Sepulchri*, see Leeney, 26–32.

Further Reading

Pethica, James. "Lady Gregory's Abbey Theatre drama: Ireland real and unreal." In *The Cambridge Companion to Twentieth-Century Irish Drama*, edited by Shaun Richards, 62–78. Cambridge: Cambridge University Press, 2004.

Pilz, Anna. "Lady Gregory's *Gaol Gate*, Terence MacSwiney and the Abbey Theatre." *Irish Studies Review* Vol. 23, no. 3 (2015): 277–91.

THE PLAYBOY OF THE WESTERN WORLD (1907)
BY J. M. SYNGE

Synge's *Playboy* is one of the most celebrated plays of the Irish theatrical repertoire. Yet at its 1907 première at the Abbey Theatre, Dublin, the play was virulently opposed by audience members claiming that it was anti-nationalist, represented the Irish peasantry as innately violent, and impugned the integrity of Irish women. There were fights and police arrests in and outside the theatre;[1] and when *The Playboy* toured in the United States a few years later in 1912, a similar level of disgruntlement saw the Abbey Theatre players temporarily arrested in Philadelphia on grounds of indecency. Despite such inauspicious beginnings, Synge's play quickly achieved canonical status, and has held the stage in Ireland and the English-speaking world ever since.

Set in a "country public house" or "shebeen"[2] in a remote area in the West of Ireland, the play opens with the publican's daughter Pegeen Mike alone on stage, writing a list of requirements for her coming wedding to her cousin, Shawn Keogh. Like Ibsen's *A Doll's House*, Synge's play begins with the focus of attention on an individual and apparently independent young woman. Pegeen is presented as an exuberant character who mocks the priest-fearing timidity of her fiancé, and bemoans the absence from the locality of law-breaking men "the like of Marcus Quinn," who "got six months for maiming ewes, and he a great warrant to tell stories of holy Ireland till he'd have the old women shedding down tears about their feet" (59). Into this isolated peasant setting walks Christy Mahon, a young man from outside the region seeking shelter and, intriguingly, afraid of the police. Under protracted questioning from Pegeen and other locals, Christy eventually reveals that he killed his father (Old Mahon). His audience is impressed and delighted by Christy's narrative. Conscious of the effect that his story of parricide has on the Mayo community, Christy quickly masters the art of storytelling and, with each new iteration, his narrative becomes more colourful and even more exaggerated. The performance practice of storytelling transforms Christy from the "slight young man" "very tired and frightened and dirty" (67) of the beginning to something altogether different: a performer at the height of his power, confident, and the eponymous "playboy of the western world." Emboldened, Christy goes on to achieve even more palpably embodied successes, winning all the prizes in the sports competition ("racing, lepping, dancing, and the Lord knows what!" (133)).

It is at this point (the beginning of Act Three) that Christy and Pegeen fall in love. They do so partly by discovering how much they have in common (a shared loneliness and isolation from their families and communities), and partly because of their joint excitement at the prospect of a future transformed by lyricism and imagination.

Christy. It's little you'll think if my love's a poacher's or an earl's itself when you'll feel my two hands stretched around you, and I squeezing kisses on your puckered lips till I'd feel a kind of pity for the Lord God is all ages sitting lonesome in his golden chair.

Pegeen. That'll be right fun, Christy Mahon, and any girl would walk her heart out before she'd meet a young man was your like for eloquence or talk at all.

(147)

Pegeen and Christy's relationship collapses, however, with the entrance of Old Mahon rushing on stage with a bandage around his head, knocking Christy to the ground and beginning to beat him. Brandishing a "loy" (or spade—the same instrument that he claimed as the original murder weapon) Christy's response is to chase his father off stage and, apparently, kill him. However, while Old Mahon's "resurrection" gives rise to moments of heightened comedy, as when Christy earlier darts behind the door after seeing what he takes to be "the walking spirit of his murdered da" (119), Christy's attempt to kill his father a second time marks a darker shift in the play's tone. Angry and disillusioned, Pegeen now rejects Christy as "an ugly liar was playing off the hero and the fright of men" (163), concluding that "there's a great gap between a gallous story and a dirty deed" (169), and demanding that Christy be sent away. Although previously entranced by his stories, the Mayo peasantry now turns violently against Christy, tying him up with rope and preparing to take him to the police. At this point, farcically and grotesquely Old Mahon, as if rising from the dead for a second time, re-enters, releases Christy from his bondage and demands his filial obedience. But Christy, now more confident than ever, exits the stage triumphantly, driving out his father in front of him: "Ten thousand blessings upon all that's here, for you've turned me a likely gaffer in the end of all, the way I'll go romancing through a romping lifetime from this hour to the dawning of judgement day" (173). However, the play's concluding vignette is of Pegeen grieving. Alone in the society of the County Mayo peasantry to which, nevertheless, she discovers that she belongs, Pegeen adopts the posture of a traditional keener pulling her shawl over her head and lamenting the new isolating loss brought about by her own rejection of Christy: "Oh my grief, I've lost him surely. I've lost the only playboy of the western world" (173). If the play began with a version of a new woman—independent and in touch with her desire—it ends with her defeat, and the celebration instead of a newly invigorated masculine individuality: Christy as a modern individual, untrammelled by traditional social attachments.

The week-long protests at the first performances of Synge's play—the so-called "*Playboy* riots"—are sometimes framed as an age-long conflict between, on the one hand, a modernist-oriented artistic avantgarde and, on the other, a theatre audience bound by convention and conservatism. On the first night the Abbey Theatre director Lady Gregory sent a telegram to her fellow director W. B. Yeats announcing that *The Playboy* was a success, and then a second telegram that retracted this message by stating that the "audience broke up in disorder at the word shift."[3] "Shift," the name for a woman's petticoatlike undergarment, is the word spoken by Christy when he tells the Widow Quin that he'd prefer Pegeen to "a drift of chosen females, standing in their shifts itself maybe, from this place to the Eastern World" (167). Audiences were dismayed at the sexual explicitness of the image, which they took as an attack on the virtue of Irish women. The wild physicality which the play calls for, the lingering traces of the stereotype of the Stage Irishman with which Christy and his father share several characteristics, the Mayo community's taste for violence and the flowery language were also resented. In 1907 *The Playboy* became "a political battleground," audiences begrudging a satirical representation of the West of Ireland, which was at the time "a contested site in the nationalist/colonial struggle."[4] In the negative reactions to the first performance of *The Playboy* there was a strong sense that by presenting an Irish peasant community as capable of turning a parricide into a hero, Synge had undermined claims for Irish national political autonomy just at the very moment when this autonomy was most being sought.[5]

After Ireland's political independence in 1922 *The Playboy* went on to become a regularly performed staple of the Irish theatrical canon. One of the reasons for its enduring vitality is the way in which it celebrates the transformative potential of different kinds of performance practices and especially of the theatre itself. It may be no coincidence, therefore, that *The Playboy* continues to have a powerful theatrical afterlife not only in Druid's celebrated hyper-realist productions since the mid-1970s, but more recently, in various intercultural adaptations including the 2006 Chinese production by Pan Pan, and the 2007 rewriting of the play by Bisi Adigun and Roddy Doyle.

Hélène Lecossois

Notes

1 Christopher Morash, *A History of Irish Theatre 1601–2000* (Cambridge: Cambridge University Press, 2002), 130–8.
2 J. M. Synge, *The Playboy of the Western World,* in *Collected Works IV: Plays II*, ed. Ann Saddlemyer (Gerrards Cross: Colin Smythe, 1982), 57. Subsequent references are entered in parentheses.
3 W. B. Yeats, "J. M. Synge and the Ireland of his Time," in *Essays and Introductions* (London: Palgrave Macmillan, 1961), 311.
4 Nicholas Grene, *The Politics of Irish Drama* (Cambridge: Cambridge University Press, 1999), 79, 97.
5 Lionel Pilkington, "The Pitfalls of Theatrical Consciousness," *Kritika Kultura* 21/22 (2014): 533–42.

Further Reading

Collins, Christopher. *The Playboy of the Western World.* London: Routledge, 2016.
Frazier, Adrian, ed. *Playboys of the Western World: Production Histories.* Dublin: Carysfort Press, 2004.
Lecossois, Hélène. "'Groaning wicked like a maddening dog': Bestiality, Modernity and Irishness in J. M. Synge's *The Playboy of the Western World.*" *Sillages Critiques* No. 20, 2016. https://doi.org/10.4000/sillagescr itiques.4441. Accessed 18 October 2021.
Synge, J. M. *The Playboy of the Western World.* Edited by Christopher Collins. London: Methuen Drama, 2021.

HARVEST (1910) BY LENNOX ROBINSON

At the opening of *Harvest*, which premiered at the Abbey Theatre, Dublin on 19 May 1910, newly-weds Jack and Mildred Hurley arrive at his family's farmhouse in Knockmalgloss, only for Mildred to express her disappointment. "But I thought it was a cottage ... a thatched cottage" she complains and seeks Jack's assurance as to the

Irish authenticity of his family: "I mean this house is really a peasant's house, and your father and Maurice are real, genuine peasants, aren't they?"[1] On seeing the interior of the house, however, her reassurance is immediate: "it's perfectly lovely. There's an open fire and a big pot hanging over it ... and there's turf! ... It's just like a scene at the Abbey Theatre" (2).

The Dublin-born daughter of a wealthy landowner, Mildred is representative of those who sentimentalised rural life in ignorance of its harsh reality. Her rhapsody about having "to get close to the soil, to get to know the great, eternal mother of us all" (3) parodies the nationalist sensibility of the time and allows audiences to laugh at a position which might be uncomfortably close to their own. The comic potential of the Irish bourgeoisie's idealisation of peasant life had already been realised in Gerald MacNamara's *The Mist That Does Be On the Bog* (1909), with its titular allusion to lines from J. M. Synge's *In the Shadow of the Glen* (1903). But despite opening on these notes of comic meta-theatricality and parody Robinson's darker intent becomes clear as the reality of the family's crippling debt is revealed. This was caused by the cost of an education for Jack and three of his four brothers which has enabled them to enter the professional class; Jack as a chemist in Dublin and the others a civil servant, a solicitor and a priest respectively. Only Maurice, the brother who has had to stay on the farm, strikes a discordant note and the act closes as he says he'd like to break the neck of William Lordan, the schoolteacher who enabled this financially ruinous upward mobility, and *"raises his arm as if to strike Lordan"* (19).

Robinson's first play, *The Clancy Name*, had been staged at the Abbey in 1908 and judged to be "a shocking and libellous picture" of Irish country people.[2] His own view was that his work "brought for the first time on an Irish stage harsh reality." Indeed, he said, "We must criticise ourselves ruthlessly."[3] When Jack points out to Mildred that "There used to be a big manure heap here (*pointing*) just in front of the door" (4) he is surely evoking the audience's memory of the earlier play which, Robinson commented, was "as realistic as the midden in front of an Irish farm-house."[4] But if the audience expected that the absence of the manure heap from the stage world of *Harvest* meant that Robinson was no longer committed to a harsh realism, Acts Two and Three of the play showed otherwise.

Act Two is set on the next day, following a night in which a fire has destroyed three farm buildings adding to the disquiet over the debt. The reality is that the father started the fire in order to claim compensation, a fact which determines Jack to leave Dublin and work on the farm, so avoiding the dishonesty of making a false claim; a plan to which Mildred readily agrees. Amidst the disruption of the fire and the disappointment that the brother who became a solicitor prefers to treat himself to a motorcar rather than help the family, the only apparent positive is the return from London of Mary, Jack's sister. But the fact that Mary is not the "country girl with a thin veneer of civilisation" (31) expected by Mildred, but something more mysterious, proves to be the controversial crux of the play.

Act Three opens three weeks later when the harsh reality of farm work has started to dawn on the newly-weds; Mildred is exhausted having spent two hours trying to churn butter while Jack has passed out while working in the fields. As Mildred acknowledges, "It's all very well to look at it from a distance, but … it's hateful to have to live it" (41). Jack's despair at failing to meet the demands of farming is alleviated by Mary's news that their brother, the civil servant, has sent fifty pounds and promised to send more. However, the mood of celebration is broken by Mary's declaration that she is returning to London and, on being pressed by Jack for details of her life, acknowledges that, dissatisfied with her work as a typist, she became the mistress of her married employer who has sent her the fifty pounds. Mary's return home was fuelled by a desire to escape her situation, but she finds that she is still "longing for that life, and its excitement and splendour and colour" (49) and determines to return to London and her lover.

Harvest opened on an August afternoon with the arrival of the newly-weds but advances to the breakup of their marriage and a destruction of all Mildred's ideas about the nobility of peasant life. She now sees Knockmalgloss as "this hole of a place" (52) while Jack brutally confronts her with the fact that "You made a mistake when you married me – damn you" (54). Mary has savaged Lordon, the retired schoolteacher, with the fact that the harvest of social successes in which he is so proud is in reality a crop of deracinated, discontented individuals. But this is a truth he prefers not to accept and readily agrees with Maurice's contention that Mary was just joking. The play closes as, based on the fifty pounds provided by Mary, the farm is saved and Maurice can marry, ignorant of the truth as to the source of the money on which his happiness is based.

W. B. Yeats coined the term "Cork Realists" to describe Robinson and fellow playwrights T. C. Murray and R. J. Ray. Far from the "ancient idealism" to which Yeats wanted theatre to be dedicated, they staged an un-idealised Ireland showing the people as "guilty of arson, steeped in trickery and jobbery."[5] The depiction of Mary was the most contentious aspect of the play as women were the idealised embodiment of Ireland, to question their virtue was to doubt that of the nation and audiences reacted with hostility to any such depictions. *Harvest*, in the words of the nationalist *Evening Telegraph*, was "repellent, repulsive, abhorrent" with the final act being "a mere seething pot of vice, filth, meanness, dishonour, dishonesty, depravity and duplicity." Indeed, said the reviewer, it "out-Synges Synge"; an allusion to his *The Playboy of the Western World* (1907) whose depiction of peasant life caused riots on the occasion of its premiere.[6]

Driven more by a sense of moral outrage than a political position, the Cork Realists were an antidote to the idealised view of Ireland. But although Robinson admired Ibsen and aspired to an equivalent rigour of analysis *Harvest* lacks the Norwegian's clarity of focus on the causes of a dysfunctional society, wielding a flail rather than scalpel. Following three nights at the Abbey in May 1910, *Harvest* was staged at the theatre on seven more occasions in the following year and was also part of a tour to England and the United States, ending its production history at Maxine Elliott's Theatre, New York, in December 1911.

Robinson progressively moved to less contentious dramas and while, as he acknowledged, there was a brief return of social criticism with Sean O'Casey's *Dublin Trilogy* (1923–26) when "The bubble of false sentimentality which we Cork realists had pricked years before was beginning to be blown up again" but the impetus was largely over and there were few plays like *Harvest* which aimed to disturb the country's increasingly self-satisfied conservatism and cultural conformity.[7]

Shaun Richards

Notes

1 Lennox Robinson, *Two Plays: Harvest; The Clancy Name* (Dublin: Maunsel & Co., 1911), 1–3. Subsequent references are entered in parentheses.

2 Robert Hogan and James Kilroy, eds, *The Abbey Theatre: The Years of Synge, 1904–1909* (Dublin: Dolmen Press, 1978), 225.

3 Lennox Robinson, *Curtain Up: An Autobiography* (London: Michael Joseph, 1942), 21–2.

4 Ibid., 18–19.

5 Ibid., 22.

6 Robert Hogan, Richard Burnham and Daniel P. Poteet, eds, *The Modern Irish Drama Vol. 4: The Rise of the Realists, 1910–1915* (Dublin: Dolmen Press, 1979), 33–4.

7 Robinson, *Curtain Up*, 140.

Further Reading

Murray, Christopher. "Lennox Robinson: The Abbey's Anti-Hero." In *Irish Writers and the Theatre*, edited by Masaru Sekine, 114–33. Gerrards Cross: Colin Smythe, 1986.

Richards, Shaun. "'We were very Young and we Shrank from Nothing': Realism and Early Twentieth-Century Irish Drama." In *The Oxford Handbook of Modern Irish Theatre*, edited by Nicholas Grene and Chris Morash, 105–20. Oxford: Oxford University Press, 2016.

AT THE HAWK'S WELL (1916) BY W. B. YEATS

First performed at the London drawing room of Lady Cunard, and that of Lady Islington soon after, in April 1916, *At the Hawk's Well* begins with musicians evoking the setting as they unfold and refold a cloth upon which appears the image of a hawk. They sing of a lonely place where an old abandoned well lies beside bare trees up to where a man climbs. The musicians describe a mountainside scene at nightfall, where a Guardian sits by that dried-up well, and of the Old Man who has been waiting "fifty years" for its waters to flow.[1] As part of Yeats's non-naturalist approach none of the physical elements are represented realistically: the well is indicated only by a square blue cloth beside which the Guardian sits, a figure covered entirely by a black cloak. This absence of stage picture was in keeping with a desire that Yeats harboured since he first became involved in writing drama: delivered with the right sense of melody and emphasis, poetic speech might not only succeed in creating the mood of a play but also convey its setting and movement. Beginning his play with musicians chanting rather than characters speaking, Yeats revives a Greek tradition of the chorus, a tradition evident also in his use of masks for the two main characters, the Old Man and the Young Man who is Cuchulain, the warrior of Irish legend. *At the Hawk's Well* is the third of Yeats's plays in which Cuchulain features as one of the central characters, but it is the first in which he has characters appear in masks. Edward Gordon Craig had planned to use them in the 1911 production of Yeats's *The Shadowy Waters* at the Abbey Theatre, but it is not until Edmund Dulac designed masks for *At the Hawk's Well* that masks were actually used in a Yeats play.

The Old Man is never given a proper name, suggesting that he is to be understood more as an archetype than an individual character. This aligns *At the Hawk's Well* with Expressionist drama of the 1900s and the years of the First World War, where such generic names as "Man," "Old Man" and "Woman" are found in plays by August Strindberg,

George Kaiser, Oskar Kokoschka and Ernst Toller. The Old Man appeals to the Guardian of the Well to move or speak, her blank stare and her unwavering stillness "enough to drive an old man crazy" (403). Her silence is interrupted by the appearance of a Young Man, who reveals himself as Cuchulain. The Old Man entreats him to "Go from this accursed place!," telling him that "I came like you/When young in body and mind," blown by what he had then thought was "a lucky sail" that would lead him to the miraculous water (405). Instead he finds himself cheated by "the holy shades/ That dance upon the desolate mountain," wasting away the years in forlorn hope that the water would eventually flow (405). When the Young Man speaks of his determination to remain at the spot so as to attain immortality, the Guardian of the Well emits the cry of a hawk. The young Cuchulain takes this as an omen, having been attacked by a hawk – "the best in the world / I had fancied" – on his way to the lonely spot (406). In keeping with Yeats's belief in birds as spirits in physical form, the Old Man believes this hawk to be "The Woman of the Sidhe her-self/The mountain witch" who is "always flitting upon this mountain-side / To allure or to destroy" (407).[2] This spirit figure has its origins in Irish folklore tradition with which Yeats was long familiar.[3] The Old Man speaks of the curse that falls on anyone who gazes into the "unmoistened eyes" of the Woman of the Sidhe: "Never to win a woman's love and keep it," "Or it may be that she will kill your chil-dren," potentially even maddening the victim to the point of killing them himself (407–8). This disturbing prospect points ahead to Yeats's controversial filicide play, *Purgatory* (1938), but more immediately, it links *At the Hawk's Well* with Yeats's first Cuchulain play of 1904, *On Baile's Strand*. This is a play in which Conchubar, High King of Uladh, worries that as Cuchulain has declared his love for Aoife, "that fierce woman" who now will leave "no army in idleness/That might bring ruin on this land you serve" he will not defend the kingdom against her.[4] It ends with Cuchulain's descent into madness, fighting the waves of the sea after discovering that the Young Man whom he has just killed in defence of the land was his own son by Aoife.

The cry of the hawk proves a fateful premonition in *At the Hawk's Well*. When hearing it a second time, Cuchulain realises that it comes from the mouth of the Guardian of the Well. The Old Man tells him that it is not the Guardian's voice that utters it, but the spirit of the Sidhe that possesses her. Cuchulain's fate is sealed when the eyes of this Guardian meet his, hers an unhuman stare. The Guardian *"throws off her cloak and rises. Her dress under the cloak suggests a hawk"* and begins to dance, *"moving like a hawk"* (409), prompting the Young Man to fall into a trance and the Old Man to fall asleep. After the dance has concluded, Cuchulain "*drops his spear as if in a dream*" and follows the Guardian off stage (410). The Old Man awakens to discover that he has missed the flow of the well's waters and curses "the shadows" that have deluded him. When the Young Man returns, he hears the name of Aoife cried out among the hills. In the stage performance, the cries are made by the musicians, thereby blurring the boundaries between their roles as commentators and participants (411).

The name Aoife also recalls *On Baile's Strand*. She was the mother of the Young Man, sent to avenge the man who had fathered him. Before the combat in *On Baile's Strand*, the Young Man tells Cuchulain "I am of Aoife's country" (501) and later the Fool reveals to him "that the young man was Aoife's son" (521). Yeats found the story of Aoife's son in Lady Gregory's *Cuchulain of Muirthemne* of 1902, based on original Irish-language manuscript sources. The story records that after defeating Aoife's army in battle in Scotland, Cuchulain fathers a child with her.[5] *At the Hawk's Well* concludes with Old Man declaring that the Woman of the Sidhe has "roused up the fierce women of the hills/Aoife and all her troop" while Cuchulain, as the hot-headed Young Man, declares "I will face them" and goes out "*no longer as in a dream*" (412).

At the Hawk's Well is remarkable in successfully rendering a scene developed from old Irish mythology through daring new experiments with the medium of theatre, working in collaboration with Edmund Dulac. Most ambitious of all was the Hawk dance of the Guardian of the Well as the moment of catharsis. It was performed in the first London and Dublin stagings by Michio Ito, a Japanese dancer who had trained with the French choreographer Émile Jaques-Dalcroze and who possessed knowledge of the medieval tradition of Japanese Noh theatre. Yeats learnt of this tradition mainly through his association with Ezra Pound in the 1910s, Pound having in his possession the papers of Ernest Fennollosa, an American expert in Japanese art history who had lived for a time in Toyko. Yeats would adapt the Noh form more consistently in subsequent dance plays like *The Dreaming of the Bones* (1919) and *The Only Jealousy of Emer* (1919) but in *At the Hawk's Well*, audiences encounter an eerily atmospheric Sino-Celtic alignment of Irish myth with Japanese form. The play occupies a pivotal position in non-naturalist European modernist theatre between the 1890s Symbolism of Maurice Maeterlinck and the 1950s minimalism of Samuel Beckett.

Michael McAteer

Notes

1   W. B. Yeats, *At the Hawk's Well*, in *The Variorum Edition of the Plays of W. B. Yeats*, ed. Russell K. Alspach (London: Macmillan, 1966), 401. Subsequent references are entered in parentheses.
2   For further discussion on bird symbolism in Yeats's work, see Nicholas Grene, *Yeats's Poetic Codes* (Oxford: Oxford University Press, 2008), 104–33.
3   W. B. Yeats, "'Irish Fairies" (1888) and "Irish Fairies, Ghosts, Witches'" (1889), in *Writings on Irish Folklore, Legend and Myth*, ed. Robert Welch (London: Penguin, 1993), 8–25.
4   W. B. Yeats, *On Baile's Strand*, in *The Variorum Edition of the Plays of W. B. Yeats*, 488–9. Subsequent references are entered in parentheses.
5   Lady Augusta Gregory, *Cuchulain of Muirthemne: The Story of the Men of the Red Branch of Ulster* (1902), 4th edn (London: John Murray, 1911), 313–19.

Further Reading

Cave, Richard. "Modernism and Irish Theatre 1900–1940." In *The Oxford Handbook of Modern Irish Theatre*, edited by Nicholas Grene and Chris Morash, 121–37. Oxford: Oxford University Press, 2016.
Ellis, Sylvia. *The Plays of W. B. Yeats: Yeats and the Dancer*. London: Palgrave Macmillan, 1999.
McAteer, Michael. *Yeats and European Drama*, 87–109. Cambridge: Cambridge University Press, 2010.

THE PLOUGH AND THE STARS (1926)
BY SEAN O'CASEY

On Thursday 11 February 1926, the performers of the Abbey, Ireland's national theatre, faced a group of unruly playgoers. Spectators booed, chanted nationalist songs and slogans, and attempted to destroy the playhouse's furniture. One rioter even attacked two of the female performers, before being clobbered from the stage. When W. B. Yeats rose to praise the interrupted play, someone lobbed a shoe at his head.

The play in question was O'Casey's *The Plough and the Stars*, the third piece in what is sometimes called his *Dublin Trilogy*. In 1923, the Abbey had premiered *The Shadow of a Gunman*; *Juno and the Paycock* appeared at the same venue in 1924; and *The Plough and the Stars* followed two years later. These three works have different characters and are non-sequential, but all take place in Dublin's tenements during the recent Irish revolutionary period (1916–23), and express sympathy towards the urban poor, dislike of British rule, as well as antipathy for the violence that Irish patriotism might inspire.

The Plough and the Stars is set in Dublin before and during the Easter Rising of 1916, a six-day rebellion during the First World War, when armed nationalists attempted to establish a Republic of Ireland. The main onstage action of O'Casey's play occurs in a tenement room occupied by the recently wedded Nora and Jack Clitheroe. Jack feels wearied by his wife's affections and excited instead by the notion of fighting for Ireland. Despite Nora's attempts to protect him, he is promoted to officer in the Irish Citizen Army, one of the militias that fought during the real-life Rising, and he dashes away to battle the British. In the second act, he and his companions thrill to the rhetoric of a nameless nationalist leader, whose words are undercut by the boozy pratfalls and prostitution of a Dublin pub. The bleak, later section of the play is set during the final phase of the failed uprising, when a pregnant Nora tries to haul Jack back into the safety of the tenement. He pushes her away and causes her to miscarry. Another young child in the tenement dies of consumption, Jack himself is killed, and Nora becomes insane with grief. At the end of the play, a Protestant neighbour, Bessie Burgess, attempts to care for Nora, and is in turn shot while dragging Nora away from a window. Finally, a group of British soldiers invade the building as Dublin blazes in flames.

The Plough and the Stars expressed exasperation with the Easter Rising and its participants, many of whom O'Casey knew well. O'Casey himself had been a member of the Irish Republican Brotherhood (IRB), the oath-bound group whose military council planned the Rising. O'Casey had even helped to organise the publicity for a theatrical pageant staged in 1913 by one of the Rising's future leaders, Patrick Pearse. O'Casey had also played a significant role in establishing the Irish Citizen Army (ICA), the group for whom Jack Clitheroe fights during the play. O'Casey penned that militia's constitution of March 1914, part of which would be recycled during 1916 in the proclamation of the Irish Republic.

But by 1926, O'Casey had lost his affinity with these groups. When police had crushed a workers' strike in Dublin during 1913, O'Casey felt appalled that nationalists had failed to support the strikers, and he abandoned the IRB. He also felt dismayed that Patrick Pearse –the best-known martyr of Easter Week – had ignored the strike and travelled by tram during that lockout. By the end of 1914 O'Casey had also abandoned the ICA after a row about the role occupied within by the aristocratic Countess Markievicz. In 1916, then, the IRB led the Citizen Army (with Markievicz) and the Irish Volunteers (with

Pearse) into the fight against the British Army. Consequently, during Easter week, O'Casey stayed at home, and later wrote *The Plough and the Stars* in response to those events.

The first performance of *The Plough and the Stars* came shortly before the tenth anniversary of the Easter Rising, in a playhouse that stood amidst the former battleground, and performed by an acting company in receipt of a subsidy from the Irish Free State. In this context, O'Casey presented a play that set high patriotic principles alongside music-hall slapstick; co-opted melodramatic techniques without the attendant drive to reconciliation; and presented a morbific version of Irish nationalism. He especially appeared to mock Patrick Pearse, with some of Pearse's best-known writings appearing in the mouth of the demagogic orator who appears, at the same time as a prostitute, during Act Two.

For those who protested against his work, O'Casey had provided a grotesque distortion of historical events: his play slandered those who had died for Ireland, and so necessitated a demonstration on the fourth night of the run. Most unfortunately for the theatre management, the riot featured a co-ordinated appearance from the real-life widows and bereaved women of 1916, including the mother of Patrick Pearse, who arrived at the theatre to protest against what was presented onstage.

This public protest and its attendant media storm gave O'Casey a reputation for being an iconoclast. Yet he always retained sympathy for the rebels and felt wounded by the hostility that his play generated. He remained particularly grieved by the objections of Hanna Sheehy Skeffington, whose pacifist husband had been murdered by a British soldier during the Rising. O'Casey, who praised and admired her husband as a socialist martyr, now decided that enough was enough. Less than one month after *The Plough and the Stars* premiered, O'Casey abandoned living in Ireland, and moved to England for the rest of his life. By 1928, the cords looked like they had been cut completely, when the Abbey rejected his next play.

O'Casey was shocked by the hostile reaction to *The Plough and the Stars*. He pointed out that the Abbey had already presented a satirical portrait of the Easter rebels in the shape of Maurice Dalton's *Sable and Gold* (1918), and argued that *The Plough and the Stars* was never intended as a direct insult to Patrick Pearse. Indeed, O'Casey's drama does not present an unmitigated attack on the rebels. At one of the most memorable moments of the play, Fluther highlights the appallingly unequal odds faced by the insurgents, asking a British soldier, "D'ye want us to come out in our skins an' throw stones?"[1]

Nationalism is scarcely the only ideology that O'Casey mocks in *The Plough and the Stars*. The play is notably cynical about O'Casey's own brand of Marxism, with the author parodying his personal left-wing beliefs through the character of The Covey. The play also expresses distaste for British imperialism: O'Casey himself, when scripting his play, avidly followed news from the high court in London, where a libel action was proceeding over the Amritsar massacre of 1919. One British general told the court that bombs, whips, and machine guns provided acceptable ways of restoring law and order in colonial situations. In Dublin, O'Casey read and retained the newspaper that reported these comments, and in *The Plough and the Stars* we hear an echo of such imperial brutality, as Corporal Stoddart declares, "We'll jab the belly aht of 'im."[2]

In one powerful later critique, Seamus Deane argues that the play's rejection of all ideology and its favouring of the realm of the maternal, offers no real solution to the political problems of twentieth-century Ireland. In the context of the "Troubles" (c.1968–98) some theatre makers had indeed made rather facile attempts to connect O'Casey's work with the later conflict. Yet, despite all the harsh comments made about O'Casey's work, Irish audiences have consistently appreciated *The Plough and the Stars*. Following the initial riots, the play helped the Abbey Theatre to stay afloat through the late 1920s, and in the later twentieth century, it become a touchstone in Irish cultural debate. By the early twenty-first century, the play triggered a political campaign to relocate the entire national theatre to the General Post Office (the rebel headquarters in 1916), and a high-profile Abbey Theatre version of the play became central to Ireland's centenary commemorations of the Easter Rising in 2016. Admirers can find in the play a piece of writing that is Shakespearean in scope, with O'Casey dramatising one of the foundational historical narratives of Ireland with humour and with humanity. Part of the reason why O'Casey's play has continued to hold the Irish stage for decades is that, whatever the political enthusiasms of the moment, *The Plough and the Stars* continues to remind audiences of the lives of the poor and neglected. But this drama is no dry tract or treatise. Rather, the play is funny and profound; it draws on music hall and melodrama, and it reminds spectators of how the best arguments against inequality can be made with pathos, laughter, and song.

James Moran

Notes

1 Sean O'Casey, *The Plough and the Stars*, in *The Complete Plays of Sean O'Casey: Vol. I* (London: Macmillan, 1984), 255.
2 Ibid., 250.

Further Reading

Deane, Seamus. "O'Casey and Yeats: Exemplary Dramatists." In *Celtic Revivals: Essays in Modern Irish Literature, 1880–1980*, 108–23. London: Faber & Faber, 1985.

McDonald, Ronan. "Sean O'Casey's Dublin Trilogy: Disillusionment to Delusion." In *The Cambridge Companion to Twentieth-Century Irish Drama*, edited by Shaun Richards, 136–49. Cambridge: Cambridge University Press, 2004.

Murray, Christopher. *Seán O'Casey: Writer at Work*. Dublin: Gill and Macmillan, 1984.

THE OLD LADY SAYS "NO!" (1929)
BY DENIS JOHNSTON

Denis Johnston's *The Old Lady Says "No!"*, the final production of the Dublin Gate Theatre Studio's second season, was one of the most stylistically radical – and politically pertinent – plays of the Free State years. The young barrister's debut play premiered on 3 July 1929, directed by Hilton Edwards and starring Micheál mac Liammóir in the lead role as "The Speaker." This opaque designation already flags one of the play's many expressionist elements, but at the same time *The Old Lady Says "No!"* is firmly rooted in both Irish history and the contemporary Free State. Indeed, the innovative staging and lighting techniques that Edwards and mac Liammóir were championing at the Gate Theatre provided the means by which Johnston could construct a multifaceted critique of the cultic veneration of Irish revolutionary history, even as he questioned the complacency of believing that the Free State truly embodied the ideals that had led to its establishment.

The play's opening scene is a far cry from the expressionist extravaganza that soon follows: the initial action is an overly melodramatic rendition of the arrest of the famous rebel leader Robert Emmet, who headed the failed 1803 insurrection but was unwilling to flee the country and leave his beloved Sarah Curran behind. As Major Sirr tries to place Emmet into custody, one of the British soldiers clobbers the rebel over the head with his musket: the stage lights flicker and the actor playing Emmet – the Speaker – remains floored, forcing the rest of the befuddled cast to break character and ask for medical assistance. As a Doctor clears the stage, mysterious figures begin to dance behind a gauze curtain and a drum starts pounding ominously. After a few moments, the Speaker seemingly regains consciousness, but the audience is actually experiencing the actor's concussed delirium, which provides a fruitful setting for reflections on how Emmet's legacy persists in 1920s Ireland.

The expressionist dreamscape that is subsequently presented includes a talking statue of the eighteenth-century politician Henry Grattan, a Flower Woman who bastardises lines from W. B. Yeats and Lady Gregory's nationalist classic *Kathleen ni Houlihan* (1902), and the Speaker, who now believes himself to truly be Robert Emmet, anachronistically declaiming a speech by Patrick Pearse, one of the leaders of the 1916 Easter Rising. This temporal chaos also marks what remains of the plot: the Speaker navigates contemporary Dublin to find a bus to Rathfarnham, the home of Sarah Curran, in a desperate attempt to rescue his love and liberate the Irish nation from British rule. Of course, Ireland has already achieved independence, and the Speaker's failure to recognise this casts shadows on the Free State's legitimacy as the incarnation of the revolutionary ideals for which Emmet gave his life.

Indeed, Grattan's statue bitterly articulates how Ireland has condemned itself to an endless purgatory, observing that his country is "Driven blindly on by the fury of our pitiable moral courage! Is there to be no rest for Ireland from her Soul? What monstrous blasphemy has she committed to be condemned to drift for ever like the wandering Jew after a Heaven that can never be?"[1] He goes on to highlight the contrast between his own attempts at parliamentary reform and the violence that later generations of Irish nationalists embraced:

Grattan. In my day Dublin was the second city of a mighty Empire. What is she now?
Speaker. No! No!
Grattan. *[with unutterable scorn]*. Free!
[He bursts into a wild peal of laughter.]

(54)

In the final part of the first act, the Speaker's revolutionary zeal is put to the test even further when his attempts to rally the Irish people for his cause are undermined by the Flower Woman, who is played by the same actor as Sarah Curran (just as Major Sirr and the Grattan statue are doubled parts). When Emmet rebukes her, she reveals his fake identity to the bystanders: "An' a nice lot a bowsy scuts youse are, God knows! Emmet! He-he-he! Up Emmet! Let me tell youse that fella's not all he says he is!" (64).

By this stage, the same doubt is growing about the revolutionary cause more generally, even if the contemporary Dubliners are likewise portrayed in an unflattering light. The act ends with the Speaker firing into the crowd that is closing in on him, thereby fatally wounding a man named Joe. In the ensuing chaos, the Flower Woman adopts Sarah Curran's voice again to speak lines from *Kathleen ni Houlihan* that celebrate martyrdom ("Do not make a great keening / When the graves have been dug tomorrow" [69]), and the curtain drops on the Speaker frantically searching for his beloved Sarah.

The second act opens with more straightforward satire: the Speaker crashes a party where the Minister for Arts and Crafts is entertaining guests who mostly excel at spouting vapid and self-congratulatory remarks about the Free State's moral rectitude. Many of these statements are parroted by a Chorus, which speaks in an expressionist stream of consciousness that modulates between mindless prattle and darker undercurrents, such as advocating censorship: "Clean and pure Art for clean and pure people" (72). Robert Emmet's appearance at the gathering causes some surprise, but he is quickly welcomed and integrated into the cacophony of voices that begin to overlap and which include wistful reflections on the good old days of revolutionary violence: "Sometimes I wish I was back again on the run with the old flying column out by the Glen of Aherlow" (82). The socialites, then, are less interested in creating a viable future for Ireland than in fetishising its bloody past.

As the scene morphs again, the Speaker finds himself in the company of a blind man who likewise observes that, in Ireland, "the ghosts of the dead and the half dead and them that will never die [...] can find lazy, idle hearts in which their withered hates may still live and burn" (86). As Sarah Curran's voice is heard once more, the lights come up and the setting is transformed to a tenement house where Joe, the man whom the Speaker shot earlier, lies dying. Sean O'Casey's *Dublin Trilogy* (1923–1926) resonates strongly here, and Johnston's characters debate the power of revolutionary rhetoric until Joe, with his dying breaths, curses his own mother, the Flower Woman, who, as both Sarah Curran and Kathleen ni Houlihan, also represents Ireland: "[*through his teeth*]. Strumpet! Strumpet!" (91).

Such obscenities return in the final scene of the play, for after Joe dies and various half-hearted mourners come to pay their respects, a mass of dancing Shadows and rhythmic Voices perform his wake. In a wild frenzy, quotations from Swift, Mangan, Yeats, Joyce, and others create an intertextual tapestry that eventually sees the Speaker resurfacing as Robert Emmet and proclaiming Dublin to be a "Strumpet City in the sunset" that nevertheless "one day will walk the streets of Paradise / Head high and unashamed" (101). This declaration ends with an appeal to the audience – "There now. Let my epitaph be written" (101) – which recasts the conclusion of the famous speech that the historical Emmet gave shortly before he was condemned to death: "when my country takes her place among the nations of the earth, then, and not till then, let my epitaph be written."[2] After Speaker falls asleep onstage, the Doctor returns from the wings to attend to him as the curtains are drawn.

The Old Lady Says "No!", then, is both satirical and harrowing, and its politics are deliberately difficult to pin down: it reveals how hollow rhetoric can boom powerfully, how blazing idealism can be dangerously beautiful, and how dreams of revolution can animate a people but also drain it of life. No less compellingly, the play employs a wide range of expressionist techniques to endow Robert Emmet with an elusive quality that embodies precisely such conflicted politics. Ultimately, it remains up to the audience to decide what Emmet's epitaph – and the place of nationalist ideology in Irish society – should be. The Doctor's final gesture is hushing the audience, but after the curtain is drawn, what do they say?

Ruud van den Beuken

Notes

1 Denis Johnston, *The Old Lady Says "No!"*, in *Plays of Changing Ireland*, ed. Curtis Canfield (New York: Macmillan, 1936), 54. Subsequent references are entered in parentheses.
2 Quoted in Patrick M. Geoghegan, *Robert Emmet: A Life* (Montreal: McGill-Queen's University Press, 2002), 254.

Further Reading

Ferrar, Harold. *Denis Johnston's Irish Theatre*. Dublin: Dolmen Press, 1973.
Pilný, Ondřej. *Irony and Identity in Modern Irish Drama*. Prague: Litteraria Pragensia, 2008.
Poulain, Alexandra. *Irish Drama, Modernity, and the Passion Play*. London: Palgrave Macmillan, 2016.
St Peter, Christine. Introduction to *The Old Lady Says "No!"*, by Denis Johnston, 1–45. Washington, DC: Catholic University of America Press, 1992.
Van den Beuken, Ruud. *Avant-Garde Nationalism at the Dublin Gate Theatre, 1928–1940*. Syracuse, NY: Syracuse University Press, 2021.

YOUTH'S THE SEASON–? (1931) BY MARY MANNING

On 8 December 1931, the Dublin Gate Theatre presented *Youth's the Season–?*, a singularly funny, scathing, and macabre play. Its author, Mary Manning, was only 26 years old when it was first produced, and with this remarkable debut, she captured that paradoxical adolescent mood of gloom and exuberance, of self-doubt and accusation. The play already signals this disposition through its truncated title, which takes its cue from the *cotillon* (a round dance) that occurs in the second act of John Gay's *The Beggar's Opera* (1728):

> Youth's the Season made for Joys,
> Love is then our Duty,
> She alone who that employs,
> Well deserves her Beauty.
> Let's be gay,
> While we may,Beauty's a Flower, despis'd in decay.
> Youth's the Season &c.[1]

Manning's adoption of these lines is profoundly – but also hilariously – cynical: the play revolves around the group of friends and family whom the aspiring but frustrated young artist Desmond Millington invites to his studio on the eve of his twenty-first birthday, "to celebrate the death of my childhood, and farewell to happiness."[2] Desmond's expectations of this darkly festive occasion immediately become clear: "It will be a beautiful party; everyone will fight; we'll all be miserable – I *love* that!" (329).

Indeed, Desmond himself is delighted to be the instigator of such wrangling, which he considers to be the inevitable result of the stifling bourgeois milieu in which he grew up: "Now let's gossip. Let's be vilely libellous. Let's be salacious and treacherous. Let's stab our best friends in the back. Let's betray our relations; let's wash our dirty linen in the drawing-room. In other words – let's be *Dublin*" (324). However, he is also a victim in a more serious sense: his father has forbidden his going to art school or becoming a designer in London, and instead orders him to take up an office job, which is Desmond's ultimate nightmare. This rejection is especially pertinent in light of Desmond's queer identity: he describes himself as a "soft, clinging, merely decorative she-man" (349) and embraces terms that others use as slurs: "My deah fellow! I *am* effeminate. It's my temperament. I was born that way" (347).

To articulate such sentiments onstage during the conservative Free State years was a daring move by Manning, and the play more generally undermines conventional ideas about propriety and decorum. At Desmond's frenzied party, which is depicted in the second of three acts, tensions mount as the youngsters down their drinks and vent their frustrations. Terence, an alcoholic writer who admits to have been a "transparent poseur from puberty" (352), realises that he and his peers are all "wrapped in his or her little cloak of egotism. Each one going his own futile wavering road – Oh Lord, what a generation!" (363). Despite their shared artistic airs, however, Desmond mostly holds Terence in low regard: he considers him "one of the many minor poets, whose names are writ in whiskey" (383).

Desmond's younger sister Connie is nevertheless infatuated with Terence, but since he declares that he can only love himself, she reluctantly accepts the desperate advances of Harry, who is in the British Colonial Service. When Terence mocks Harry for being a spineless collaborator, the pair come to blows, as do Desmond's elder sister Deirdre and her fiancé Gerald, who had been trying to goad Deirdre by flirting with another girl. During this altercation, Desmond gleefully cries "Up the repuberlick!" (372): he orchestrated Gerald's behaviour, believing that Deirdre's jealously would soon turn into obsessive love (and, eventually, he is proved right).

The party, then, is precisely the disaster that Desmond had been wishing for, and there is also more than enough ridicule for the audience to enjoy. The American tourist Priscilla, for example, tells everyone that she is "crazy about Dublin" (361) after having been there for a single day. This fervour appeals strongly to Europa, whom the stage directions describe as "*a plump young woman of twenty; a living, breathing mass of Celtic embroideries and hand-woven tweeds [... who] speaks with an extreme [sic] cultured Anglo-Irish accent*" (356). Revealing their vacuous and self-centred natures, Europa enthusiastically offers to show Priscilla "round the slums tomorrow" – a "divine" (363) offer in the American's eyes.

These caricatures are offset, however, by the darkness that is at the heart of *Youth's the Season–?*, and which the entirely mute character of Horace Egosmith embodies. Included at the suggestion of Samuel Beckett – a close friend of Mary Manning's – Egosmith is Terence's *Doppelgänger*, his ever-present shadow, who keeps the poet's violent despair at bay with his deferential, empty manners. Terence manages to shake off Egosmith after the party and when he returns to the Millingtons' house in the third act, he forces Desmond and his friend Toots, who are nursing their hangovers, to lock the door in an attempt to stop Egosmith – and soulless conformity – from subjugating him. When Terence believes Egosmith is coming up the stairs for him, he announces that there is only one route of escape left for him:

Terence. [...] Now I hope you don't mind – I'm bumping myself off here, because I think this house needs to be shaken to its bourgeois foundations. I swear that if anyone attempts to stop me I will take them with me. Terrible is he who has nothing to lose! [*His voice grows louder. Toots realises his intention too late, and rushes towards him.*] Santa Teresa, pray for this sinner now, and in the hour of his death! [*He shoots himself through the heart, and very slowly falls forward off the sofa.*] (403–404)

While Desmond is generally dismissive of – though, at times, also intimidated by – Terence, he actually shares this bleak outlook on the prospects of adolescents growing up in the Free State. Moments before Terence's suicide, Desmond had articulated the same overwhelming feeling:

Desmond. Twenty-one years have I looked out on this square, and I see us all here, struggling to escape from our environment, fighting against it, refusing to conform; and Life, like a big sausage-machine, descends upon the raw material, grinds it up, moulds us into the required shape, and throws us out again as nice, pink, conventional little sausages—
Connie. I *won't* give in!
Desmond. You'll be the first to give in – you weak piece of voluptuous affectation.
Connie. [*viciously*]. At least I'm normal. (395)

It is, of course, painful that Connie tries to wound Desmond by disparaging her brother's queerness, but, tellingly, he is used to such barbs: "I know exactly what people say about me here – it all goes around in a vicious circle" (395), much like the dance in *The Beggar's Opera*.

Youth's the Season–? is a play that hits many different notes, from uproarious put-downs to harrowing self-hatred, and from bitter indictments to heartfelt sympathy. There are moments when Manning's young Dubliners seem on the verge of breaking free from their constraints and buoyantly striking out for themselves. At other times, and certainly in the final scene, they can only be described as a lost generation, whose dreams are shattered by a conservative society that will not condone idiosyncratic ambitions, let alone alternative gender roles or sexual identities. With her barbed wit, black humour, and deep compassion, Mary Manning painted a picture of her generation in tragicomical colours that remain vivid almost a century later.

Ruud van den Beuken

Notes

1　John Gay, *The Beggar's Opera* (Oxford: Oxford University Press, 2013), 30.
2　Mary Manning, *Youth's the Season–?*, in *Plays of Changing Ireland*, edited by Curtis Canfield (New York: Macmillan, 1936), 3. Subsequent references are entered in parentheses.

Further Reading

Lanters, José. "Desperationists and Ineffectuals: Mary Manning's Gate Plays of the 1930s." In *The Gate Theatre, Dublin: Inspiration and Craft*, edited by David Clare, Des Lally and Patrick Lonergan, 97–110. Dublin: Carysfort/Peter Lang, 2018.

Lanters, José. "Queer Creatures, Queer Place: Otherness and Normativity in Irish Drama from Synge to Friel." In *Irish Theatre in Transition: From the Late Nineteenth to the Early Twenty-First Century*, edited by Donald E. Morse, 54–76. New York: Palgrave Macmillan, 2015.

Leeney, Cathy. *Irish Women Playwrights, 1900–1939: Gender and Violence on Stage*. New York: Peter Lang, 2010.

Meaney, Gerardine, Mary O'Dowd, and Bernadette Whelan. *Reading the Irish Woman: Studies in Cultural Encounter and Exchange, 1714–1960*. Liverpool: Liverpool University Press, 2013.

van den Beuken, Ruud. *Avant-Garde Nationalism at the Dublin Gate Theatre, 1928–1940*. Syracuse, NY: Syracuse University Press, 2021.

Vroomen, Grace. "'Let's Be Gay, While We May': Artistic Platforms and the Construction of Queer Communities in Mary Manning's *Youth's the Season–?*" In *A Stage of Emancipation: Change and Progress at the Dublin Gate Theatre*, edited by Marguérite Corporaal and Ruud van den Beuken, 57–75. Liverpool: Liverpool University Press, 2021.

KATIE ROCHE (1936) BY TERESA DEEVY

When Teresa Deevy's *Katie Roche* first opened at the Abbey Theatre on 16 May 1936, Deevy was one of the theatre's most prolific playwrights. In the previous six years, she had had four plays performed at the Abbey – *The Reapers* (1930, now lost); *A Disciple* (1931), *Temporal Powers* (1932), and *The King of Spain's Daughter* (1935) – with *The Wild Goose* due later in 1936. "My knowledge of Miss Teresa Deevy's previous work had prepared me for a vital and unusual play," wrote the *Irish Independent* when *Katie Roche* opened; "but not for a masterpiece. Masterpiece is a word to be used sparingly, but I have no hesitation in applying it to Miss Deevy's 'Katie Roche.'"[1] And yet, *Katie Roche* was performed only twenty-two times over the course of 1936, 1937, and 1938, and not staged again until Ria Mooney mounted a new production in the Peacock in 1949. After that, when Judy Friel directed the play for the Abbey in 1994, it was virtually unknown, and certainly not out of keeping for the Mint Theatre in New York – which specialises in "worthy but forgotten plays" – to stage it in 2013 as part of its wider project of reviving Deevy's work.

The question with *Katie Roche* must first be: how do we go from "masterpiece" to "worthy but forgotten"? The answer in part lies in an undated letter Deevy wrote to a friend (probably in 1940 or 1941), after having submitted a new play to the Abbey's director, Ernest Blythe, only to have it refused: "Blythe's letter, when returning it, showed clearly that he has no use for my work – never asked to see any more."[2] From that point onwards, apart from Mooney's 1949 revival of *Katie Roche*, Deevy fell out of the Abbey repertoire, and apart from a few productions by small companies or by amateurs, most of her writing was for now for radio. In one respect, this was not remarkable for the time. Indeed, even before her fall from grace with the Abbey, her plays were being produced on radio, and a production of *The King of Spain's Daughter* for the pre-Second World War phase of BBC television in 1939 makes it one of the first television dramas ever broadcast. However, what was remarkable about Deevy writing for radio was the fact that from about 1920 she had been deaf. Given that the first Irish radio broadcast took place in 1926, radio was a medium of which she had no direct experience.

From the outset, Teresa Deevy's deafness and her playwriting were closely connected in ways that help to explain the continuing power of *Katie Roche*. Deevy was not born deaf; she gradually lost her hearing during her late teens as a consequence of an hereditary condition, Ménière's disease, and was sent to London to learn lip-reading, where she "went very often to the theatres," as she later wrote, "reading the plays first, when possible, then following them on the stage. [...] One night returning from the theatre I felt very strongly the urge to put 'the sort of life we live in Ireland' into a play."[3] Returning to Ireland, as a deaf woman in a society that made few allowances for disability, her correspondence shows her frustration at not being able to carry on conversations with fellow writers she admired, such as Lennox

Robinson. And it is that daily experience of the obduracy of language that is transformed in her plays into a floating sense of the impossibility of true communication between two people. And it may be that because that sense of the privacy of the self is most often to be found in her strong female characters – such as Katie Roche – that her plays sat uneasily in the repertoire of the Abbey in the 1930s, ultimately leading Blythe to have "no use" for Deevy's work.

What makes Deevy a playwright easily under-estimated is that on the surface her plays look like examples of conventional stage realism. In this respect, *Katie Roche* is typical: its single set is "the living room of Amelia Gregg's cottage in Lower Ballycar. It is a pleasant little room, time-worn now and scantily furnished."[4] With few exceptions, the world of Deevy's plays is the "pleasant," sunlit respectability of the middle classes of Ireland's small rural towns. Likewise, the narrative seems simple enough. The first Act opens on an August afternoon with Katie Roche, who is "not quite twenty," formally greeting Stanislaus Gregg; "a short stoutish man of about forty-five" (57), who is an architect and brother of Katie's employer, Amelia; it ends with Katie agreeing to marry Stanislaus. The second Act takes place the following December, with Katie and Stanislaus excitedly examining architectural plans that Stanislaus has drawn up. When Stanislaus goes out, Katie invites in Michael, a young man we encountered in Act One, offering him a drink. Stanislaus arrives back, is annoyed, and announces that he will be spending more time away from home. The final act takes place the following August; Stanislaus returns, and admits that when he left the previous winter, it was because "I had to be on my own" (100). The play ends with Stanislaus and Katie leaving to travel.

None of this, however, captures the sheer strangeness of *Katie Roche*. At key moments in each Act, there is an appearance by Reuben, a wandering holy man, who is more like a cautionary figure from a folk tale than a character from a domestic realist drama. In Act One, in a disturbing moment, he beats Katie, warning her that "Christ left no doubt. He was at war with this world, worldly thoughts and worldly values" (63). In the second Act, he arrives just as Katie is offering Michael a drink; and in the final Act, he reveals that he is Katie's long-lost father. At the core of the play's enigma is Katie herself, whose sense that she can be "grand" is at odds with the stage world; Deevy writes of her that "perhaps the most remarkable thing about her is a sort of inward glow, which she continually tries to smother and which breaks out either in delight or desperation according to circumstances" (57). In Act One, Katie tells Stanislaus that she intends to enter a convent, "Wouldn't it be a good thing to save my soul – and to more than save it – so what else can I do?" (58). Later, however, after the scene with Reuben in Act Two, she announces: "I'll make my own goodness" (79). And, finally, as she exits, Amelia (whose role up to that point has largely been to bake scones), assures Katies that if she is "brave" she can make her life "grand" (102) – something Katie receives as if it were a revelation.

The effect is of a more complex play in which issues of salvation and "greatness" are being determined, taking place just out of sight in the gaps of language. Catherine Byrne's 2017 staging at the Abbey tried to capture this by moving away from a realist setting to find a visual language for Katie's interior conviction that she'll be "a great woman" (79). Joanna Scotcher's set for Byrne's production juxtaposed soaring architectural shapes with a soil-covered stage, positioning an altar-like table between them. Byrne's production led audiences to read *Katie Roche* in terms of the patriarchal world of 1930s Ireland, where many women felt their true selves to be trapped in the dirt; or, in terms of a deaf artist in a hearing world, where "grand" things can be imagined but only obliquely communicated. Theatrically, it also suggested that we can read *Katie Roche* as an implicit critique of the realism so dominant on the Irish stage at the time, in which to be seen is to be known. None of these possibilities are mutually exclusive. However, beyond these specific contexts, *Katie Roche* deals with the fundamental inadequacy of language and the ultimate privacy of the imagined self. As a character in a late, unpublished play, *The Cellar of My Friend*, puts it: "there's no two people who can to the full com-pre-hend one another ... not fully."[5]

Chris Morash

Notes

1 D.S., "A masterpiece at the Abbey: Miss Deevy's new play," *Irish Independent*, 17 March 1936. *Teresa Deevy Archive*. 2021. http://deevy. nuim.ie/items/show/108. Accessed 16 September 2021.
2 Teresa Deevy, Letters to Florence Hackett (undated; 1941/2?). TCD Ms. 10722.
3 Matthew Hoehn, *Contemporary Catholic Authors: Biographical Sketches* (New Jersey: St. Mary's Abbey, 1952), 121.
4 Teresa Deevy, *Katie Roche*, in *Teresa Deevy Reclaimed: Volume One*, ed. Jonathan Bank, John P. Harrington, and Christopher Morash (New York: Mint Theatre Company, 2011), 57. Subsequent references are entered in parentheses.

5 Teresa Deevy, *In the Cellar of My Friend*, in *Teresa Deevy Reclaimed: Volume Two*, ed. Jonathan Bank, John P. Harrington, and Christopher Morash (New York: Mint Theatre Company, 2017), 120.

Further Reading

Leeney, Cathy. *Irish Women Playwrights 1900–1939: Gender and Violence on Stage*. New York: Peter Lang, 2010.
Richards, Shaun. "'Suffocated in the Green Flag': The Drama of Teresa Deevy and 1930s Ireland." *Literature and History* Vol. 4, no. 1 (1995): 65–80.

PURGATORY (1938) BY W. B. YEATS

"I hope to be here [Dublin] for the first night of Yeats's new play *Purgatory* next Wednesday week at the Abbey," wrote Samuel Beckett to a friend.[1] As the young Beckett sat in the auditorium that evening on 10 August 1938, he saw a play acted out by two ragged tramps on a stage empty of all but a dead tree and the shell of a ruined house. Not surprisingly, more than one commentator has since found echoes of Yeats's play in Beckett's own work, notably *Waiting for Godot* and *Endgame*.[2] On that evening in 1938, if Beckett was near the beginning of his writing life, Yeats was near the end of his. *Purgatory* is then not simply yet another of the twenty-six plays that Yeats wrote during his lifetime; it is effectively the culmination of his experiments with theatre going back to the 1890s. Indeed, it may be that *Purgatory* most resembles Beckett's theatre in its compacted intensity and in the deliberate poverty of its stage image. It is, in effect, a distillation of ideas percolating in Yeats's writing for almost fifty years, not only in the poetry for which he is best known, but most strikingly in the arcane work *A Vision* (1937), the great unclassifiable text he had finally finished revising just before he wrote *Purgatory*.

The original version of *A Vision* (1925) has one of the most remarkable origins of any work in modern literature. "On the afternoon of October 24th, 1917, four days after my marriage, my wife surprised me by attempting automatic writing," Yeats later wrote.[3] Automatic writing involves spirit messengers responding to questions posed by a medium in a trance – in this case, Yeats's wife, George. The answers that the Yeatses received during these trances confirmed for Yeats his own beliefs about the afterlife, which he had already formulated in a short essay published earlier that year entitled *Per Amica Silentia Lunae*. "The toil of the living is to free themselves from an endless sequence of objects," Yeats explains, "and that of

the dead to free themselves from an endless sequence of thoughts."[4]
From his reading of the mystic Emmanuel Swedenborg, philosophers
such as Plato and Plotinus, his study of Irish folklore, and – most
crucially for his theatre – his encounter with Japanese Nōh theatre, in
which ghosts feature strongly, Yeats had developed his own eschatology. He believed that after death the soul continues to exist in what
he calls a "dream," re-acting over and over again the events of the life
past, until it eventually purges itself. Over time, Yeats's beliefs grew
into a complex system of catastrophic collapse and rebirth, embracing not just individual lives but all human history. It was this system
that burgeoned into the labyrinthine diagrams, tables, poems, and
speculations of *A Vision*.

Purgatory collapses all of this material into a play that is as simple
and concise as *A Vision* is arcane and digressive. "I have a one-act
play in my head, a scene of tragic intensity," Yeats wrote to a friend in
March of 1938 – with "intensity" being the operative word.[5] The play
opens with two ragged wanderers, identified only as the Old Man and
the Boy, stopping in front of the ruins of an old house. "Study that
house,"[6] the Old Man instructs him:

> Great people lived and died in this house;
> Magistrates, colonels, members of Parliament,
> Captains and Governors, and long ago
> Men that had fought at Aughrim and the Boyne.
> (1043)

The Old Man then goes on to explain that his father had been a groom
in the stables, had married the heir, and then proceeded to drink and
gamble away everything she had, until the trees were cut down to pay
his debts, and the house left ruined. "He killed the house; to kill a
house/ Where great men grew up, married, died,/ I here declare the a
capital offence" (1044). The Old Man means this literally, claiming to
have killed his father: "I stuck him with a knife,/ That knife that cuts
my dinner now" (1045).

At that point, the Old Man hears hoofbeats, which he immediately
identifies as the ghost of his father "riding from the public-house,/
A whiskey-bottle under his arm" (1045). Now the play becomes a
haunting in its own right. One of the windows in the ruined house
lights up, and the image of a young girl – the Old Man's mother –
appears, seen by the Old Man and the audience, but not by the Boy.
"There's nothing but an empty gap in the wall," jeers the Boy. "You

are getting madder every day" (1045). The Old Man, however, continues to speak, staring at the window, articulating Yeats's own belief:

> The souls in Purgatory that come back
> To habitations and familiar spots [...]
> Re-live their transgressions; and that not once
> But many times.
>
> (1042)

His mother, he insists, "must live/ Through everything in exact detail,/ Driven to it by remorse" (1046). As the Old Man speaks, the Boy tries to steal from him, and the image of the girl fades, to be replaced by that of a man pouring a glass of whiskey. This time, the Boy sees the image, and cries out in horror: "A dead, living, murdered man!" (1048). Then, in a moment that never fails to shock an audience, the Old Man stabs the Boy, "again and again" (1048), killing him with the same knife with which he had killed his own father.

Where the play begins with the injunction to "study that house," it ends with the Old Man, alone on the stage, the window again grown dark. "Study that tree," he tells us. "It stands there like a purified soul,/ All cold, sweet, glistening light." He explains that he "killed that lad because had he grown up/ He would have struck a woman's fancy,/ Begot, passed pollution on." Having killed his son and his father, the Old Man thinks, "I finished all that consequence" (1049). And yet, as the play ends, he hears the relentless hoof-beats once again, realises the murders to have been pointless, and knows his mother's soul must continue to "animate that dead night/ Not once but many times!" The play ends with a final desperate plea:

> O God
> Release my mother's soul from its dream!
> Mankind can do no more. Appease
> The misery of the living and the remorse of the dead.
>
> (1049)

Yeats wrote to a friend that into *Purgatory* he had put "my own conviction about this world and the next."[7] In Ireland in 1938, Yeats's convictions about this world, always inclining towards the catastrophic, increasingly saw the Ireland of aristocratic largesse that he had idealised disappearing forever, as its big houses fell into ruin. "I know of old houses, old pictures, old furniture that have been sold without apparent regret," he told an interviewer. "In some few cases a house has been destroyed by a mesalliance. I have founded my play on this exceptional case."[8] However, beyond staging the end of a civilisation (as he saw it), *Purgatory* stages the fate of the soul after death, in which the afterlife is an exact reproduction, over and over again, of the life lived on earth, where spiritual existence is inextricably dependent upon the material world. What is more, if we believe – as Yeats did – that the soul after death must return to "habitations and familiar spots," and there act out, night after night, the same emotionally intense series of actions to a precise script, we have an eschatology that is fundamentally theatrical. And so, at the end of his own life, in *Purgatory* Yeats created a play that attempts – and necessarily fails – to end not only a cycle of dreaming and remembering, but also theatre itself. In that sense, *Purgatory* is theatre at its end – which is effectively where Beckett begins.

Chris Morash

Notes

1 *The Letters of Samuel Beckett: Vol. 1, 1929–1940*, ed. Martha Dow Fehsenfeld and Lois More Overbeck (Cambridge: Cambridge University Press, 2009), 640.
2 Michael McAteer, *Yeats and European Drama* (Cambridge: Cambridge University Press, 2010), 176; Katherine Worth, *The Irish Drama of Europe from Yeats to Beckett* (London: Athlone Press, 1978), 253.
3 W. B. Yeats, *The Collected Works of W. B. Yeats: Vol. XIV: A Vision: The Revised 1937 Edition*, ed. Margaret Mills Harper and Catherine E. Paul (New York: Scribner's, 2015), 7.
4 W. B. Yeats, *Per Amica Silentia Lunae*, in *The Collected Works of W. B. Yeats: Vol. V. Later Essays*, ed. William H. O'Donnell (New York: Scribner's, 1994), 23.
5 W. B. Yeats, *The Letters of W. B. Yeats*, ed. Allan Wade (London: Rupert Hart-Davis, 1954), 907.
6 W. B. Yeats, *Purgatory*, in *The Variorum Edition of the Plays of W. B. Yeats*, ed. Russell K. Alspach (London: Macmillan, 1966), 1041. Subsequent references are entered in parentheses.
7 Yeats, *Letters*, 913.
8 "Mr. Yeats Explains Play: Plot of 'Purgatory' is its Meaning," *Irish Independent*, 13 August 1938, 9.

Further Reading

McAteer, Michael. *Yeats and European Drama*. Cambridge: Cambridge University Press, 2010.
Morash, Christopher. *Yeats on Theatre*. Cambridge: Cambridge University Press, 2021.

AN APPLE A DAY (1942) BY ELIZABETH CONNOR (UNA TROY)

At first glance *An Apple a Day* by Elizabeth Connor might appear to be an unremarkable comedy typical of the Abbey in the 1940s and 1950s. It has a three-act structure with the action of the play all set in one location: the dispensary room of a rural doctor's house. The comedy is for the most part character-driven, often relying on the audience's recognition of familiar Irish country types. These include the garrulous servant, the self-serving politician, the trusted and reliable doctor, and drunken villagers. It also includes a romance and ends with a marriage proposal. However, on closer inspection Connor's play is revealed to be a bold theatrical experiment that uses comic license, parody, and role reversal as a means to challenge patriarchal structures and constructions of female types.

The play begins with the news that the Local Appointments Office has assigned a new doctor, Dr Gavin Barry from Dublin, to the town of Carrigmahon, County Waterford. The town is not pleased with this young doctor being forced upon them when they have a Dr Burke already practising in the town. Dr Burke's son is a medical student in Dublin and the townsfolk believe him to be the right doctor to take over the practice. The entire action of the play takes place in Dr Burke's Dispensary House, in which the doctor's two servants, Lizzie and Jeremiah Power, live with his sister Tottie and his two daughters, Janet and Ann. In Act One, Dr Barry moves into the Dispensary after Dr Burke goes to visit his son in Dublin. The residents of the house begin to torment the young doctor to discourage him from staying. They puncture his bicycle wheels, serve him inedible food, and force him to walk miles in the rain for trivial errands. In Act Two, the three Burke women decide to perform as extreme characters in order to drive the doctor from the house. Aunt Tottie tries to terrify him when she assumes the role of a psychic medium and harbinger of death, Ann wishes to irritate him in her playing of a rude, precocious child who has been brought up without conventional boundaries, and Janet wishes to repulse him by casting herself as a nineteenth-century romantic heroine who has had a sexual encounter with a ghost. Despite all their efforts the doctor lasts the week in the house and becomes fond of its inhabitants. The women also become fond of him and his gentle and kind manner. Indeed, both young daughters fall in love with him and he falls in love with Janet. In Act Three the men of the community, led by the self-serving local politician, T. D. Sarsfield Clancy, come to the Dispensary to drive the young doctor from the community by force. They are thwarted in their efforts, however, as the women turn on their men and protect him. Dr Burke then arrives home and reveals that his son has married an elderly widow for financial gain and has no wish to return to Carrigmahon. Dr Barry is then accepted by all as the new doctor and he tells an approving Dr Burke of his wish to marry Janet. The play ends with the local T. D. ridiculed, and peace restored.

The masquerade by the Burke women in Act 2 is designed as a "man-scare-ade" to frighten and drive the young doctor away. As such the parts played by the Burkes are deliberately those of "improper" and "mad" women in terms of 1940s Irish standards of morality and decency. They play grotesque versions of traditional female types of wife, daughter, and mother. Janet's performance is a twist on the love-interest/wife figure who is found to be lustful rather than dutiful; Ann plays a grotesque child who through her outspokenness and in her terrible violin playing proves to be the opposite to the Victorian "good daughter" who should be seen and not heard. Aunt Tottie in the character of a psychic medium is an otherworldly "unnatural mother" figure who speaks to the doctor as though he were a child and pretends to protect him from evil spirits. In all this exaggerated playacting they reveal these roles and femininity itself to be a performance. As Mary Russo writes of masquerade: "Deliberately assumed and foregrounded, femininity as a mask, for a man, is a take-it-or-leave-it proposition; for a woman, a similar flaunting of the feminine is a take-it-*and*-leave-it *possibility*. To put on femininity with a vengeance suggests the power of taking it off."[1]

Connor's comic twist is that the young doctor is not turned off or driven out by the women's pretence but instead plays along with them. He is not morally outraged or embarrassed by Janet's behaviour but instead is attracted to her. When Ann plays the violin manically and claims to want to write a novel only for it to be banned, her behaviour does not shock him. In Act Three it is reported that he smiles during the violin playing and is encouraging of Ann's writing. He finds Aunt Tottie's encounters with the spirit-world entertaining rather than terrifying.

The women also begin to take on the characteristics of their invented personas or are emboldened by them. By Act Three Aunt Tottie confesses that she is beginning to have visions and see "real ghosts,"[2] while Ann, made brave by her outspoken persona in Act Two, has a very open and direct dialogue with Gavin about her feelings for him. Janet through her character is allowed to express her desires and sexuality in an open manner and as a result the doctor wishes to meet her desires rather than simply possess her so she can meet his needs. The masquerade of Act Two can thus be read as an act of becoming. During the performance in the playing of their roles Ann and Tottie remake the space they are living in, transforming it from a home (in an Irish context a place of containment for women, in light of de Valera's Constitution of 1937 which declared that women should not "neglect […] their duties in the home")[3] into a theatre – a space of play and becoming. This is even explicitly signalled in Act Two, when Lizzie's footsteps are heard on the stairs, Gavin comments to Tottie that "You'd feel it could be almost anything in this house wouldn't you?" to which she replies "Oh, my dear young man, in this house anything can be anything" (63). Such a space where anything can be anything is the theatrical space.

Many comedies afford female characters freedoms only to shut these down in the ending which traditionally sees a woman wed and patriarchal control re-established. True to its form *An Apple a Day* ends in the future marriage of Janet and Gavin. This suggests that instead of critiquing the status quo the play presents unruly women only to laugh at them, safe in the knowledge that such women will be put in their place by the end of the drama when conventional structures are reinstated. However, *An Apple a Day* sees traditional roles reversed in its ending, rather than a return to the norm. Consequently, the freedom afforded to the women in Act Two is not fully crushed. The play ends in the future marriage of Gavin and Janet but it also ends with the marriage of Dr Burke's son, Bill, to a wealthy older lady. Dr Burke comments "Well – she's not very young but there's plenty of money there" (97). It is Bill's marriage that brings closure to the play's primary conflict: who will be the new doctor of Carrigmahon? In Bill's marrying and consequently staying in Dublin this conflict is resolved and Gavin can stay on as doctor to the community, who now accept him. The fact that Bill marries an older woman for her wealth reverses the traditional role of the woman marrying for financial gain. This comes after the reversal of power in Act Three, where the women have saved the doctor from the men's violence and have proved themselves to be the "stronger" sex. At the close of the drama the men of the community accept the doctor but only do so because their wives have told them to. The happy ending of Connor's play is one where the women are in charge and the restricted patriarchal roles imposed on women are reversed, mocked, and challenged.

Ian R. Walsh

Notes

1 Mary Russo, *The Female Grotesque: Risk, Excess and Modernity* (London: Routledge, 1995), 70.
2 Elizabeth Connor, *An Apple a Day*, unpublished script, National Library of Ireland, Una Troy Papers, MS 35,687. 69. Subsequent references are entered in parentheses.
3 See Melissa Sihra, ed., *Women in Irish Drama: A Century of Authorship and Representation* (Basingstoke: Palgrave, 2007), 1–22.

Further Reading

O'Dowd, Ciara. "The Premiere Staging of Mount Prospect (1940) by Elizabeth Connor (the pen name of Una Troy) at the Abbey Theatre." In *The Golden Thread: Irish Women Playwrights, Volume 1 (1716–1992)*, edited by David Clare, Fiona McDonagh, and Justine Nakase, 211–22. Liverpool: Liverpool University Press, 2021
Walsh, Ian R. "Experiments in Gender: Elizabeth Connor." In *Experimental Irish Theatre: After W.B Yeats*, 74–94. Basingstoke: Palgrave, 2012.

TOLKA ROW (1951) BY MAURA LAVERTY

When *Tolka Row* premiered at the Gaiety Theatre, Dublin on 8 October 1951, Maura Laverty was still enjoying the success of her first play, *Liffey Lane*, which had opened only seven months previously. Already a household name in Ireland for her novels, short stories, journalism, cookery books, and radio programmes, Laverty had embarked upon playwriting at the suggestion of Hilton Edwards who saw the dramatic potential offered by the portrayal of tenement life in her novel *Lift Up Your Gates* (1946), adapted as *Liffey Lane*. Prompted by its success, Edwards asked Laverty for another play for his and Micheál mac Liammóir's Dublin Gate Theatre Productions.[1] The resulting *Tolka Row* offered mac Liammóir one of his most memorable roles playing the elderly Dan Dempsey and, as Christopher Fitz-Simon has noted, *Tolka Row* was the Gate's "great reliable" in the five years following its first production when the theatre was beset with financial difficulties.[2]

In Laverty's second work for the stage, the tenements of Liffey Lane are replaced by a Corporation housing scheme that provides homes for Dublin's working class, Tolka suggesting a location adjacent to that river on Dublin's northside. The setting is a three-bedroomed house: "It is one of a thousand similar houses in a slum-clearance scheme on the fringe of Dublin."[3] The Gaiety premiere, and subsequent transfer to the Gate, used a realist design by Michael O'Herlihy, and was lit and directed by Edwards. The parlour takes centre stage, but the set includes the hallway and front door, and the external area of paths from the street to the front door and to that of the neighbouring house. A railing divides the two neighbouring paths, and many conversations take place in this shared space over the railing – a hark back to the closer-knit living of the inner city.

Tolka Row features the Nolans and their neighbours, the Feeneys, both families having moved from the inner-city to give their children a better life. As Rita Nolan says: "sure they had to have a home they could be proud of. When we were living in Clanbrassil Street, I always kept it before me to do that for them. Always" (Act 1). At a time of the rapid expansion of Dublin's working-class suburbs, Laverty is thus staging the experience of many families who moved from inner-city slum dwellings to the less communal environment of low-density estates. The play opens after the recent death of Dan, Rita's father, but the cause of his death is unknown to the audience as the action unfolds in the form of a three-act flashback to the events that led to his tragic demise.

The Nolan household is a busy one. Rita has raised three children: Eileen, recently married, and living in England with her Irish husband, Paddy; Sean, an apprentice fitter; and the dance and fashion-mad Peggy who works as a tobacconist's assistant. Rita's long-suffering, but good-natured, husband, Jack, works as a fitter. Rita also keeps home for Jack's sister, the embittered Statia, a laundry-worker and religious zealot. It is already a crowded household of five adults when Dan, a retired canal boatman, comes to live with them following an illness. Now hale and hearty, Dan, although good natured, is Statia's nemesis and they regularly spar, not least because Statia had to surrender her bedroom to Dan and share with Peggy instead. As there is no bedroom for Sean, he sleeps on a chair-bed in the parlour. Domestic tension is already close to breaking point when Eileen returns from Liverpool, having left her husband. As the pressure builds, it is Rita who suffers most as she loses control over her home and her family.

The play is firmly rooted in an urban and female domestic space, and can be considered a drama of space, or rather the lack of it. This theme, of both physical and emotional space, is successfully integrated with the experiences of the family, and with the decisions taken by Rita. Her dual roles as both daughter and mother are confounded by lack of space in the house and the intergenerational strife that results: "Maybe it's a hard thing to be old. And the young have their own hardships. But it's a hard thing, too, to be neither young nor old, but to be standing between the generation that's going before you and the one that's coming after you and to be torn asunder between the two" (Act 1). Rita's domestic harmony is also disrupted by having Dan live with her, and his very presence censors her private conversations, as she says to Mrs Feeney: "Anything to get him out from under my feet for a minute. I wouldn't hurt his feelings for the world. But you know how awkward it can be with a man around the house all day" (Act 1). When the two women manage to chat out of Dan's earshot, the talk turns to birth control, or lack thereof, as Mrs Feeney laments her situation with eight daughters under the age of fourteen, and her concern that "unless it's the mercy of God, maybe as many times more" (Act 1). While *Tolka Row* was very well received by the critics, the frank, and very humorous, conversations between the women were criticised, and all reviewers called for these scenes to be cut.

In staging marital breakdown and women's lack of control over their fertility, both of which were under the strict control of the Catholic Church in 1950s Ireland, Laverty is unafraid to tackle taboo subjects. While Rita and Jack are concerned about Eileen's return to the family home, it is left to Dan to point out the harsh reality of the situation: "But you married him, Eileen. Even if he wasn't able to give you the kind of home you wanted, isn't he your husband? You're an Irish Catholic. You can't change that" (Act 1). Dan encourages Eileen to write to Paddy and make up, and when Paddy agrees to return to Dublin and to move into the Nolan home, Rita is torn between her children and her father: "To tell you the truth, there's been times this past couple of weeks when I found myself envying daughters that never married, that kept on with one love only, the love they were born with" (Act 3). When Rita takes the difficult decision to move her father out, so that Paddy can move in, she must ask her belligerent cousin, Mary Loughlin, to have Dan live with her. Peggy suggests tricking Dan into thinking the move back to his home place of Ballyderrig is only for a holiday, and this is successfully achieved by means of a fabricated letter. By chance, Statia comes upon the truthful letter from Mary to Rita: "A pound a week is little enough for taking on the care and annoyance of a troublesome old man. But I'm giving you due warning that if you fail in the money or if your father gets laid up, he can go out of this and into Mullinagarry Union" (Act 3). Statia's hatred of Dan drives her to reveal the letter to him, and his subsequent acute distress leads to his death by drowning in the canal that was once such a large part of his life.

Tolka Row's success led Hilton Edwards to declare 1951 to be one of the best seasons the Gate had ever had. Additionally, Laverty's depiction of urban working-class life found success beyond the Dublin stage: *Tolka Row* has been a constant on the Irish amateur dramatic scene since the St Philomena's Drama Group's production won the first ever All-Ireland Amateur Festival in 1953. The play also found an afterlife as the basis for Telefís Éireann's first soap opera, also called *Tolka Row*, and Laverty wrote all the scripts from its first television broadcast in January 1964 until her untimely death in 1966.

Deirdre McFeely

Notes

1 Dublin Gate Theatre Productions shared the Gate Theatre with Longford Productions, each company having it for six months a year. It is for this reason that *Tolka Row* premiered at the Gaiety Theatre, with revivals taking place at the Gate Theatre
2 Christopher Fitz-Simon, *The Boys: A Biography of Micheál MacLiammóir and Hilton Edwards* (Dublin: Gill & Macmillan, 1994), 172–3.
3 Maura Laverty, *Tolka Row* (Unpublished play script), stage directions. As the script is unpaginated references relate to the Acts and are entered in parentheses.

Further Reading

Leeney, Cathy and Deirdre McFeely. *The Plays of Maura Laverty: Liffey Lane; Tolka Row; A Tree in the Crescent*. Liverpool: Liverpool University Press, 2022.

Leeney, Cathy and Deirdre McFeely. "Social Class, Space, and Containment in 1950s Ireland: Maura Laverty's 'Dublin Trilogy' (1951–1952)." In *The Golden Thread: Irish Women Playwrights, Volume 1 (1716–2016)*, edited by David Clare, Fiona McDonagh, and Justine Nakase, 233–55. Liverpool: Liverpool University Press, 2021.

McFeely, Deirdre. "Maura Laverty at the Gate: Theatre as Social Commentary in 1950s Ireland." In *A Stage of Emancipation: Change and Progress at the Dublin Gate Theatre*, edited by Marguérite Corporaal and Ruud van den Beuken, 39–53. Liverpool: Liverpool University Press, 2021.

HOME IS THE HERO (1952) BY WALTER MACKEN

First produced by the Abbey at the Queen's theatre, Dublin, in July 1952, *Home is the Hero* was a popular success running for seventeen weeks, with the *Evening Herald* reporting that 92,000 people had seen the play.[1] It was also subject to some media controversy after a letter from a US visitor, James J. Munro, criticising how Irish people were being represented in the drama, was printed on the front page of the *Evening Mail*. This in turn lead to further letters defending Macken's play and others in support of Munro's position.[2]

The popularity of the play may strike us as odd given its dark subject matter and its gritty, realistic treatment. It tells an intense tale of the return of a brutish criminal to his family home and his subsequent expulsion from it. In its harsh reality and disruption of the family home, it captures the disillusion of mid-century Ireland tired of tales of an ancient mythic heroic past when faced with a dire present of poverty and mass emigration due to the failure of disastrous isolationist economic policies of self-sufficiency. The play offers hope and renewal in the weak and oppressed delivering themselves of heroes and deciding their own future. The media controversy over the representation of the Irish character in the piece is redolent of that caused by J. M. Synge's *The Playboy of the Western World* (1907) and the play in its plot and theme could also be viewed as a revision of that seminal Irish drama.

Home is the Hero similarly begins with a west of Ireland community ready to celebrate a criminal as a hero and ends with them happy with his departure. However the trajectories of the protagonists of the two plays are quite different. Synge's work concludes as the initially timid Christy Mahon becomes "a likely gaffer in the end of all"[3] through the rural community's false belief that he has killed his father. Macken's urban drama opens on Paddo O'Reilly's return from prison to his home in Galway city after he has served time for the manslaughter of a neighbour after a drunken test of strength went too far. Paddo's transformation is not that of Christy who is made into "a mighty man [...] on the power of a lie,"[4] instead the lie of Paddo's heroic status is revealed to be based on brutalising the weak and defenceless. On Paddo's exit the young lovers of the piece are set to marry and a new future free of past wrongs made possible.

Before we meet Paddo he is described in heroic terms. Daylia, his wife, speaks of his superhuman strength: "Couldn't he lift a hundredweight in each hand?"[5] While Lily, the daughter of the man he killed, comments on his size: "I thought he was a giant" (15). These qualities are those of the heroes from Irish legend such as Finn Mac Cool, who was often described as a giant with the strength of a hundred men. Even Willie who does not view his father as a hero reluctantly admits that "he was like holding a charge of electricity" (16). At the opening of the play we learn that Paddo's old friend Dovetail has organised a hero's welcome for his return with the local children to sing songs in Paddo's honour. But Paddo spoils the festivities by slipping in the backdoor to avoid the crowd and refuses "to be a hayro, in the eyes of the nobodies" (39). On his entrance he immediately begins to dominate, chastising Daylia for her drinking and for allowing Dovetail and his wife Bid to rent the upstairs of the house. He shows no sympathy for his family's struggle while he was in prison and thinks only of the shame they have brought to him in their desperate actions to survive. Paddo speaks with Mrs Green, the widow of the man he killed, seeking forgiveness from her which she gives, but requests that she not be made to remember the events that led to her husband's death. Selfishly Paddo ignores her plea and recounts all the details of the night the killing was committed. His belligerence continues into the following scenes where he refuses to accept his son Willie's engagement to Lily Green, on the grounds that it is unnatural for his son to marry the daughter of the man he killed. Then after his daughter Josie defies his dictum that she should not be seen with a local small-time gangster Manchester Monaghan he viciously attacks her, tearing her frock and beating her with a strap. Paddo's savagery continues to escalate. He assaults his wife Daylia in their room offstage. Her return onstage all the more horrific in its quiet torment. The final brutal act of the play sees Paddo knock Dovetail down the stairs after the drunken lodger taunts him for not being a hero, for having no friends and for being "no bloody good" (102). Dovetail does not move after his fall. Paddo, believing him dead, panics and tries to convince all present that it was an accident. Dovetail regains consciousness but with the shock of almost killing a man again Paddo decides to leave his home and family knowing he will only destroy it if he stays. With his exit a happy ending is made possible. Willie and Lily are free to marry and Josie and Manchester can continue to be together. The home is no longer threatened by the hero. A younger generation are liberated of the past that had wronged them. The marriage of Willie, who was crippled by his father as a child, and Lily, who lost her father due to Paddo's drunken antics, signifies rejuvenation of the home place. Willie is the opposite of his father in being hard-working, selfless, caring, and modest. While Lily is forthright and determined. They will make a stable loving home together.

Macken's message is clear: after the destructive years of the War of Independence (1919–21) and the Civil War (1922–23) there is no place for Paddo's fierce destructive energy in the new Republic of Ireland which was less than four years old at the time of the play. Although he presents a happy ending for the O'Reilly family, in the final moments of the play Macken is keen to sound a cautionary note that people will continue to look for heroes, often choosing badly who to lionise, as the children light bonfires at the closing of the play and sing songs in honour of Dovetail, who has acquired heroic status in surviving Paddo's attack.

With the realism of his characters and their urban, poverty-stricken situations, Macken's early plays have more often been compared to O'Casey's *Dublin Trilogy* than to Synge. Christopher Murray has identified how *Home is the Hero* is particularly "indebted" to *Juno and the Paycock*[6] while Robert Hogan has pointed out how "the O'Reilly family like the Boyle family, in *Juno*, is composed of a false-hero father, a long suffering mother, a son and a daughter" adding how Josie is "as headstrong as Mary Boyle" and Willie "maimed like Johnny Boyle."[7] However, Macken's characters differ from those of Synge and O'Casey in their language which contains none of the poetic stylisation of the earlier playwrights and is instead a restrained attempt to reproduce the pattern of Galwegian speech that is permeated with Irish words. The realistic presentation of the characters, with the exception of the "Joxerish Dovetail," in their language, motivations and actions are powerfully made "truer to life than the theatre."[8] Paddo, for instance, despite his brutal actions is well-meaning in his previous misdeeds, he wants Daylia to stop drinking and is right to try to distance her from the corrupting influence of Bid and Dovetail. Likewise, Manchester Monaghan is corrupt and it is reasonable that Paddo would not want Josie to be with him. Although he is not likeable Paddo is sufficiently complex in his desires for audiences to understand and relate to him. They cannot simply dismiss him as a melodramatic villain, which makes his fierceness so terrifying. Despite his theme that preaches against the creation of heroes, Macken himself in Paddo O'Reilly created one of Irish theatre's most memorable and affecting stage characters.

Ian R. Walsh

Notes

1 *Evening Herald*, 29 November 1952.
2 For a full account of this controversy and the published letters see James E. Reid, *Walter Macken (1915–1967): Playwright, Actor and Theatre Manager* (Dublin: Carysfort Press, 2012), ebook.
3 J. M. Synge, *The Playboy of the Western World*, in *Collected Works IV: Plays II*, ed. Ann Saddlemyer (Gerrards Cross: Colin Smythe, 1982), 173.
4 Ibid., 165.

5   Walter Macken, *Home is the Hero: A Play in Two Acts* (London: Macmillan, 1966), 1. Subsequent references are entered in parentheses.

6   Christopher Murray, "Where are they now: Plays of the 1940s and 1950s," in *Players and Painted Stage: Aspects of the Twentieth Century Theatre in Ireland*, ed. Christopher Fitz-Simon (Dublin: New Island, 2004), 61.

7   Robert Hogan, *After the Renaissance: A Critical History of Irish Drama since The Plough and the Stars* (London: Macmillan, 1968), 68.

8   Ibid.

Further Reading

Heinen, Sandra and Rennhak, Katharina, eds. *Walter Macken Critical Perspectives*. Cork: Cork University Press, 2022.

THE WOOD OF THE WHISPERING (1953)
BY M. J. MOLLOY

The Wood of the Whispering was staged at the Gaiety Theatre, Dublin, in 1953. This was a period when "The protracted post-war Irish economic crisis had created a situation in which the country was unable to provide for vast numbers of the rural poor" and across the decade some 400,000 people, nearly a sixth of the population, emigrated.[1] The Ireland of this play is then shattered by poverty and gutted by emigration; sanity is tentatively held, religion is a formality with little material or spiritual comfort, and marriage is not an act of love but of economic necessity.

The play takes place in the west of Ireland, Molloy basing the varying registers of Hiberno-English spoken by his characters on his own experience of Irish-inflected English spoken in Connaught – an area which experienced high levels of female emigration. The set is the ramshackle campsite of Sanbatch Daly overshadowed by the demesne wall of Castle D'Arcy, a once imposing Norman castle that would have provided employment for locals like Sanbatch who has been living at this camp since his house collapsed after years of neglect. Comedic and unkempt, living in fear of being taken to the poor house to die in poverty, Sanbatch meets Con Kinsella, who has come to cut the trees as part of the sale of the property by the last remaining family member of the estate and lays the scene for him: how poverty has driven so many to leave the area that those who remain have collapsed under the pressure of material destitution and overwhelming loneliness. Those who never married, like Sanbatch, are coming to realise how much they have lost in years of partnership and the ability to encourage the next generation to maintain the community. The neglected castle stands as a monument to a lost class, lost social mobility, loss of employment and, with the loss of the "wood of the whispering" – a once-popular courting place for young couples, the final loss of a carefree and romantic time for the community. With the sale of the castle and the realisation that no help is coming, Sanbatch turns his attention to reviving the dying village.

The first two acts of Molloy's play are characterised by an oppressively dark story told with humour, much being wrought from scenes with older bachelors Jimmy and Paddy King, preening and arguing about marrying the one eligible woman left in the area. The younger, Mark Tristnan, comments on their having "gone as silly as geese"[2] but gradually his own fretful stories of ghosts and his visible ill-health indicate he is similarly in danger of descending into an isolation that will destroy his ability to function in society, and which could prevent him from ever improving his situation. He is viciously critical of Irish women like Sheila Lanigan, shortly returned from England to care for her dying father, for having left Ireland and deserting people like him for material comfort. Sheila stands her ground and argues that to stay in Ireland is to risk destitution.

Between them, the men try to convince Sheila to stay in Ireland and marry one of them. She remains pragmatic about opportunities in England, and moreover is anxious to return lest her suitor there move on and marry someone else. She finds herself torn between securing her economic status through marriage as quickly as possibly or staying with her father through a long illness that could lead to a drawn-out death.

The cautionary tale of this predicament is represented by Sadie Tubridy, a woman in her forties, who is the most pitiful example of the spiritual and mental damage of failing to marry. Sadie was too poor to marry her love interest Hotha Flynn, a farmer now in his fifties, and withdrew from society to the extent that she has, by the time of the play's events, been non-verbal for two years and is regarded with pity and concern by those around her. For Sanbatch:

> The time she was in her bloom th' oul' Depression was on, and no farmer around could afford to marry a girl that had no fortune. So she had to stop with her father and mother till they died, and then she was left alone and the lonesomeness and the darkness and the trees defeated her at last. 'Tis two years now since she spoke to anywan or went out amongst the neighbours. She spends the day and night within there thinking and ever thinking about how she lost herself.
>
> (119)

Characters like Sanbatch, Jimmy and Paddy King, and Hotha Flynn are comical bachelors – familiar figures from many twentieth-century Irish plays, but for them, oppressive poverty and social exile has undermined their humanity and sanity. Despair is the undercurrent in every moment of humour. The men joke that had they married, a wife would have cared for them but also driven them to care for themselves and they have come to this knowledge too late. Much is made of the lack of women to care for men as proxy parents, co-workers in running farm and home, or to offer emotional support. Sexism aside, Molloy appeals to the value of partnership and community. Isolation is destructive to the individual as well as the community.

The County Home, the only formal help forthcoming, is a threat. The Church is often invoked, but more credence is given to the words of dead villagers than the living priest. In practical terms, the villagers can barely attend mass on Sundays:

Sanbatch. [...] The young priest was talking to me about it and about the unsane. "A lot are in the asylum for leading a bad life," he said. "Father," I ses, "there's more in the asylum from want of married life." Tis easy for the priests and nuns to live straightforward; they have God every morning. But we can't go to Mass on a Sunday itself, we're gone so old, some of us, and more of us are so starved and raggedy.

(135)

Sanbatch, in despair of Church or State intervention, turns his remaining energy to trying to encourage as many marriages as he can, while trying to make money with a device to make illegal poteen. He also strives to reintegrate Sadie into society, and to make her "marriageable." In addition to coaxing her with kindness, he encourages Hotha to play music to help Sadie emerge from her isolation. While this develops, Kitty Wallace, a local young woman who has generally cared for Sadie, begins a relationship with Con. Sheila's father dies, and she decides to stay.

Sanbatch's invention briefly succeeds, before it and all the poteen he has brewed are seized by the police. Invention lost, and money spent, Sanbatch finally loses hope which leads to his great gesture of tying himself Christ-like to a tree so that he'll be taken to the asylum in Ballinasloe. After this, the remaining characters can sell his land and make use of his meagre resources. Here his attentiveness to Sadie pays off, as she agrees to marry Hotha only if everyone can help

Sanbatch. The villagers cease to struggle with individual decisions, and devise plans to marry and economically sustain one another.

Mark and Sheila are hastily betrothed as Kitty says: "Give Mark your ring finger, and you'll save Sanbatch. Wance he sees two young couples here and the village coming to life again, Con's lorry and ropes won't be strong enough to drag him from it" (173). Kitty and Con will also marry, moving into Hotha's house and looking after Sanbatch and his land. The play then ends like a typical traditional comedy, with the promise of multiple marriages, the integrity of the community intact and the possibility of better things ahead with the problem-solving something that emerges as a result of a shared sense of community and ownership. Molloy's characters compel action and change around them with humour and romance being not just a distraction, but a roadmap to salvation. Sanbatch's will to live returns at the thought of the regeneration of the village and the final lines of the play are his: he will die happy "because we will be leaving room for more" (177).

When the play was produced by Druid Theatre, Galway, in 1983, director Garry Hynes described it as "undoubtedly quirky and difficult, bizarre almost" but said that her understanding of it crystalised when she "became aware of the place the play occupied in our theatrical history, forty years after *The Playboy of the Western World* and three years before *Waiting for Godot*. It seemed to me that *The Wood of the Whispering* stands in direct line between these high points of our drama."[3]

Lisa Coen

Notes

1 Clair Wills, *The Best Are Leaving: Emigration and Post-War Irish Culture* (Cambridge: Cambridge University Press, 2015), 1.
2 M. J. Molloy, *The Wood of the Whispering*, in *M. J. Molloy: Selected Plays* (Gerrards Cross: Colin Smyth, 1998), 125. Subsequent references are entered in parentheses.
3 Garry Hynes, "Whispering the Leaving of the West," *Theatre Ireland* 4 (1983): 29.

Further Reading

Coen, Lisa. "Urban and Rural Theatre Cultures Collide: M. J. Molloy, John B. Keane, and Hugh Leonard." In *The Oxford Handbook of Modern Irish Theatre*, edited by Nicholas Grene and Chris Morash, 307–21. Oxford: Oxford University Press, 2016.

WAITING FOR GODOT (1953) BY SAMUEL BECKETT

Written in French in postwar Paris, *Waiting for Godot* has gone on to become the most influential Irish play of the twentieth century, cited during political revolutions as well as on episodes of *Sesame Street* and *Game of Thrones*. When Samuel Beckett wrote the text, he had very little theatre experience and was living in straitened financial circumstances, but its success launched his career as a globally influential writer and director. Crucially, it was the material poverty of *Godot*'s stage – with its small cast of five playing against a simple outdoor backdrop containing a tree and a moon – that facilitated the play's premiere at the experimental Théâtre de Babylone (*En attendant Godot*, 1953), as well as the many restagings and adaptations that have fuelled its huge cultural influence in the almost seven decades since.

Due to the non-arrival of its titular character across two acts, *Godot* has famously been described as a play in which "nothing happens, *twice*."[1] As we hear in the first spoken line, there is a general sense of "Nothing to be done" in this play, with its two main characters Vladimir (Didi) and Estragon (Gogo) largely occupying themselves with comedic crosstalk as they await their appointment with the never-to-be-seen Godot.[2] However, Beckett did subtitle his English translation "*A Tragicomedy in Two Acts*" and there is a strong echo of Greek tragedy in Estragon's joke that he and Vladimir should repent "being born" (13).[3] If anything can be said to happen, it is their encounter with the domineering, whip-wielding Pozzo – who claims to own the land on which they stand – and his helper, Lucky, tied to his master by a rope around his neck. Though Pozzo fancies himself as an orator, it is Lucky who gives the most memorable monologue of Act One, termed by the other characters his "think" (39). This largely unpunctuated stream of speech can last over four minutes in performance, providing a climactic counterpoint to the blather and banter which surrounds it. However, it offers little in the way of explicit thematic development, and fittingly ends with the word "unfinished …" (43). Soon after, Pozzo and Lucky leave and a Boy arrives, telling Vladimir and Estragon: "Mr Godot told me to tell you he won't come this evening but surely tomorrow" (49). Act Two features a similar scenario played out by the same characters, only this time Pozzo is blind and Lucky (apparently) dumb. When they leave, the Boy re-enters, claiming not to remember Vladimir and making the same promise about Godot's arrival tomorrow. Further repetitions abound as the play ends: Didi and Gogo – as they did in Act One – consider hanging themselves from the tree, before replaying the final tableau of the opening act:

Vladimir. Well? Shall we go?
Estragon. Yes, let's go.
　[*They do not move.*]

(88; see also 52)

What are we to make of a play in which so little happens? At a symposium held after a 1957 New York production, one audience member suggested that interpretations of *Godot* tell us more about interpreters' own predispositions than the content of the text itself: "Isn't *Waiting for Godot* a sort of living Rorschach [inkblot] test?" he asked rhetorically.[4] Indeed, the history of *Godot*'s critical reception can serve as something of a guide to postwar Eurocentric thought. Early readings were influenced by the dominance of existentialism, and focused on Didi and Gogo's predicament as a comment on the human condition, led in the Anglophone world by Martin Esslin's bestselling monograph *The Theatre of the Absurd* (1961). Such readings have since been forcefully challenged by a range of critical perspectives, from postcolonial readings of Pozzo's dominance over Lucky to a queer reading of the play which places it in the broader context of homoeroticism across Beckett's writing.[5] Though existentialism has long since fallen out of critical favour as a frame with which to make sense of *Godot*'s stage action, recent research on Beckett's compositional manuscripts show that the author did consider including a long passage structured around an existential question as to whether "it" is worthwhile [Est-ce que c'est la peine?].[6] While such manuscript discoveries by no means simply validate an existentialist reading, they may serve as a useful reminder to keep testing our critical predispositions against evidence from the play.

The practice mentioned by the New York audience member of reading one's own experience into this open-ended text is by no means limited to critics. Theatre practitioners have brought their own contexts to bear on *Godot*'s skeletal plot, the play's transportability enabled by its bare setting and lack of elaborate stage machinery. Soon after the Paris premiere, male prisoners in Lüttringhausen, Germany put on their own version, with one of them telling Beckett by letter that his non-developmental plot reflected their own incarcerated situation. Male prisoners in San Quentin, California, staged *Godot* in 1957, eventually leading to the development of the San Quentin Drama Workshop which Beckett assisted when it toured his work globally. These prison productions may have influenced Beckett's own directorial work. When he directed the German-language *Godot* in Berlin (1975), Didi and Gogo wore striped clothing reminiscent of prison uniform – this in spite of Beckett's repeated refusal to answer questions about what his play meant.

As the cultural capital of *Godot* grew, the play became a lens through which performance practitioners have reflected on a variety of situations of extreme distress, from productions in apartheid South Africa (1980) and occupied Palestine (1984) to a wartime production in Sarajevo (1993) and another staged in New Orleans in the wake of Hurricane Katrina (2007). Such productions draw on the capacity of the play for "reanimation," the power dynamics between the characters shedding new light on the spaces in which it is performed, with these spaces also reanimating the text via their own specific resonances.[7]

There are legal limits to how the play is performed: Beckett himself attempted – unsuccessfully – to block an all-female Dutch production in 1988, a responsibility now taken on by his estate. However *Godot*'s cultural significance extends far beyond authorised versions of the play. Especially outside the Anglosphere, there have been radical adaptations of Beckett's text. A number of these have the eponymous character arriving onstage, with Alan Titley's Irish-language *Tagann Godot* (Godot Arrives; 1987) seeing him killed by Estragon, before coming back to life in a fridge![8] That *Godot* can be stretched and extended in this way is testament to the play's wide-ranging cultural influence: such sequels depend upon audience awareness that Godot's arrival is a significant, almost impossible event. Even in Beckett's country of birth, then, the global impact of his most influential play can be seen in the radical way in which it is adapted.

By the time Beckett died in December 1989, his debut play had already achieved iconic status. That same winter, which saw the collapse of communist regimes across Central and Eastern Europe, it was reported that the phrase "Godot is Here" could be seen on a poster outside the pro-democracy opposition headquarters in Prague, where the Czechoslovak communists had just relinquished their grip on power.[9] In this way, Godot's arrival was used to encapsulate the unexpected nature of the defining political event in late-twentieth-century European history. Will *Waiting for Godot* continue to hold such resonance for its next generation of readers and stage interpreters? For the answer to that question, we just have to wait.

James Little

Notes

1 Vivian Mercier, "The Uneventful Event," *The Irish Times*, 18 February 1956, 6. Emphasis in original.
2 Samuel Beckett, *Waiting for Godot*, in *The Complete Dramatic Works* (London: Faber & Faber, 2006), 11. Subsequent references are entered in parentheses.
3 See Sophocles, *Oedipus at Colonus* (lines 1225–8). With thanks to Burç İdem Dinçel for bringing this to my attention.
4 Vivian Mercier, *Beckett/Beckett* (Oxford: Oxford University Press, 1979), vii.
5 Peter Boxall, "Beckett and Homoeroticism," in *Palgrave Advances in Samuel Beckett Studies*, ed. Lois Oppenheim (London: Palgrave Macmillan, 2004), 110–32.
6 Dirk Van Hulle and Pim Verhulst, *The Making of Samuel Beckett's "En attendant Godot / Waiting for Godot"* (Brussels and London: University Press Antwerp and Bloomsbury, 2017), 237–46.
7 Rónán McDonald, "Global Beckett," in *The Oxford Handbook of Modern Irish Theatre*, ed. Nicholas Grene and Chris Morash (Oxford: Oxford University Press, 2016), 585.
8 Alan Titley, *Tagann Godot: Coiméide Thraigéideach Dhá Ghníomh* (Dublin: An Clóchomhar Tta, 2002).
9 "Editorial: The New Europe, the New World," *Performing Arts Journal* 12, no. 2/3 (1990): 6.

Further Reading

Beckett, Samuel. *The Theatrical Notebooks of Samuel Beckett, Vol. 1, Waiting for Godot*. Edited by Dougald McMillan and James Knowlson. London: Faber & Faber, 1993.
Little, James. *Samuel Beckett in Confinement: The Politics of Closed Space*. London: Bloomsbury Academic, 2020.
Simpson, Hannah. "Trying Again, Failing Again: Samuel Beckett and the Sequel Play." *New Theatre Quarterly* 37, no. 3 (2021): 258–72.

THE HOSTAGE (1958) BY BRENDAN BEHAN

First performed at the Theatre Royal, London, on 14 October 1958, *The Hostage* is haunted by another play, Behan's more naturalistic *An Giall* (June 1958). This simpler, Irish-language drama, staged earlier that year, would mutate into the English-language *The Hostage*, though not by any simple process of translation. Some would see the result – a markedly different play – as a travesty. The two pieces share broadly the same plot, but were so different in terms of dialogue, characters, style and content that Behan stood accused of producing, or rather, allowing to be produced, an absurd farce tailored to the tastes of London audiences. This accusation of kow-towing to "perfidious Albion," levelled at a playwright who was also a former IRA volunteer, reveals something of the complexities of mid-century British–Irish relations.

Behan's message in *The Hostage* was, however, vehemently decolonial.[1] It lambasted essentialist notions of nationhood, casting the more chauvinist elements of Irish nationalism as themselves suffering a colonial hangover. It was also deeply critical of the British empire – its portrayal of a poor, naive English soldier sent abroad to do the bidding of London's elites denounces the classism inherent to imperialism, recalling also the commonalities Behan had felt with English working-class fellow prisoners in *Borstal Boy* (1958).

The action of *The Hostage* takes place in a 1950s Dublin lodging house that doubles as a brothel. Its caretaker, Pat, is a cynical, war-weary IRA veteran of the revolutionary period (1916–1923), its owner, Monsewer, another aged volunteer, but a less perspicacious one: myopic in mind and body, he literally and figuratively can't see what is going on around him. With his French-sounding name that also amusingly suggests the proprietorship of a sewer, Monsewer, like the house itself, connotes high notions and lowly realities. He is thrilled his home is commandeered as part of the IRA's Border Campaign (1956–1962), imagining himself once again part of a heroic independence struggle, but revealingly, Monsewer doesn't recognise the real business of the brothel. This short-sightedness allegorises the remoteness of nationalist Ireland's "owners," his brothel the poor condition of their state.

Without directly depicting any real historical event, Behan's plot invokes the IRA's ongoing military operations during a recent, intense period of guerrilla warfare. Recalling the 1942 hanging of IRA volunteer Tom Williams (who tellingly shares a surname with Behan's captured British soldier), in *The Hostage* a young IRA volunteer is to be hanged in Belfast following capture by Crown forces. Affable British solider Leslie Williams has been captured in retaliation by the IRA, and will be secretly imprisoned in the brothel, his safety to be traded for the safe return of their volunteer. Here, the play echoes Frank O'Connor's short story "Guests of the Nation" (1931) – its tension between soldierly duties and natural affections as an IRA unit is ordered to execute its likeable English captives. Like O'Connor, Behan poignantly questions war's rationalisations. And he questions the transformations envisaged by the contemporary IRA. If the IRA Border Campaign Proclamation of 12 December 1956 declared a "new Ireland will emerge, upright and free […] a country fit for all our people to live in,"[2] Behan's brothel is an emblem of failed freedom – its denizens mostly neither "upright" nor "free", their home hardly fit for habitation: "*Like the house,* [brothel staff] *have seen better times. As the curtain rises, pimps, prostitutes, decayed gentlemen and their visiting 'friend'*" appear.[3] If Taoiseach Éamon de Valera's famous St. Patrick's Day speech in 1943 had envisaged a pious, wholesome land of "people who, satisfied with frugal comfort, devoted their leisure to the things of the spirit,"[4] Behan's opening scenes of sex-workers "*dancing a wild Irish jig*" (1), in a place where bodies are traded for cash, could hardly have been more satiric.

This gap between grand aspirations and degrading realities is the key conceit of the play. As with much of Behan's work, *The Hostage* reveals its themes through a series of ironic contrasts: the permissive brothel madam solemnly declaring "the old cause is never dead" (3); the civil servant and social worker, Mr Mulleady and Miss Gilchrist, whose hectoring, "sterilized" (23) piety is belied by their vulgar minds; the working-class orphan and British soldier, Leslie, who has more in common with the marginalised Irish than do the various zealous patriots we encounter. Those patriots espouse an austere, otherworldly idealism and worry about "sin[s] of impurity" (73) in the brothel, but the real-world love Leslie feels for the play's most Irish of colleens, brothel maid and fellow orphan, Teresa, is far purer than anything the patriots espouse. We follow Leslie's growing affection with Teresa, alongside the uproariously comic, frequently bawdy comings and goings of prostitutes, religious extremists, patriots and homosexuals. Behan had raised issues around state repression of homosexuality in his play *The Quare Fellow* (1954) and his short story "After the Wake" (1955). The action then culminates on a tragic note, with safe-house discovered by police and an ensuing gun-battle precipitating Leslie's death. In a typically Behanesque turn to farce, Leslie presently arises from the dead, the assembled cast singing a jolly tune.

Beneath the mirth is indignation; as Behan had said of his own stagecraft, while audiences "were laughing their heads off, you could be up to any bloody thing behind their backs; and it was what you were doing behind their bloody backs that made your play great."[5] His comic ironies critique an Ireland enmeshed in religious hypocrisy and second-hand imperialist ideology. His most prominent patriot, Monsewer, is after all English-born, "*looks like Baden Powell in an Irish kilt*" (5) and sounds like a member of the British upper classes: "That's the trouble with the fighting forces today. No background, no tradition, no morale" (62). Here, the play anticipates the trajectory of an increasingly socialist IRA of the 1960s, after Behan's friend, Cathal Goudling, takes over as its Chief of Staff. Through the conflict-thwarted love of poor English and Irish orphans, *The Hostage* stresses that class solidarities are struggling to emerge from jaded nationalist reflexes.

To some in Ireland, the new play was a "blown-up hotch-potch compared to the original."[6] Behan's alleged obliviousness to Joan Littlewood's London workshopping was blamed for the transformation of a simple Irish-language tragedy into a riotous, sexed-up extravaganza. Was it "calculated to appeal to Princess Margaret and the raucous fashionable, *avant-garde* first-night audience?"[7] A more apt question, perhaps, is did Behan feel too restricted by the context of the Gael Linn-sponsored Irish-language version at An Halla Damer, Dublin, to mount the kind of provocative lampooning that appeared four months later? *The Hostage* has seven new characters. Prostitutes Colette and Ropeen, though mentioned, do not appear in the earlier play, but are integral to *The Hostage*, along with gay navvy, Rio Rita, and his black boyfriend, Princess Grace. The introduction of significantly more song, dance, metatheatrical jesting, and the breaking of the fourth wall that saw Behan drawn into spontaneous banter with actors, all departed significantly from the serious tone of *An Giall*. But the suggestion that Behan had simply been conned into an experimental travesty fails to give reasonable consideration, among other things, to Behan's own evolving experimentalism, as Ian R. Walsh's analysis shows.[8] It also fails to recognise similarities of tone and style in Behan's *The Big House* (1957) and *Richard's Cork Leg* (unfinished; adapted and performed 1972), for example. In this context, it is instructive that a boy who had left Dublin to bomb England in 1939 was, less than two decades later, making the same journey, possibly, to find greater freedom to do what he wanted with his play.

Michael Pierse

Notes

1 I use the term "decolonial" here, as Catherine E. Walsh does, to describe "the recognition and undoing of the hierarchical structures of race, gender, heteropatriarchy, and class that continue to control life, knowledge, spirituality, and thought." C. E. Walsh, "Decoloniality as/in practice," in *On Decoloniality: Concepts, Analytics, Praxis*, ed. W. D. Mignolo and C. E. Walsh (London: Duke University Press), 17.

2 Qtd. in J. Bowyer Bell, *The Secret Army: The IRA* (London: Transaction, 2004), 291.

3 Brendan Behan, *The Hostage* (London: Methuen, 2000), 1. Subsequent references are entered in parentheses.
4 Quoted in Maurice Moynihan, ed., *Speeches and Statements by Eamon de Valera, 1917–73* (Dublin and New York, 1980), 466.
5 Brendan Behan, *Brendan Behan's Island* (London: Corgi, 1965), 17.
6 Ulick O'Connor, *Brendan Behan* (London: Coronet, 1970), 219.
7 Declan Kiberd, *Inventing Ireland: The Literature of the Modern Nation* (London: Vintage, 1996), 520.
8 Ian R. Walsh, *Experimental Irish Theatre: After W. B. Yeats* (Basingstoke: Palgrave, 2012), 170–5.

Further Reading

Behan, Brendan. *An Giall: Poems and a Play in Irish.* Loughcrew: Gallery Press, 1981.
Brannigan, John. *Brendan Behan: Cultural Nationalism and the Revisionist Writer.* Dublin: Four Courts Press, 2002.
Ní Ríordáin, Clíona. "Brendan Behan's *The Hostage*: Translation, adaptation or recreation of *An Giall?*" In *Reading Brendan Behan*, edited by John McCourt, 117–26. Cork: Cork University Press, 2019.
Pierse, Michael. "'*A dance for all the outcasts*': Class and postcolonialism in Brendan Behan's *An Giall* and *The Hostage.*" *Irish University Review* Vol. 44, no. 1 (Spring–Summer 2014): 92–115.

OVER THE BRIDGE (1960) BY SAM THOMPSON

Sam Thompson's *Over the Bridge*, with its echoes of Elia Kazan's Oscar-Winning *On the Waterfront* (1954), broaches a subject for many years taboo in Northern Ireland: religious bigotry and the violence it breeds. Much of its dynamic derives from dramatic action, but also from verbal confrontations, clashes of ideology and personality between individuals, families, generations, and within communities. It sets out to burst a fiction long fostered by the Ulster Unionist party and government, that Northern Ireland's Protestants constituted a single homogeneous entity which was encouraged to believe that its survival depended on rejecting any form of accommodation with the Catholic minority.

The play opens in the Belfast shipyard with a deeply ironic hymn which anticipates its dark, disturbing outcome: "Lead kindly light/ Amid the encircling gloom."[1] What stirs Rabbie White, an elderly shipyard worker, into song, is the hope that divine guidance will help him achieve a big win on the football pools. Though this provokes laughter, seconds later the mood changes with the entry of Warren Baxter, an ambitious young shop steward. His initial remark

"Man, you're a bloody old hypocrite," along with Rabbie's sardonic response, establish a core theme in the play: "You know, Warren, hymn singing ... [is] the only time you'll get people together in loving harmony. Then after the *Amen*, they're at each other's bloody throats again" (22).

Moments later, Baxter challenges Rabbie over a decision by Davy Mitchell, the union's elder statesman who becomes progressively central role to the drama, to hold an unofficial meeting addressing the resurgence in sectarian tensions in the shipyard. In a subsequent row between Rabbie and Baxter we discover how much Davy's ethical and political perspectives were shaped during the 1930s, a decade when Northern Ireland's shipbuilders and their families starved. Despite Baxter's disdain for religious bigotry he feels no qualms about exploiting it to advance his union career: "Seventy-five percent of our members are Prods. They'll vote for me because I'm a Prod ... it proves my point about men. Never depend on them. Never *sacrifice* yourself on their behalf" (36). Convinced of his superior judgement, he remarks of his prospective father-in-law, "Davy has *faith* in his *principles*. I have *faith* in my common sense. I've learnt the grim lesson of Davy's life without having to give a repeat performance" (38). However, the clash that proves pivotal to the play's tragic outcome concerns a Protestant, Archie Kerr, and a Catholic, Peter O'Boyle. Its ugliness becomes apparent when a young apprentice reports that "a Prod vigilance committee" (29) has threatened him with a beating, should he continue to make tea for Peter. What appals Kerr is not just the fact that the "Papist" O'Boyle serves on the union district committee, but that democratic processes allowed this to happen.

Act One's closing scene transfers to the Mitchell household where Martha, Davy's daughter, is humming contentedly while ironing, until suddenly she is compelled to stop, "*alarmed, at the sound of an explosion*" (49). On entry, Martha, Rabbie's wife, urges her not to imagine the worst but Baxter bursts in, reporting that an explosion in the shipyard has left one worker seriously injured. The assumption that an IRA bomb caused it has taken an immediate hold, with the result that an enraged Protestant mob has already forced every Catholic to quit their workplace.[2] Baxter anticipates that Peter O'Boyle will be their principal target the following day, and that every effort must focus on persuading him to stay away.

At the start of Act Two Thompson establishes that events are accelerating towards a terrible conclusion with the revelation that the sole Catholic worker to present himself for work is Peter. As a result, the play's principal male characters – Rabbie, Baxter, Davy, his brother

George, and the management's head foreman, Fox – find themselves under siege in one of the shipyard's offices. What has inflamed the angry mob is a rumour that their fellow worker, injured in the previous day's explosion, had died on the way to hospital. Conscious of their vulnerable position each man repeatedly endeavours to coax Peter into leaving.

To the audience, Davy appears the only figure capable of defusing the crisis, yet it quickly becomes clear that his authority and room for manoeuvre are extremely limited. Deftly, Thompson ratchets up the tension, first by having Davy smack Peter's face to stop his defiant shouts carrying; next by adding the sound of breaking glass to the swelling noise off-stage; and lastly by staging a face-to-face encounter between Peter and the mob leader. Neither verbal abuse nor physical threats lessen Peter's resolve to stay put, though the psychological strain is evidently telling.

Fearful of what lies in store for them, the trapped officials cannot agree on a course of action. Baxter displays almost complete indifference towards Peter's fate, arguing "It's about time we thought of ourselves and got out of here before that mob goes into action" (81). When Fox urges Peter to leave immediately and do exactly whatever the mob leader demands, George questions the wisdom of such advice: "That mob didn't come all this way to let him walk through the gate unmolested" (81). Disregarding Peter's refusal "to be chased out of my employment because I'm a Catholic" (81) Rabbie, like Baxter, rejects Fox's order that everybody should stay together:

> If he's not prepared to walk out through that gate, I am- I'm not goin' to be a witness to a scene where a man is stupid enough to offer himself as a sacrifice.

Thompson's stage directions read "Fox, Peter *and* Davy ... *stand their ground.*" Though others are prepared to forsake a core premise of trade unionism, collective solidarity, Davy cannot:

> All my life I've fought for the principles of my union and Peter here fought for them too. Would you want me to refuse to work with him, because he upholds what is his right, to work without intimidation?

> (82)

From the outset Thompson has prepared the ground for such a decision which is entirely consistent with Davy's political beliefs and moral constitution. In positioning himself literally and metaphorically alongside Peter, Davy reaffirms his socialist ideals and articulates what was and remains an overarching need in Northern Ireland, a need for spaces and structures which will bring its diverse constituencies together.

Thompson has not always received sufficient credit for his stagecraft, though his skill in creating mood through theatrical effects are considerable, as the end of this scene shows. The sounding out of a shipyard horn signals more than an end to the lunch-break, since it acts as the overture to violence, "*the banging of hammers and angry voices*" (83). In a further irony, it is Baxter, who most wanted to distance himself from the spectacle, who is compelled to describe it for the audiences on- and off-stage. His account of the two men walking out to their bench and beginning work "as if nothing was going to happen" and of the mob "closing in" is punctuated by a scream, a brief but "*terrifying din*" and then a silence stopped by his own sobbing (84). At the scene's close a single figure is exposed on stage, Archie Kerr, who initiated the tragic process, but who now has nothing to say.

Although the Ulster Group Theatre's young artistic director, James Ellis, was enthusiastic about the play and its Reading Committee endorsed his decision to proceed with rehearsals, the staunchly conservative Board of Directors first demanded major script changes, then axed the production. A letter to the *Belfast Telegraph* spelt out their reasons:

> The Ulster public is fed up with religious and political controversies. This play is full of grossly vicious phrases and situations which would undoubtedly offend and affront every section of the public. ... It is the policy of the directors of the Ulster Group Theatre to keep political and religious controversies off our stage.[3]

In response to this attempt to stifle debate, the majority of the actors and three directors resigned, and Thompson and Ellis formed their own company, Ulster Bridge Productions, and raised enough funds to hire Belfast's Empire Theatre, which had capacity of over one thousand. Following the play's first performance there on 26 January 1960, it enjoyed a six-week run. A local newspaper estimated that 42,000 people must have seen it, far more than any other play in the city's history. As Seamus Heaney wrote, Thompson was a man "whose passion for justice transfigured plays that might otherwise have been regarded as clumsy or old-fashioned into urgent tracts for the times."[4]

Michael Parker

Notes

1 *Sam Thompson: Over the Bridge and Other Plays*, ed. John Keyes (Belfast: Lagan Press, 1997), 21. Subsequent references are entered in parentheses.
2 The composition and production of Thompson's play coincided with "Operation Harvest," an IRA campaign of violence which lasted from December 1956 until February 1962.
3 "Why *Over the Bridge* was withdrawn," *Belfast Telegraph*, 14 May 1959.
4 Seamus Heaney, "Out of London: Ulster's Troubles," *New Statesman*, 1 July 1966, 23–4.

Further Reading

Devlin, Paddy. "The 'Over the Bridge' Controversy." *The Linen Hall Review* Vol. 2, no. 3 (Autumn 1985): 4–6.
Mengel, Hagal. *Sam Thompson and Modern Ulster Drama.* Zurich: Peter Lang, 1986.
Parker, Michael. *Northern Irish Literature and the Imprint of History 1956–75.* Basingstoke: Palgrave, 2007.

STEPHEN D. (1962) BY HUGH LEONARD

"Hugh Leonard" is a pseudonym for John Keyes Byrne (1926–2009), a prolific writer destined for success in television, the West End and Broadway. *Stephen D.* is an adaptation of Joyce's novel *A Portrait of the Artist as a Young Man* (1916) and Joyce's earlier *Stephen Hero*, not published until after his death. Leonard later described *Stephen D.* as "no more than a scissors-and- paste affair with nothing of myself in it."[1] Modesty aside, this description is misleading: *Stephen D.* is a tour de force, showing how close in spirit Leonard felt to the rebellious Joyce.

It was a timely production, undertaken by the annual Dublin Theatre Festival established in 1957. In 1958 the Festival was cancelled because the local Archbishop found the programme scandalous, containing an adaptation of *Ulysses* and a new play by Sean O'Casey. The power of the Irish clergy at this time was a major threat to the freedom of the stage. In 1957 the Pike Theatre production of Tennessee Williams's *The Rose Tattoo* was raided by the police and the director arrested for public indecency. In 1959, a production of J. P. Donleavy's *The Ginger Man* was ordered to close after three nights. Hugh Leonard was a brave man to try again with *Stephen D.* Fortunately, this time there was no opposition. As the producer enthused, "When the curtain fell, there was a silence, and then pandemonium broke loose with cheers and countless curtain calls. On the following day the reviews were favourable beyond our wildest dreams."[2] In February 1963 the play moved to St Martin's Theatre in London; in 1967 it had an Off-Broadway production, with Joyce's grandson Stephen as one of the three Stephens in the cast, a good omen.

Robert Hogan described *Stephen D.* as "one of the most impressive plays to appear in Dublin since the [Second World] war."[3] This is because Leonard brought Joyce's work to an audience mainly ignorant of Joyce's writings. Joyce's *Portrait* became available in Penguin paperback only in 1960, while *Stephen Hero*, available in the United States since 1944, was not available in England until the Panther edition in 1977. It is clear Leonard studied these texts closely, and worked with his director Jim Fitzgerald to bring out the meaning dramatically.

In the published text, Leonard deliberately kept stage directions at a minimum because "*Stephen D.* is a most difficult and intricate play [to stage], which will stand or fall depending upon its director's imagination."[4] Basically, he wanted a bare stage with platforms, Stephen to act as narrator locating settings, and lighting to arrange the scene changes. The play is written in two acts (unusual at the time), performing a perfect circle. The opening stage direction reads: "*The curtain rises on a dark stage. The wail of a ship's siren is heard. A long line of passengers moves slowly towards the waiting ship.* Stephen *comes forward and regards an open suitcase. We hear the cries of seabirds.*" The adult Stephen speaks: "My mother is putting my new secondhand clothes in order. She prays now, she says, that I may learn in my own life and away from home and friends what the heart is and what it feels. (*He closes the suitcase.*) Amen. So be it" (11). He moves towards the gangplank, searches for his ticket, hears a sailor's hornpipe, whistles in tune and then sits in reverie, moving into the opening lines of Joyce's narrative. The staging recalls the experimental style of Hilton Edwards and Micheál mac Liammóir at the Gate, where, indeed, *Stephen D.* premiered. Like Tom in Williams's *The Glass Menagerie*, the elder Stephen moves in and out of the play as narrator and participant. *Stephen D.* is thus a modernist memory play.

Leonard's craftsmanship lies in the coherence of scenes that flow into each other with a focus on the major episodes in Stephen's progress from childhood to early adulthood. In his production note Leonard refers to the issues Stephen struggles with as "the four great 'F's' of Ireland: faith, fatherland, family and friendship" (5). Act 1 concludes with the sermon on hell, Stephen's repentance of his sexual sins and his confession to Old Priest, from whom he immediately receives Holy Communion. Then the light changes expressionistically to suit Stephen's cynicism. Alone, he announces: "Chastity, having been found a great inconvenience, was quietly abandoned. *He lights a cigarette*. Curtain" (29).

Act 2, set in University College Dublin and other locations exterior and interior, dramatises Stephen's growth towards independence from those "nets" mentioned towards the end of *A Portrait*: "You talk to me of nationality, language, religion. I shall try to fly by those nets."[5] There were fishermen's nets on stage, thrown into relief by the cyclorama extending across the upstage area. Joyce's metaphor underlies a play about existential freedom. Leonard identifies with Joyce over clerical oppression and uses *Stephen Hero* to focus in Act 2 on Joyce and Ibsen as a means of highlighting censorship. For his lecture to the Literary and Historical Society Stephen chooses the topic "Drama and Life," which gets him into an argument with the President of University College Dublin, and fellow-students more interested in nationalism, the Irish language and what McCann (based on Francis Sheehy-Skeffington) calls "the question of universal peace" (35). In choosing to promote Ibsen and modernism Stephen alienates just about everybody. The president cautions him: "I am afraid I cannot allow you to read your paper before the Society. [...] It represents the sum total of modern unrest and modern freethinking." When he realises that Stephen intends to publish the text he firmly forbids it: "I should not care for anyone to identify the ideas in your essay with the teaching in our college. [...] Our people have their faith and they are happy" (39–40). The scene switches to the delivery of the paper, after which McCann jumps onto the platform and denounces Ibsen: "We want no foreign filth. [...] If we are to have art, let it be moral art, art that elevates, above all, national art" (41). Stephen is silenced but Leonard sympathised, believing that Ibsen and Strindberg created twentieth-century drama.[6]

An argument with his mother provides further evidence of Stephen's alienation. She wants him to prepare for his Easter "duty." Instead, Stephen argues with her over Christ's ascension. "It's absurd: it's Barnum. He comes into the world God knows how, walks on the water, gets out of his grave and goes off up the Hill of Howth. What drivel is this?" (42). She blames third-level education. "It's all the fault of those books. [...] I'll burn every one of them. I won't have them in the house to corrupt anyone else." To this threat Stephens responds: "If you were a genuine Roman Catholic, Mother, you would burn me as well as the books," reducing her to tears (43).

The death of Stephen's sister Isobel soon after deepens his refusal to believe in "an all-wise God calling a soul home" (53). His grief is mixed in with disappointment that his girlfriend Emma Clery disapproves of his "heretic" tendencies. But he tells Cranly, his closest friend: "I do not fear to be alone or to be spurned for another [man] or to leave whatever I have to leave. And I am not afraid to make [...] a lifelong mistake" (50). He is ready to abandon Ireland since Ireland has abandoned him.

In the final scene the play returns to its opening. The ship's siren sounds *"for the last time"* as Stephen moves towards the gangway, reciting the opening of *A Portrait*, "Once upon a time and a very good time it was," but after three lines switches savagely to Joyce's poem "Gas from a Burner," registering rejection:

> This lovely land that always sent
> Her writers and artists to banishment—
> O Ireland, my first and only love
> Where Christ and Caesar are hand in glove.

Leonard then adds the curtain line, "I will not serve!" from *A Portrait* (54), before Stephen steps into exile.

Christopher Murray

Notes

1 Hugh Leonard, *Out after Dark* (London: André Deutsch, 1989), 169.
2 Phyllis Ryan, *The Company I Kept* (Dublin: Town House, 1996), 174–5.
3 Robert Hogan, *After the Irish Renaissance: A Critical History of the Irish Drama since The Plough and the Stars* (London: Macmillan, 1968), 187.
4 Hugh Leonard, "Production Note," *Stephen D* (London and New York: Evans Brothers, 1964), 2. Subsequent references are entered in parentheses.
5 James Joyce, *A Portrait of the Artist as a Young Man* (Harmondsworth: Penguin, 1960), 203.
6 Hugh Leonard, "Drama. The Turning Point," in *Ireland at the Crossroads: The Acts of the Lille Symposium June–July 1978*, ed. Patrick Rafroidi and Pierre Joannon (Lille: Publications de L'Université de Lille III, 1978–9), 77–85.

Further Reading

Lanters, José. *Missed Understandings: A Study of Stage Adaptations of the Works of James Joyce*. Amsterdam: Rodopi, 1988.

Pine, Emilie. "Leonard's Progress: Hugh Leonard at the Dublin Theatre Festival." In *Interactions: Dublin Theatre Festival 1957–2007*, edited by Nicholas Grene and Patrick Lonergan, 47–60. Dublin: Carysfort Press, 2008.

THE FIELD (1965) BY JOHN B. KEANE

John B. Keane, a playwright and novelist from Co. Kerry, emigrated to England like many of his generation, experiences which informed plays such as *Hut 42* (1962). He returned to open a pub in Listowel in 1955 and his first play, *Sive*, performed by his local amateur drama group, won the All-Ireland Drama Festival in 1959. *The Field* was first staged at the Olympia Theatre in Dublin in 1965, with Ray MacAnally playing Bull McCabe. It was adapted for a film in 1990 starring Richard Harris.

Where J. M. Synge was an outsider listening through a chink in the floorboards, Keane was an insider, absorbing stories and dialogue and, like Synge, giving voice to rural Ireland and the clash of old values with modernisation. Along with Brian Friel, Tom Murphy, Thomas Kilroy, and Hugh Leonard, Keane would become a key figure in the "second renaissance" of Irish drama which coincided with "the sudden and exciting changes (economic, social, cultural) which the country itself underwent after 1958."[1] Lionel Pilkington suggests that the "unprecedented flourishing" of drama in this period "arises partly because of the way in which the inadequacy or inappropriateness of traditional nationalist verities is rendered not satirically (as in Macken and O'Donovan), but as an existential trauma."[2]

Written and set in 1965, *The Field* begins in a public house in the small rural village of Carraigthomond. The play follows the growing tension and eventual violence between the village's domineering quasi-leader, Bull McCabe, whose nickname links him to cattle and, by extension, the land on which they graze, and William Dee, an emigrant returned from England who wants to buy the same field as Bull.

The field in question is a piece of land about to be sold by Maggie Butler, a local widow. The site is attractive to any buyer due to its position, access to roads and water, but in particular it is of use to McCabe, as it borders his land and he has been using it to graze cattle. Bull has worked the field for five years and invested much time and work – and this is where the audience has an opportunity to experience a kind of understanding for Bull and his claim – but Maggie puts it up for auction to seek a high price because it is clear that Bull would underpay. However, Bull is confident that no one would bid against him in an auction, until William Dee enters.

The characters in the pub, Bird, Maimie, her husband Mick, establish with witty exchanges that the village is small and the people pious – in Mass if not always in practice. There is a biting poverty and a resentment of small-town life where cabbage is too often on the menu. Physical and emotional abuse are accepted as the norm. Bull enters with his son Tadhg, and both behave in an imposing, bullying manner, complaining about Maggie's decision to have the field auctioned.

Bull warns Mick that "Half of the village is related to me and them that isn't is related to my wife."[3] This is why he can be sure of loyalty when the auction happens, and he solidifies his position by threatening to organise a boycott of Flanagan's pub if Mick refuses to participate in a sham bidding on the day of the auction. Bull's manipulation of his community is the combination of an appeal to the recent past and a need for Irish rural people to take ownership of their land on one hand, and simple brute intimidation on the other. Shortly after, the local police sergeant comes to question Bull about a dead donkey. It becomes clear that Bull and Tadhg were responsible for beating the animal to death, but their denial is supported by Bird, and it is clear that the sergeant has no real power in Carraigthomond.

William Dee makes a different kind of entrance. He is polite, circumspect in his responses to small-talk, and generously buys drinks. Dee is originally from Galway, but has lived in England for twelve years and asserts his preference for living there. His interest in the field is less romantic than Bull's; as the site is "on a river with first-class gravel" (122) he intends to use it as a site for developing building materials. This is shocking to the residents, as Bull articulates: "Tis a sin to cover grass and clover with concrete" (130). Dee can easily be seen as a signifier of the imposition of industry on rural Ireland. He is not a flat token of capitalism, though, as his main motivation in moving back to Ireland is his wife's euphemistically described mental illness and her wish to come home to recover. Crucially, however, he lacks familial knowledge of the land, and, as his claim is purely material, it is seen as less legitimate. Bull tried to intimidate Dee, who holds his ground, and the auction proceeds. It is clear that Dee has the means to outbid McCabe, so he is thwarted by Mick who adjourns until the next day.

The tension of this scene is balanced with a comedic scene in the pub between Leamy, one of the Flanagan children, and visiting relatives of Bull who have come to show support. Bull then instructs everyone that the intimidation of Dee will escalate, and swears them to silence. Throughout his career, Keane would skilfully deploy violent, disturbing subject matter in humorous circumstances, using witty dialogue and well-timed humour as a Trojan horse for an important excoriation of contemporary Ireland and the cracks in the façade of Catholic respectability. Characters like Maimie Flanagan offer a robust indictment of the abuse of women by nominally respectable characters. Her husband Mick is a good man, trying to do honest work in the face of Bull's intimidation, but he is also someone who once struck his wife so violently that he thought he had killed her. The governing reality is that violence has its place, and Bull cannily appeals to his community on atavistic terms when he calls for loyalty: "A total stranger has come and he wants to bury my sweat and blood in concrete" (136).

In Act 2, set by a road at night, Bull and Tadgh wait for Dee. In their conversation we learn that Bull's wife hasn't spoken aloud to him in eighteen years because of another brutal attack on an animal. When Dee enters, the ensuing dispute results in Bull's savagely beating him with Tadhg's help (and Bird looking on). The crucial final blow is delivered by Tadhg, however, while Bird and Bull call for him not to go too far. This last savage kick by Tadhg is the result of years of Bull's instruction and justification for his own violent behaviour, as well Tadhg's need to impress his father.

Five weeks later, no one has been held accountable. Leamy Flanagan wants to report his suspicions about Bull to Sergeant Leahy, but is sworn to secrecy by his terrified mother. Thereafter, a monologue is given by the Bishop about hypocrisy, criticising the collusion of the villagers in the conspiracy to protect Dee's murderer. In an attempt to destabilise the villagers' loyalty to Bull, the bishop gives a sermon on the "hunger for land" (149). The speech evokes the sustained trauma of poverty and hunger that causes obsession with land and ownership, while still rejecting this as an excuse, and insisting upon Christian values. Meanwhile, Bull buys the field for £350 – more than he was willing to pay, but significantly less than Maggie would have received from Dee.

The final act does not see the play resolve this injustice, instead a series of interviews are conducted by the sergeant and priest. Each witness evades or lies to avoid incriminating Bull McCabe, who in his turn argues against the legitimacy of church or state in the village. The concluding image, once Bull exits, is of Leamy, emerging from a hiding place, and seemingly struggling with indecision, resigning himself to clearing the tables.

Tending towards melodrama (for instance in *Sive*), Keane's work can suffer if a production overly depends on humour. But thoughtful staging can emphasise his discreet and underrated feminism, and his canny eviscerations of dated ideologies and the damage they can inflict on people hemmed in by poverty and unquestioning obedience. And though Keane's themes now seem well-worn, Robert Welch argues that after Padraic Colum's *The Land* (1905), which treats the trauma of the illegitimate transfer of land ownership in Ireland in the nineteenth century, we have to wait until Keane's *The Field* "before we encounter an Irish play adequate to this powerful obsession with land."[4]

Lisa Coen

Notes

1 Christopher Murray, *Twentieth-Century Irish Drama: Mirror up to Nation* (Manchester: Manchester University Press, 1997), 162.
2 Lionel Pilkington, *Theatre and the State in Twentieth-Century Ireland: Cultivating the People* (London: Routledge, 2001), 160.
3 John B. Keane, *The Field and Other Irish Plays* (Dublin: Roberts Rinehart Publishers, 1994), 104. Subsequent references are entered in parentheses.
4 Robert Welch, *The Abbey Theatre 1899–1999: Form and Pressure* (London: Oxford University Press, 1999), 38.

Further Reading

Herr, Cheryl. *The Field*. Cork: Cork University Press, 2002.
Richards, Shaun. "'Saved in the man and in the nation': the Sacralisation of the Soil in Twentieth-Century Irish Drama." *Worldviews: Environment, Culture, Religion* Vol. 5, no. 1 (2001): 80–95.

FAMINE (1968) BY TOM MURPHY

Tom Murphy's *Famine*, a play depicting the Great Famine of the nineteenth century, premiered on the Abbey Theatre's Peacock stage, Dublin, in March 1968. The play's genesis dated to 1962, when Murphy first read about the Irish Famine in Cecil Woodham-Smith's *The Great Hunger*. After intensive research on the topic Murphy (re) created the cosmology, or the "feeling of life" of the common people who suffered during the Famine.[1]

The play is set in the fictional village of Glanconor, between the autumn of 1846 and the spring of 1847. It centres on the family of John Connor, descended from kings of the clan after which Glanconor is named. An imminent famine is looming in the opening scene where the villagers gather to mourn the daughter of John and Sinéad ("Mother") who died of starvation. However, the Connors could still afford a traditional wake in which *"people laugh, smoke, eat and drink."*[2] This is the final glimpse of a well-functioning community, from which the play evolves to present its utter disintegration. As food becomes scarce, anything edible is desperately pursued, while a convoy of corn-carts is sent to England as rent. In a scene where the villagers meet to discuss solutions at his house, John insists on sharing whatever he has with his neighbours, observing the custom of pre-famine days. In contrast to her husband who wants to do what is right, Sinéad, the mother of two starving children, is focused on the practicalities of keeping the family together. She unwillingly follows her husband's demand and gives their food to the neighbours at her children's expense. The contrast between the traditional culture and the people's plight during the Famine is captured through the disparity between John and Sinéad, the king and the queen. John could have been a noble and reliable leader in a different context; however, he is an obstinate and incapable one in these circumstances. Conversely, it is Sinéad who suggests a pragmatic plan such as to produce coffins with trap-bottoms to sell across the countryside. However, the excess of motherly selfishness leads her to steal from a neighbour who dies as a consequence. Meanwhile, the Relief Committee decides to introduce an emigration policy as a solution to help the peasants. Since it is an official form of eviction, John refuses to accept the plan that will send him and his family to Canada. The majority of villagers abide by his decision. However, the refusal of the offer does not prevent eviction for John and the others. The houses are demolished and unroofed, because of their inability to pay the rent. In the rubble of their ruined house, Sinéad confesses her theft to John, who cannot accept her act of wrongdoing. However, in her final moments, her previous bitterness is transformed into the noble defiance of a tragic heroine and she is ready to be killed by her husband. Sinéad dies as a proud queen. Murphy refuses to pass moral judgement on Sinéad or John, who, after the killing of his wife and son, wanders about the village in his frenzy.

Famine is unmistakably a historical play; however, it also presents a playwright's response to the Irish society of the 1950s and 1960s. Murphy, after working on the play for several years, concluded that he was "a victim of the Famine" and felt "the need to write about the moody self and [his] times" (xi), which stem from the Famine as a racial memory. Indeed, as Murphy states, "it takes nine generations to get rid of the racial memory."[3] In order to accept his present moment, in *Famine* Murphy references the time span of 120 years between the historical famine and his contemporary times. This inner history and racial memory amalgamated in the play can be traced through images and phrases taken from the canonical plays of modern Irish theatre.

For example, villagers in *Famine*, thinking of an off-stage figure, repeat that "he will be remembered" (75). This is a line that echoes the sentiment in Lady Gregory and W. B. Yeats's *Kathleen ni Houlihan* (1902): the eponymous heroine, as an old hag, sings the following line: "they shall be remembered for ever."[4] The play, set at the time of the United Irishmen's rising of 1798, is a reminder that its failure eventually led to the Act of Union in 1800. This political moment was the background of the historical famine. In addition, Maeve, John's sixteen-year-old daughter, who appears on stage as "a bitter old hag" (43), is subtly likened to the old woman in *Kathleen ni Houlihan*. Maeve becomes a young girl again by devouring an apple (45), while Kathleen is transformed into a queen by devouring the blood of young patriots. Both Maeve and Kathleen symbolise a starving Ireland – Maeve starved for food and Kathleen for blood.

The phrase "the dirty deed" (17) evokes the speech of Pegeen Mike in Synge's *The Playboy of the Western World* (1907). Indeed, Murphy's peasants, with their violence and harshness, are the literary descendants of those of Synge who in turn are the imaginative off-spring of the people who suffered the Famine. This allusion to *The Playboy* objectifies and visualises the historical sense of continuation as the national trauma had been transferred to modern Ireland through the early 1900s of *The Playboy* and on into the 1950s and 1960s.

The most contemporary Irish play alluded to in *Famine* is Beckett's *Waiting for Godot* (1953). The opening tableau in which one villager, who is "sitting on a ditch by the roadside" (5), is joined by another, presents a striking resemblance to a similar instance in *Waiting for Godot*. John asks to himself: "How am I to overcome it?" (7), which could be a question answerable in the first speech of *Godot*, "Nothing to be done." Seeing elements of the Irish Famine in this avant-garde play is not as absurd as it initially seems. The prevailing apathy of *Godot* is a racial memory, the feeling of inertia that has been passed down from the Famine period as a national trauma.

In 1985, two plays of Murphy about a fictional village called Bochtán, *A Thief of a Christmas* and *Bailegangaire*, were premiered by the Abbey and Druid Theatres respectively. *A Thief,* set in the 1950s, the backdrop of Murphy's "moody self," presents the sense of continuation from the Famine in its poverty-stricken Irish peasants.

In *Bailegangaire*, set in 1984, Mommo, a senile old woman, repeats a story about what happened in *A Thief*. In these plays Murphy further expanded the time span covered in *Famine* to include the 1980s. The two plays about Bochtán and *Famine* are imaginatively connected.[5] They deal with the misfortunes of a family, of a community, of the country.

Famine, as one of the important plays of Irish theatre, has been revived in the twenty-first century. Two prominent examples are the Abbey production in 2001, as part of the Tom Murphy season, and the Druid production in 2012 as part of DruidMurphy. The social context of each production was, however, very different. The former was produced in the period of affluence during the Celtic Tiger era, and the latter under what Garry Hynes, the director, termed "the pressure of a debt crisis that has become an identity crisis" following the economic collapse in 2008. In her words, *Famine* stages "an inner history of Ireland" and sets the "interrogation of where [they] take up [their] futures, [their] lives."[6]

Famine concludes with Maeve's tears, Murphy's little angry Kathleen ni Houlihan. The rage and bewilderment crystallised in her tears become a sense of purgation, a form of catharsis, as Murphy states even more revealingly: "There is always hope at the end of the play. [...] I seem to be looking for hope, always."[7]

Hiroko Mikami

Notes

1 Tom Murphy, "Introduction," in *Tom Murphy Plays 1* (London: Methuen, 1992), ix.

2 Tom Murphy, *Famine*, in *Plays 1*, 16. Subsequent references are entered in parentheses.

3 Eric Grode, "A Dark Irish Voice Revisits His Rage," *The New York Times*, 27 June 2012. www.nytimes.com/2012/07/01/theater/druidmurphy-three-tom-murphy-plays-at-lincoln-center.htlm. Accessed 1 September 2021.

4 Lady Gregory (and W. B. Yeats), *Kathleen ni Houlihan*, in *Lady Gregory: Selected Writings*, ed. Lucy McDiamid and Maureen Waters (Harmondsworth: Penguin, 1995), 309.

5 In 1984 Murphy became the Writer-in-Association of Druid Theatre Company, which revived *Famine* in 1984, before he wrote *Bailegangaire* for the company.

6 Garry Hynes, "Director's Note," in *DruidMurphy: Plays by Tom Murphy* (London: Methuen Drama, 2012).

7 John Waters, "The Frontiersman," *In Dublin*, 15 May 1986, 28.

Further Reading

Mikami, Hiroko. "*Famine* in Context." In *Alive in Time: The Enduring Drama of Tom Murphy*, edited by Christopher Murray, 39–55. Dublin: Carysfort Press, 2010.

Troupe, Shelly. "Tom Murphy and Druid Theatre's *Famine*: Developing Images and Contexts, 1984 and 2012." In *The Great Irish Famine: Visual and Material Culture*, edited by Marguerite Corporaal, Oona Frawley, and Emily Mark-Fitzgerald, 165–82. Liverpool: Liverpool University Press, 2018.

TRANSLATIONS (1980) BY BRIAN FRIEL

In *Translations* Brian Friel traces the roots of Ireland's complex linguistic identities. Set in the fictional Donegal townland of Ballybeg in 1833, the plot centres on the convergence of two key developments in the nineteenth century: the establishment of National Schools that were free and open to Catholics, to replace the informal network of "hedge schools" that had existed since the days of the Penal Laws; and the introduction of the first Ordnance Survey, carried out by the British government to draw standardised maps of the entire island of Ireland. Into this historical moment, Friel placed characters who were caught at the crux of these pivotal events. Ageing teacher Hugh O'Donnell conducts a hedge school in a disused hay shed, instructing his peasant students in Latin, Greek, and mathematics. Hugh's assistant is his son Manus, who hopes to marry one of those students, the beautiful and outspoken Maire Chatach, herself the eldest of eleven children, who dreams of emigrating to America. As the play opens, the hedge school class is interrupted by the arrival of Hugh's second son, Owen, returning home with two British soldiers, members of the Royal Engineers, for whom he is serving as interpreter as they survey and map the surrounding area.

As the action unfolds, Friel charts the communication lapses between the two linguistic communities on stage. Although the script is almost entirely in English, when the soldiers – stern Captain Lancey and starry-eyed Lieutenant George Yolland – appear, their confusion alerts the audience that Hugh, his sons, and his students are in fact speaking Irish, as would have been the case for Donegal residents in 1833. Friel's technical virtuosity in managing this feat culminates in Act II with a love scene between Yolland and Maire, when, after meeting at an evening dance, they guess at each other's meaning while drawing closer and closer:

> *She holds out her hands to* **Yolland**. *He takes them. Each now speaks almost to himself/herself.*

Yolland.   I wish to God you could understand me. […]
Maire.   Don't stop—I know what you're saying.
Yolland.   I would tell you how I want to be here—to live here—always—with you—always, always.
Maire.   "Always"? What is that word—"always"?[1]

The connections created in this scene become all the more poignant in Act III, when the audience learns that Yolland has disappeared and is presumed the victim of foul play, perhaps at the hands of the absent Donnelly twins, whose rebellious activities have been alluded to at previous points in the dialogue. Suspicion also falls on Hugh's son Manus, who jealously went after Yolland with a stone in his hand, only to be stilled upon seeing the lieutenant together with Maire outside the dance.

As Act III opens, Manus packs his clothes and his most treasured books – "the Virgil and the Caesar and the Aeschylus" (475) – and flees Ballybeg before the final entrance of Captain Lancey, who gathers the hedge school students and demands that Owen translate his orders: his troops will shoot all livestock, evict all residents, and raze the surrounding townlands unless they receive information about Yolland's whereabouts. Chaos ensues offstage as the British camp is set afire, but an eerie calm descends within the hedge school as master Hugh and his eldest pupil, the bachelor Jimmy Jack Cassie, muse on their shared history as "young gallants with pikes across their shoulders and the *Aeneid* in their pockets" during the United Irishmen uprising of 1798 (490). As the lights dim, Hugh recites the opening lines of Virgil's epic in Latin and translates them into English – an ambiguous ending to a complicated play.

Names and naming provide a consistent theme throughout the script, and it is important to bear in mind that the first production of *Translations* was staged in Derry/Londonderry, a city with two names used by two divided communities even today. The region itself is known by many names, none of them neutral – Northern Ireland, the North, Ulster, the Six Counties – signifying conflicting political and cultural stances, as Friel knew well. When Owen explains that Lieutenant Yolland will anglicise and standardise the names on the Ordnance Survey map, his brother Manus challenges: "What's 'incorrect' about the place names that we have here?" (466). The Name Book that Owen and Yolland work on in Act II is an historical artefact; one such book can be viewed today in the Tower Museum, Derry, where its ledger columns show the multiple Irish-language names for each place surveyed, along with their literal translations into English and the eventual standardised name bestowed on each location. The play opens with Manus coaching the stammering Sarah Johnny Sally to voice her name despite her speech impediment. Heritage and identity are further underscored by the offstage birth and death of an infant whose christening and wake Hugh attends in the first and final acts; the unwed mother "was threatening she was going to call it after its father," a point of gossip among the hedge school students (427). Even Owen is known by two names until Act II, when he corrects his friend Lieutenant Yolland, who, along with Captain Lancey, has been mistakenly calling him Roland since the start of their mapmaking mission. Yolland's love scene with Maire pivots on their shared recitation of local place names in Irish, which Yolland has been trying to learn – and Lancey's ultimatum to the hedge school students requires the recitation of the same names in both English and Irish, as the captain lists the townlands to be razed, and an abject Owen translates for listeners he has known since birth.

Friel drew upon multiple historical and linguistic sources while writing *Translations*, including memoirs by Colonel Thomas Colby, director of the Ordnance Survey, and the letters of John O'Donovan, an Irish speaker and scholar on whom Owen's character is modelled. *A Paper Landscape* by J. H. Andrews and *The Hedge Schools of Ireland* by P. J. Dowling further fuelled the playwright's imagination. Friel directly excerpted sentences from George Steiner's book *After Babel: Aspects of Language in Translation* to embed them in dialogue throughout the play, as when Hugh warns Yolland that "a civilization can be imprisoned in a linguistic contour which no longer matches the landscape of … fact" (459).

Translations premiered in a landscape where facts were contested and dangerous. The play was the first performance of the Field Day Theatre Company, a project initiated by actor Stephen Rea to which Friel signed on as partner in 1980. The pair chose to stage their début in a political space, Derry's Guildhall, historic home to the mayor's parlour and the Londonderry Corporation; it had been bombed twice by the IRA in the late 1970s as the "Troubles" grew more and more violent. British troops had patrolled Northern Ireland since 1969, and off-duty soldiers were frequently ambushed, so Yolland's disappearance signified more than a history play to the audience. Daily news reported the increasingly intractable blanket and dirty protests at the Maze prison, which would soon evolve into hunger strikes that claimed the lives of ten young IRA members in 1981. Murmurs about the never-seen Donnelly twins echo the invisibility of para-militaries within Northern Irish society, and Maire's romance with Yolland evokes the danger for young Catholic women who consorted with British soldiers: many were tarred and feathered by members of their own communities, and were left tied to lampposts or railings as warnings to other girls.

Field Day evolved into a larger critical project with a mission to "contribute to the solution of the present crisis by producing analyses of the established opinions, myths and stereotypes which had become both a symptom and a cause of the current situation."[2] Its theatre com-pany premiered plays in the Guildhall annually for the next decade, each of which then toured the island of Ireland, performing in cities and towns north and south of the border. *Translations* is Field Day's longest enduring production, despite controversy over the play's histor-ical accuracy following its début. In the early 1980s it was performed in divided societies such as South Africa and West Berlin, and it has been staged in Welsh, Estonian, and Basque, as well as German, French, Polish, and others. In 2018 – at the height of debates over Brexit, borders, and national identities – the National Theatre, London, presented *Translations* on a set that resembled scorched earth, with an apocalyptic red scrim for a backdrop as Friel's characters struggle to confront their shared and individual turning points.

Kelly Matthews

Notes

1 Brian Friel, *Translations*, in *Collected Plays Vol. II* (Loughcrew: Gallery Press, 2016), 471. Subsequent references are entered in parentheses.
2 "Preface," *Ireland's Field Day*, ed. Field Day Theatre Company (London: Hutchinson, 1985), vii.

Further Reading

Deane, Ciarán. "Brian Friel's *Translations*: The Origins of a Cultural Experiment." *Field Day Review* Vol. 5 (2009): 6–47.
Kiberd, Declan. "Friel Translating." In *Inventing Ireland: The Literature of the Modern Nation*, 614–23. London: Vintage, 1996.
Roche, Anthony. "Friel's *Translations*: An Inquiry into the Disappearance of Lieutenant George Yolland." In *Brian Friel: Theatre and Politics*, 130–51. New York: Palgrave Macmillan, 2011.
Whelan, Kevin. "Between: The Politics of Culture in Friel's *Translations*." *Field Day Review* Vol. 6 (2010): 6–27.

THE GREAT HUNGER (1983) BY TOM MAC INTYRE

Described retrospectively as "the inescapable production of the 1980s,"[1] Tom Mac Intyre's *The Great Hunger* marked a highly significant moment on the Irish stage when it opened on the Abbey's Peacock stage in 1983. Challenging the dominance of word-based theatre, *The Great Hunger* shocked audiences in a series of vivid and abstract images of the cruel reality of life in rural Ireland using Patrick Kavanagh's poem of the same name as its subject matter. Despite initial negative criticism *The Great Hunger* was revived at the Peacock in October 1986 and in November staged at the Belfast Festival. In December 1988 it toured to New York where a reviewer commented that "In its theatrical style, *The Great Hunger* resembles the theatrical pieces of Tadeusz Kantor and the Cricot 2 Theatre of Poland."[2]

Staged in collaboration with director Patrick Mason, designer Bronwen Casson, and a cast led by the actor Tom Hickey, the performance of the play took audiences through the day-to-day experiences of the isolated and tragic figure of Patrick Maguire, the poem's central character. Middle-aged and unmarried, Maguire is terrified of the opposite sex and yet bursting with unfulfilled desire. Duty bound to his emotionally distant mother and paralysed under the rigid laws of the Catholic Church, he is desperate for release. Capturing the visceral experience of Maguire's spiritually deprived psychological state, the play uses Kavanagh's words sparingly and as rhythms or tones as well as having communicative value between the characters on stage. Through movement and gesture the audience is offered a window into Maguire's everyday existence, his back-breaking work on the land, his immature antics with pals, and his comical awkwardness in the presence women. Resembling American and European dance theatre, theatre of the image, and occasionally silent film, the mood of the play in performance is one of claustrophobic isolation or disconnection, interrupted by episodes of dark comedy, frivolity, and exuberant theatricality. In the performance, characters make utterances into thin air, bodies shuffle up to each other, dance around each other, but never fully communicate. In appealing to the senses and not solely to the intellect the play connects audience and the environment, subject and object, "clay" and "flesh", as in the words of Kavanagh's poem.[3] Sounds and the use of objects have a powerful impact in this regard, standing in for words and heightening the impoverished status of the relationships between the characters in the play. In Scene Three, for example, Maguire's sister, Mary Anne *"converses with"* Maguire *"by her mode of pouring water very slowly from bucket to kettle. Squeaks from the bucket handle are an aid to articulation. She takes forever at pouring the water.*"[4]

In Bronwen Casson's minimalist stage design three strategically placed objects give shape to the overlapping zones of Maguire's psychological dysfunctionality and the perverse world in which he lives. Choreography surrounding these objects interlinks the semiotics of religion with that of the desire for transcendence. In the action that takes place on and around a traditional five-bar farm gate sitting centre stage, Maguire and his friends engage in juvenile horse-play, ogle women who pass by, or watch others engage in seductive acts with members of the opposite sex. In the course of such action one of the male characters stands on the gate "*as the risen Christ, arms outstretched, palms spread wide*" (28). On another occasion Maguire reverses this image by "*flatten[ing] himself upside down on the upstage side of the gate, face on view through the lower bars, legs a V sprouting from the top*" (39) as he watches a young woman try to seduce a male friend.

In similar action surrounding a metallic tabernacle on a tubular plinth positioned stage-right, one of Maguire's male counterparts is caught by the priest in the highly symbolic act of stealing a key. As described in the stage directions:

> **The Priest** [...] *Searches in the folds of his vestments for the tabernacle key. Roots in his pockets. Key not to be found – until an embarrassed* **Packy** *produces it from his pocket.* **The Priest** *(with a look of chastisement for* **Packy***) takes the key, kisses it. Addresses himself to the tabernacle door. Insertion of the key in the lock. Turning of the key. Opening of the door. Curtains of red silk visible. Delicately,* **The Priest** *parts these. He takes out a small dingy chalice, tarnished, but it contains mystery. He extends it to the congregation. Worshipful, they yield.*
>
> (22)

Denigrating the patriarchal order at other moments in the play and following in the funerary tradition in Irish theatre this choreography and use of stage objects foregrounds masculinity as "suspended in an intermediary zone where the boundaries between truth and fraudulence, sanity and lunacy, sainthood and domesticity are fluid and ever-shifting."[5] For example, The Priest plays card tricks and falls asleep in the middle of hearing The Mother's confession. In another scene he mumbles incoherently through the liturgy at Sunday Mass whilst his congregation respond with an *"orchestrated din of coughing"* and "a *chorale of farmyard noises"* (21).

Opposing the zone of transcendence on the other side of the stage (stage-left), meanwhile, the looming presence of a life-sized wooden effigy casts a shadow over the entire action of the play. Carved into the shape of a statue of the Madonna with a mid-section consisting of a seat with hidden drawer that holds cleaning equipment, the effigy is cast to play the role of Maguire's Mother and treated as a flesh-and-blood woman by the other characters in the play. At various points she is spoken to, cleaned, dressed, and undressed and this silencing and immobilisation highlights her subservience to the other characters. In turn, her presence in the form of a wooden effigy reinforces Maguire's disturbed psychological condition, lack of agency, and emasculation. Under her gaze Maguire *"flops to the floor, [...] legs extended, repetitively banging his feet together"* (16). Then, having removed a bellows from the Mother's drawer, he *"works it to climax in an image of masturbation"* (17).

The response to such images on the stage of the Peacock was one of anger, shock, and dismay, and, in America, as cast member Dermod Moore described it, audiences were "insulted, affronted, disgusted" by the play's "refusal to give in one inch to American-Irish sentimentality or nostalgia" and in witnessing Ireland's "insanity [...] on display for all to see," all *"that* dirty laundry."[6] For some of the critics, however, this was "one of the best things the Abbey [had] done in recent years" and "the sort of play Synge might have written."[7] Others urged that "on no account [should the play] be missed by anyone who cared more than tuppence about the development of Irish theatre."[8]

As part of a protracted period of collaboration Mac Intyre went on to stage four other plays with Mason, Casson, Hickey, and various cast members at the Peacock Theatre, concluding in 1988. Influencing a host of playwrights, directors, actors, and other theatre practitioners in succeeding years, this work is now widely recognised as "a landmark in Irish theatre history" and Mac Intyre's entire and diverse *oeuvre* as a "benchmark against which Irish theatre has defined itself."[9]

Marie Kelly

Notes

1 Christopher Morash, *A History of Irish Theatre 1601–2000* (Cambridge: Cambridge University Press, 2002), 258.
2 Joel G. Fink, "Review of *The Great Hunger*," *Theatre Journal* Vol. 4, no. 2 (December 1988): 550.

3 Patrick Kavanagh, "The Great Hunger," in Patrick Kavanagh and Tom Mac Intyre, *The Great Hunger: Poem into Play* (Mullingar: Lilliput Press, 1988), 3.

4 Tom Mac Intyre, *The Great Hunger*, in *The Great Hunger/The Gallant John-Joe* (Dublin: Lilliput Press, 2002), 22. Subsequent references are entered in parentheses.

5 Nina Witoszek and Patrick Sheeran, *Talking to the Dead: A Study of Irish Funerary Traditions* (Amsterdam and Atlanta: Rodopi, 1998), 123.

6 Dermod Moore, "The Lunatics in the Basement: Madness in Mac Intyre," in *The Theatre of Tom Mac Intyre: Strays from the Ether*, ed. Marie Kelly and Bernadette Sweeney (Dublin: Carysfort Press, 2010), 142.

7 Augustine Martin, "Great Hunger," *Irish Times*, 30 May 1983, 9.

8 David Nowlan, "Prompts," Review of *The Great Hunger*, *Irish Times*, 27 May 1983, 10.

9 Fiach Mac Conghail, "Preface," in *The Theatre of Tom Mac Intyre: Strays from the Ether*, xxvi.

Further Reading

Ryan, Caitriona. *Border States in the Work of Tom Mac Intyre: A Paleo-Postmodern Perspective*. Newcastle upon Tyne: Cambridge Scholars Publishing, 2012.

Sweeney, Bernadette. *Performing the Body in Irish Theatre*. Basingstoke: Palgrave Macmillan, 2008.

TEA IN A CHINA CUP (1983) BY CHRISTINA REID

Tea in a China Cup was the first of Christina Reid's plays to be professionally staged, and it brought her almost immediate public and critical attention. The *Irish Times* described the work as "finely judged, beautifully written"[1] and the *Belfast Telegraph* judged it to be "thought-provoking and entertaining."[2] It premiered at the Lyric Theatre, Belfast, on 9 November 1983, having had a staged reading by the Royal Shakespeare Company a year earlier. Directed by Leon Rubin, the cast included a number of prominent actors including Margaretta D'Arcy and John Hewitt, with Paula Hamilton as the protagonist Beth and Stella McCusker as her mother Sarah.

Set in Belfast between 1939 and 1972, the play uses the Twelfth of July[3] as one of its motifs to explore the lives of working-class Protestant women in three generations of the same family. In interview, Reid has spoken of her desire to put women's stories on the stage, noting that female characters tend to lack depth and complexity in many male-authored plays, and are often primarily defined as "mothers, sisters, and wives." She comments that women behave differently when men are not present, becoming "more relaxed, bawdier, full of life and banter."[4] Indeed, by dramatising the women's private behaviour Reid transgresses the central rule that governs her characters' lives: that they must always censor themselves to ensure that they maintain that essential respectable veneer by not revealing any secrets beyond the immediate family circle. The metaphor of the fine china cup represents respectability, cleanliness, and hard work; but also not "whining and complainin' and puttin' a poor mouth on yourself" like the Catholics.[5] Reid introduces this symbol of identity alongside the Sash, the Twelfth parades, banners and military service, so inserting women into an otherwise exclusively male set of signifiers. This also facilitates the recognition that this family stands metonymically for an entire community.

The play is in two acts. In Reid's characteristic style, lighting and sound create multiple times and spaces simultaneously on the stage. This approach allows her to juxtapose scenes and fragments of the characters' lives, encouraging the audience to question and to draw conclusions. For example, the first act opens with the rousing sound of an Orange band playing the sectarian song *Up Come the Man*; as the sound builds to a crescendo Sarah enters and lies on a sofa, listening with enjoyment. The stage directions state that she is clearly ill. In another area of the stage, Beth is buying Sarah's cemetery plot from the council clerk, as Sarah wants to know where she is going to be lying. This opening scene establishes the relationship between Sarah and Beth, but also allows the sectarian music to comment upon the absurdity of the cemetery, which separates the dead by religion. The clerk explains that this is new; the old cemetery wasn't segregated "but the people sort of segregated it themselves ... There's clumps of Catholics and clumps of Protestants. The odd one buried among the wrong crowd stands out like a sore thumb" (7). When Beth relays this information Sarah "laughs delightedly" and replies "God, isn't it great to know that you'll be lying among your own" (10).

The women's attitudes are not uniform, and Reid illustrates a diversity of opinion even within the small family group. Sarah sings along with the Orange bands, but Beth jokes with the clerk about the graveyard, asking if mixed marriages are buried under the footpath. When she returns home her mother expresses her longing to see one last Twelfth of July; and as the older woman leaves the stage Beth walks towards the front of the stage to address the audience directly with a story her mother told her about bringing her to the Twelfth celebrations when she was only an infant. The pride her mother took in the story leads Beth to another family story from before her birth: the departure of her uncle Samuel to fight in the Second World War.

This segue into the past illustrates both the values of the community – allegiance to Britain, loyalty to the crown, pride in military service – and a gendered split that is clearly articulated within the private domestic space. Samuel and Sarah's father fought in the First World War and is proud to see his son in his Army uniform, getting ready to leave. But their mother is fearful and angry and she sharply contradicts her husband's cliches about the war "making a man of him" (12). Referring to the "last great war" the stage directions state: *"She says the word 'great' with contempt"* (12). Later, Beth's brother will join the British Army and will be unable to come home to Belfast to see his dying mother, lest he be shot by the IRA.

Although the main focus of the play is on the words and actions of the women, it is the men and their values that order the world they all inhabit, in public and in private life. Beth's father is a gambler who plunges the family into poverty, but her mother never admits this: to do so would be a failure of respectability. To pay his debts she has to sell all her fine china and the cabinet that displays it; she sells them to Theresa's mother. She cuts down her clothes to make clothes for the child Beth and blames herself for her husband's failings. Beth argues with her, saying, "No matter what a man does wrong it's always some woman's fault, isn't it?" (39). In another scene from Beth's childhood, her Aunt Maisie comments on a neighbour that "He was a vindictive oul bastard all his life, treated his wife and childer like dogs" (36). There is no escape for the woman trapped in such a marriage. Even the adult Beth hides the breakdown of her marriage from her mother, while her friend Theresa hides her child, born outside of marriage, from her family in Belfast.

The respectability that the women fetishise depends on their silence; and it also depends on the suppression of sexuality. This is illustrated by the shame attendant on Theresa's situation, and in Beth's reminiscences of her wedding night. She has reluctantly married a wealthy businessman, partly to please her mother, and on the wedding night he stays at the hotel bar leaving her alone in her room. She calls Theresa, but cannot bring herself to say what is happening; instead she pretends that everything is fine. In another key scene, Beth and Theresa as children compare what they have found out about sex. Their mothers are reluctant to impart any information; Theresa's mother slaps her and sends her to confession whenever she asks a question. At school, she tells Beth, girls are sent to the "sin room" for having impure thoughts, and they are made to sew up the pockets on their skirts. Theresa doesn't know why, but it is clearly motivated by anxiety about masturbation.

In another comic yet poignant scene, Sarah tries to prepare Beth for menstruation, but the vagueness of her language leaves the child more confused. She initiates the conversation while she is ironing, using this as a displacement activity to cover her embarrassment: "You know where you go to the toilet," she says, "down there ... a drop of blood comes out of there ... don't go telling your father or our Sammy ... and another thing, Beth, when you do get older and maybe go out with boys ... don't ever let them do anything that's not nice" (29–30). When the puzzled Beth agrees, Sarah folds up the ironing board and departs with an air of relief.

Tea in a China Cup was not Reid's first play but it is the one where she finds her voice and her focus, attending to the particular histories of women in Northern Ireland and putting their stories on the stage. Using an episodic structure that juxtaposes different events, direct address to the audience, and music, Reid creates a distinctive style of political theatre that gently encourages her audience to reflect upon prejudice, gender, and patriarchal concepts of decency and respectability.

Lisa Fitzpatrick

Notes

1   Ray Rosenfield, *"Tea in a China Cup* at the Lyric, Belfast," *Irish Times*, 14 November 1983.
2   Jane Bell, "A Skilful Blend," *Belfast Telegraph*, 10 November 1983.
3   The 12th of July is an Ulster Protestant celebration of victory at the Battle of the Boyne organised through the Orange Order. This is an explicitly sectarian organisation that excludes Roman Catholics and women from membership.
4   Imelda Foley, *The Girls in the Big Picture* (Belfast: Blackstaff Press, 2003), 61.
5   Christina Reid, *Tea in a China Cup*, in *Christina Reid Plays 1* (London: Methuen, 1997), 25. Subsequent references are entered in parentheses.

Further Reading

Fitzpatrick, Lisa. "Disrupting Metanarratives: Anne Devlin, Christina Reid, Marina Carr, and the Irish Dramatic Repertory." *Irish University Review* Vol. 35, no. 2 (Autumn–Winter 2005): 320–33.

Luft, Joanna. "Brechtian Gestus and the Politics of Tea in Christina Reid's *Tea in a China Cup.*" *Modern Drama* Vol. 42, no. 2 (Summer 1999): 214–22.

Roll-Hansen, Diderik. "Dramatic Strategy in Christina Reid's *Tea in a China Cup.*" *Modern Drama* Vol. 30, no. 3 (Fall 1987): 389–95.

Tracie, Rachel. *Christina Reid's Theatre of Memory and Identity.* London: Palgrave Macmillan, 2018.

NORTHERN STAR (1984) BY STEWART PARKER

In *Northern Star*, Stewart Parker exposes contradictions in modern republican thinking about Ireland and urges audience members to reject the roles history has assigned to them. Like other Northern Irish writers of his generation, Parker felt called upon to respond to the late-twentieth-century political and sectarian violence in his birthplace between unionists, primarily Protestant, who wanted Northern Ireland to remain in the United Kingdom, and nationalists, mainly Catholic, who favoured the idea of an Irish state consisting of the whole island of Ireland. He resisted, however, the compulsion to make violence itself the subject of his plays, seeking instead to get behind the symptoms of social and political dysfunction and find new and unexpected angles from which to examine them. In *Northern Star*, Parker abandoned both the present time and a realistic mode of presentation to explore the historical dimension of Ireland's recurring "Troubles."

Northern Star was the only Parker play to premiere in Belfast, and he took advantage of the commission from the Lyric Theatre to speak directly to Northern Irish people. The play's protagonist is Henry Joy McCracken, a Belfast Presbyterian and one of the most radical leaders of the United Irishmen, who instigated the 1798 rebellion in Ireland; the audience witnesses his soul-searching in the hours leading up to his capture, trial, and execution. The United Irishmen, the first modern revolutionaries to envision a future for Ireland as an entity independent of Great Britain, inspired the Provisional IRA (responsible for much of the violence Parker witnessed), who saw in their ancestors' resort to arms justification for their own, but they are also venerated by liberal republicans, who embrace their goal of "a cordial union among *all the people of Ireland.*"[1] In focusing on McCracken, Parker aimed to reinsert Belfast into the story of the Irish nation.

Parker wanted his fellow Northern Protestants to understand that, not only had they not always been unionists in the past, but they had invented Irish republicanism. Simultaneously, he offered a critique of Irish republican ideology. The United Irishmen's greatest contribution, he believed, was their attempt to separate nationality from sectarian allegiance. However, their ultimate decision to pursue political ends by military means was, in Parker's view, a tragic mistake. In *Northern Star*, he suggests that the United Irishmen were responsible not only for the ideal of republicanism, but also for its tradition of violence. Looking back on the entire United movement with the benefit of hindsight, Parker's McCracken worries that "all we've done, you see, is to reinforce the locks, cram the cells fuller than ever of mangled bodies crawling round in their own shite and lunacy, and the cycle just goes on, playing out the same demented comedy of terrors from generation to generation."[2]

Part of the historical McCracken's legend is that he intended to make a speech from the gallows but, as an eyewitness recounted, "Hoarse orders were given by the officers, the troops moved about, the people murmured, a horrible confusion ensued and in a minute or so the handsome figure was dangling at a rope's end."[3] Parker imagines what McCracken would have said to the crowd if he had been allowed to speak. In the theatre, the citizens of Belfast addressed by McCracken merge into the present-day citizens of Belfast in the audience, and one question that preoccupies him is the use that future generations will make of his legacy. In Parker's view, a man of McCracken's generous spirit could not have failed to see that this legacy might be malevolent, and his McCracken vigorously rejects the role of martyr for Irish freedom.

Because the United Irishmen were playing to posterity, Parker's play is filled with theatrical figures of speech, with McCracken as an actor rehearsing for his "positively last appearance" (18). He tries out his rhetorical flourishes on his lover, Mary Bodle, who has little patience for the exercise, urging him instead to escape to America and begin a new life with her and their child; she represents the life force battling with McCracken's desire for a heroic death – a desire symbolised in the play by a literal ghost, the Phantom Bride. The scenes between McCracken and Mary, which express Parker's opinions most directly and exemplify his distinctive voice, alternate in *Northern Star* with a series of seven flashback scenes of events leading up to the rising: each, in keeping with the theatrical metaphor, represents one of the ages of man: "They have their exits and their entrances and one man in his time plays many parts, his acts being seven ages" (16).

Parker wrote each of the seven flashback scenes in the style of a different Irish playwright, and the manner of expression chosen for each scene is appropriate to the matter being presented. The Age of Innocence, set in a tavern and illustrating the origins of the United Irishmen in the aptly named Mudlers' Club, is presented in the style of Richard Brinsley Sheridan. The Age of Idealism, in which McCracken is shown "uniting the rabble in a common love for his shining youthful ardour" (29) is cast as a melodrama after the manner of Dion Boucicault. A passage about cultural renewal (the Age of Cleverness) is written in the epigrammatic mode of Oscar Wilde. A political debate between McCracken and the British officer who attempts to arrest him (the Age of Dialectic) is haunted by the ghost of George Bernard Shaw. The Heroic Age, in which McCracken and several of his friends first pledge themselves to "the republic of United Irishmen" (55), mimics the inflated poetic language of John Millington Synge. The Age of Compromise, "of finally taking sides" (59), pays tribute to Sean O'Casey, another dramatist who chronicled the underbelly of revolutionary politics. And the Age of Knowledge, which depicts the backbiting and betrayal of jailed United Irishmen, recalls Brendan Behan's prison drama *The Quare Fellow*.

What Parker termed "theatrical ventriloquism"[4] serves political as well as aesthetic ends. In *Northern Star*, Parker, a Protestant writer from a unionist background, deliberately positions himself within an Irish literary tradition. By imitating great Irish writers in turn, he indicates that he sees himself as their inheritor. Moreover, the Irish authors he invokes, like the pantheon of Irish revolutionaries the play is about, are overwhelmingly Protestant. Parker's McCracken argues that the truly radical contribution of the United Irishmen was a new answer to the question "What did it mean to be Irish?": "When you distilled it right down to the raw spirit? It meant to be dispossessed, to live on ground that isn't ours, Protestant, Catholic, Dissenter, the whole motley crew of us, planted together in this soil to which we've no proper title" (16). What in the 1790s was an uncommonly generous attitude towards Catholics looked by the 1980s like a plea for reciprocal generosity. The multiplicity of voices in the play underlines Parker's pluralistic vision of Irish identity while simultaneously commenting on the fact that the past and present in Ireland continue to shape each other. The technique of pastiche, he maintained,

> allowed me to march the play throughout the decades towards the present day and say to the audience, forget about historical veracity, forget about realism, I'm going to tell you a story about the origins of Republicanism and I'm going to offer you a point of

view on what's gone wrong with it and why it's become corrupt and why it's now serving the opposite ends to what it set out to serve.[5]

Most of the many characters in *Northern Star* are played by a chorus of actors who might changes roles "merely by a change of hat, coat or wig" (13); the only ones with dedicated actors assigned to them are McCracken (who barely leaves the stage), Mary, and McCracken's comrade James Hope, whose proto-socialism Parker regarded as the best "hope" for Northern Ireland's future. Parker shared both Hope's faith in the common man and McCracken's doubts regarding when the inhabitants of Belfast would come to their senses. The play ends with McCracken mounting the platform one last time and placing a noose around his neck. He declaims, "Citizens of Belfast ..." (76) but gets no further before the beating of a Lambeg drum (symbolic of twentieth-century unionist triumphalism) drowns out his words and the lights fade to black. In place of resolution, Parker offered a challenge to his original audience to arrest the cycle of retribution.

Marilynn Richtarik

Notes

1 Jonathan Bardon, *A History of Ulster* (Belfast: Blackstaff, 1992), 220.
2 Stewart Parker, *Northern Star*, in *Three Plays for Ireland: Northern Star, Heavenly Bodies, Pentecost* (Birmingham: Oberon, 1989), 65. Subsequent references are entered in parentheses.
3 Quoted in the programme for the Lyric Theatre production of *Northern Star*, Belfast, 1984.
4 Stewart Parker, programme note for the Lyric Theatre production of *Northern Star*, Belfast, 1984.
5 Stewart Parker, quoted in Ciaran Carty, "Northern Star Rising On the Tide," *Sunday Tribune*, 29 September 1985.

Further Reading

Richards, Shaun. "'Into the Future Tense': Stewart Parker's Theatre of 'Anticipatory Illumination'." *Irish University Review* Vol. 42, no. 2 (Autumn–Winter 2012): 351–65.

Richtarik, Marilynn. *Stewart Parker: A Life*. Oxford: Oxford University Press, 2012.

Richtarik, Marilynn. "Stewart Parker, Belfast Playwright." *The Princeton University Library Chronicle* Vol. 68, no. 1–2 (2007): 526–59.

BAILEGANGAIRE (1985) BY TOM MURPHY

An old woman, Mommo, bed-ridden, senile, talking mostly to herself or people of her imagination, with a granddaughter, Mary, trapped as caregiver, looking after her needs and often driven to desperation by her antics, does not promise great drama. The setting, a country cottage kitchen, is the most stereotypical, over-used place that the Irish stage had for decades. And yet, that kitchen transforms into a womb-tomb-like space, the narrow world of *Bailegangaire* broadens to the historical and social landscape of Ireland while profound psychological and spiritual issues surface as Mommo's story unevenly, fragmentarily, but eventually unfolds.

Mommo's obsessive storytelling seems to have no connection whatsoever with the present and with those present. Her tale tells how Bochtán – the "village of poor people" as the Irish name translates – "came by its new appellation, Bailegangaire, the place without laughter,"[1] just like in origin-myths, or the specifically Irish genre of *dinnseanchas*: the lore of placenames. Mommo used to be a professional storyteller, a "seanchaí" in her community, but now she has great difficulties in proceeding with her story that she keeps starting and restarting again and again, delivered in ornate, archaic language, interspersed with Gaelic.

The heroes of Mommo's tale: herself and her husband, distanced as the "strangers," a "decent man with his decent wife the same" (119), returning from a dismal fair where they sold nothing, stopped at a pub while waiting for a thaw so the horse could pull the cart uphill over the frozen road. This prolonged homeward journey with unexpected obstacles and great adventures leading to tragic consequences, provides the structure and frame to the narrative as well as the whole play. The husband got involved in a laughing contest with Costello, the "giant" laughing champion of the local community and, like in folktales, he "must slay [the giant] in order to reach home."[2] The grotesque, desperate, defiant laughter of the contestants is fed by "misfortunes" that Mommo and the other listeners – "despairing, ragged an' dirty, impoverished, hungry, emaciated and unhealthy" (164) – provide: an endless list of disasters, deaths, tragedies of their nearest and dearest.

Dire poverty reigns over the rural people and the struggle for survival ruins families, relationships, mentalities in the time of the story, the 1950s, some thirty years prior to the time of the play In contrast, outside the cottage cars and helicopters are heard passing to and from a Japanese-owned computer plant – the noises of global capitalism in the Ireland of the 1980s. The play is set at the time when the Irish were becoming disillusioned with the 1960s' promises of modernisation and affluence. Dolly, Mary's sister, a beneficiary of that affluence, for instance, is quite cynical about her house, equipped with all the paraphernalia of modern life that her husband's salary from his work in England allows.

Intermittently, with Mommo's storytelling, the granddaughters, Mary's and Dolly's life stories reveal the still existing ills of emigration that embittered the Irish for many generations. Murphy addressed the distortions of the emigrant psyche in a number of other plays, further highlighting the essential need for the quest for home. Homesickness drove Mary home from London where she had worked successfully as a nurse, only to find her home destitute due to Mommo's unwillingness to recognise her, despite all Mary's efforts. Dolly, in her turn, suffers from a loveless marriage, with her husband violent and abusive on his yearly homecomings. She finds, if not pleasure, then revenge on men in brief sexual encounters in the ditches and now, in her unwanted pregnancy, mortally afraid of her husband's Christmas return, proposes that Mary adopt the child. Both sisters – two very different personalities – sharing a love–hate relationship, now at the end of their tethers, suffer from a sense of failure, loneliness and emotional, ontological, metaphysical homelessness. One of the unique strengths of the writing is the way Murphy creates the dramatic reality of two historical moments with the first evoked only in words, of two generations (actually three, with the middle, that of the young women's parents', missing), layering two storylines, separate and colliding, parallel and overlapping, clashing and converging.

Mommo's plight embodies Ireland's struggle to come to terms with the past, accept the painful memories of sufferings and responsibilities, and find the right proportion of remembering and letting go. Dramatising "the inner history of Ireland" in the second half of the twentieth century[3] that carries the long-term consequences of earlier catastrophies, Murphy in *Bailegangaire* not only evokes the 1950s but also harks back to the greatest trauma in Irish history, the mid-nineteenth-century Great Famine. Of the many lasting warps in the Irish psyche caused by the Famine the playwright himself identifies one as "Womanhood becomes harsh. Love, tenderness, loyalty, generosity go out the door in the struggle for survival."[4] Mommo has to take the hard step to move beyond her harshness to reach out to her beloved – in the tale and then in the "reality" of the play. In Bochtán her motivation in insisting that her husband continue the contest was rooted in her frustration, anger, and desire to take revenge for their estranged marriage. And yet with an unexpected turn, she suddenly arrives at a moment of great tenderness and love re-emerging between them: "An' then, like a girl, smiled at her husband, an' his smile back so shy, like a boy he was in youth. An' the moment was for them alone" (161–2). In narrating her tale she noticeably tries to escape facing the painful truth and to evade details that prove related to her responsibility and guilt, but with Mary desperately prompting and helping her to finish the story, she now admits that, but for her, they "could have got home" (140) before the contest became fatal. That delay caused a triple death: that of Costello, her husband and her five-year-old grandson, Tom, who had a fire accident with his two young sisters – Mary and Dolly – while waiting for their grandparents.

When the play-long story eventually arrives at its conclusion with Mary's contribution, Mommo becomes able to face her huge, repressed, unspoken trauma and admit her guilt, which liberates her from the burden of the past. Even her dementia is lifted, that was, at least partly, a disguise, greatly connected to her guilty conscience. Act Two ends in "tears of gratitude" in Mary's eyes for Mommo recognising her at last and becoming able to pray: "To thee do we cry. Yes? Poor banished children of Eve. [...] Mourning and weeping in this valley of tears" (169). As in many Murphy-plays, the resolution of crises happens not so much as a gradual developmental process, but more like a divine miracle shining through the humans: the transformation that theatre can produce. The emotional and spiritual rebirth is accompanied by a prospective physical one as Mary agrees to adopt Dolly's baby, to be named Tom. The closing theatrical image of the women's trinity, joining in bed for sleep, with the grandmother in the middle, depicts an extremely hard-earned re-finding of home in love and peace. The final words sum up a restoring of the order of the world: "In the year 1984, it was decided to give that – fambly ... of strangers another chance, and a brand new baby to gladden their home" (170).

With great courage, Murphy dared to trust storytelling to carry the drama. Although radically original, *Bailegangaire* fits into the Irish dramatic tradition with its echoes of Mother-Ireland figures such as Maurya in J. M Synge's *Riders to the Sea* (1904) or the titular character in Lady Gregory and W. B. Yeats's *Kathleen ni Houlihan* (1902). A restless, passionate truth-sayer, a fearless explorer of the deformations of the Irish psyche under various historical circumstances, an always ready-to-risk searcher for adequate dramatic forms, success came to Murphy in violent jumps and abrupt haults. *Bailegangaire*, however, immediately gained high critical acclaim in Ireland and since then he has been celebrated as one of the two giants of contemporary Irish drama, along with Brian Friel. The legendary premiere with Siobhán McKenna in the role of Mommo by the Druid Theatre in Galway, directed by Garry Hynes, was followed by a number of revivals in Ireland and abroad, including one which Murphy himself directed as part of the 2001 tribute the Abbey Theatre gave his work, and the 2014 Druid production at Dublin Theatre Festival when it was paired with *Brigit*, the ur-text of the life of Mommo.

Csilla Bertha

Notes

1   Tom Murphy, *Bailegangaire*, in *Tom Murphy Plays Two* (London: Methuen, 1993), 92. Subsequent references are entered in parentheses.
2   Fintan O'Toole, *The Politics of Magic* (Dublin: Raven Arts, 1987), 189.
3   Ibid., 16.
4   Tom Murphy, "Introduction," in *Tom Murphy Plays One* (London: Methuen, 1993), xi.

Further Reading

Grene, Nicholas. *The Theatre of Tom Murphy*. London: Bloomsbury, 2017.
Grene, Nicholas, ed. *Talking About Tom Murphy*. Dublin: Carysfort Press, 2002.
Murray, Christopher, ed. *"Alive in Time": The Enduring Drama of Tom Murphy*. Dublin: Carysfort Press, 2010.
Richards, Shaun. "From *Brigit* to *Bailegangaire*: The Development of Tom Murphy's Mommo Trilogy." *Irish University Review* Vol. 46, no. 2 (Autumn–Winter 2016): 324–39.

OBSERVE THE SONS OF ULSTER MARCHING TOWARDS THE SOMME (1985) BY FRANK MCGUINNESS

Observe the Sons of Ulster Marching Towards the Somme is the most important play in Irish political interventionist theatre. It was Frank McGuinness's first major success and was directed by Patrick Mason on the Peacock stage at the Abbey Theatre in 1985. The play creatively illuminates the historical tragedy of the 36th Ulster Division of the British Army who fronted the assault on German forces in the Battle of the Somme in the First World War, eventually capturing a large section of the frontline. However, the Division's success came at a devastating expense of human life, as over 100,000 British soldiers died while serving the Crown. In Northern Ireland their well-detailed gallantry has sustained an epic patriotic memory of bravery and sacrifice that has defined protestant nationalism for decades. The Battle of the Somme took place between 1 July and 18 November in 1916, and has served as a parallel mythology to the Easter Rising in the Republic on 16 April 1916 in Dublin; with the former memorialising Unionism in Northern Ireland and the latter Republicanism in the Republic of Ireland. In fact, many of the Ulster Division who fought in the Battle of the Somme voluntarily enlisted for service in the First World War in opposition to the Irish Republican insurrection against the British occupation of Ireland.

In *Observe the Sons* McGuinness uses the conventions of the theatre to examine and interrogate aspects of history and identity in Northern Ireland. In particular, he uses Pyper, the gay protagonist, to disturb concepts of heteronormativity, part of a complex series of cultural, political, and religious ideologies which, in formation with one another, support and maintain cultural normativity in all its exclusiveness and division. McGuinness highlights the radical instability of the way in which we imagine social, political, and sectarian identities. He then disrupts them just enough to allow new ideas to enter where old ideas have become simultaneously stagnant and pugnacious. Pyper is a veteran of the war, functioning as a type of anti-hero in this epic recounting of Northern Irish patriotism. As the protagonist and as a protestant, he lacks the vainglory of the venerate veteran, elevated to the status of martyr to the Union Jack. Pyper's perspective of the past is anything but straightforward:

Pyper. Again. As always, again. Why does this persist? What more have we to tell each other? I remember nothing today. Absolutely nothing [...] There is nothing to tell you [...] Those willing to talk to you of that day, to remember for your sake, to forgive you, they invent as freely as they wish. I am not one of them. I will not talk, I will not listen to you. Invention gives that slaughter shape.[1]

Instead, he is uncertain, troubled, and haunted by the accepted mythology of an event which saw the death of so many young men.

In *Observe the Sons* McGuinness's dramaturgical form also effects a broader critical interpretation of reality in its non-naturalistic structural complexity. The play is divided into what McGuiness describes as Parts: Remembrance; Initiation; Pairing; and Bonding. In Part One: Remembrance, McGuinness begins in what the audience would understand as the present. Elder Pyper, years after the Battle of the Somme, is lying in bed, tormented by the memory of the past and speaking with history as he addresses the men he fought alongside with the play's central question: "Answer me why we did it. Why we let ourselves be led to extermination? In the end, we were not led, we led ourselves" (100). McGuinness creates a theatrical experience where the audience can revisit the past by dreaming backwards, and ask challenging questions about war, death, and the meaning of life.

McGuinness's unique contribution to Irish theatre remains the central position he gives to queer subjectivity. Part Two: Initiation, sets the tone for the introduction of the queer character as a dramaturgical strategy of disruption. The audience is led from the present to the past, where we meet Younger Pyper on the first day of his military service. Pyper immediately meets David Craig in a "makeshift barracks," bleeding from a self-inflicted thumb wound while peeling an apple. He boldly asks Craig if he will "kiss it better" (103). McGuiness conceals seduction in this Part, leading to Pyper suggestively enticing Craig, "Like a piece of Apple ... I can't tempt you?" (104). In this rather Old Testament moment, Pyper's veiled orientation is significant when you consider that at the time of the original production in 1985 homosexuality was juridically illegal in the Republic of Ireland under antiquated British sodomy laws. Subsequently, McGuinness codes through innuendo and intimation the interaction between the two men, hiding diversity within the dramatic tensions. Pyper advances this subversion of identity using metaphors of flesh and desire. Eventually, Craig calls Pyper "rare," a word that in Northern Ireland is generally understood as strange, odd, or unusual.

McGuinness favours textual allegory in substantiating his queer dramaturgy, a technique which culminates in Part Three: Pairing. He portrays eight individual men in the memory sequence of the play, each representing different attitudes and politics. Here McGuinness embodies within his characters the virtues and vices of complex sectarian politics. Each pairing represents an ideological binary, materialising an interrogation of the issues essential to searching for an answer to the question proposed by Elder Pyper at the opening of the play: the reality of divisive and rigid sectarian politics, the role of religion, bravery, and sexuality. The actors are all placed in different spaces and on different levels on the stage, as the men of the company symbolically enjoy a weekend apart from the greater company before heading to battle. The action is local and specific, and yet each location is placed within the greater frame of the single stage.

The audience is given a theatrical image in which many of the issues that divide Northern Ireland politically and culturally are represented within a single frame. Through the theatre, McGuinness creates a unique public conversation that reimagines what was unimaginable politically in 1980s Ireland, literally fragmenting the artificial unity of the myth of the 36th Division and the legend of the Battle of the Somme by the very structure of the play and its necessary refusal of a central perspective or "reality." This section of the play offers a symphonic cacophony of voices, united and yet separate, performing simultaneously the complexity and unity of Northern Irish identity.

While the politics abound still today, the attention McGuinness gives to queer subjectivity is the first of its kind in the Irish dramatic tradition, theatrically placing a queer character in the middle of a heroic national narrative, changing the character to the subject rather than the object. In Part Three, Craig and Pyper are on Boa Island in county Fermanagh surrounded by megalithic carvings, and at this point in the production the audience witness the heart of McGuinness's queries in this play. The past and the present meet in this moment as the audience is given insight into the shared intimacy between Pyper and Craig. The ghost of Craig asks Pyper what he wants from him, and as the dialogue seems to transfer from the past to the present, we capture a moment that encompasses all the gains and losses of this epic moment in Irish history:

Craig. I wanted to save somebody else in war, but that somebody else was myself. I wanted to change what I am. Instead I saved you because of what I am [...] But when you talk to me, you see me. Eyes, hands. Not carving. Just seeing. And I didn't save you that day. I saw you. And from what I saw I knew I'm not like you. I am you.

(164)

The dialogue here turns into a poetic recitation of self-truth, delivered by each of the eight characters together, in turn. Curiously, the published text and the Abbey archive video of the early performance of this play conspire to capture the bravery of McGuinness's dramaturgy of diversity in a sectarian world. What the stage directions omit textually, as the lights fade, the production video captured: Pyper and Craig kiss. Culturally and politically this was an epic moment in Irish theatrical and social history.

Inclusion, belonging, and liberation are political and emotional sentiments which permeate McGuinness's plays. Who is written in and who is written out of our collective stories are embodied in his dramatic representations and his dramaturgical techniques, as his narratives broach new topics and his bodies exhibit new actions never before shown by Irish playwrights.

David Cregan

Note

1 Frank McGuinness, *Observe the Sons of Ulster Marching Towards the Somme*, in *Frank McGuinness Plays 1* (London: Faber & Faber, 1996), 97. Subsequent references are entered in parentheses.

Further Reading

Cregan, David. *Frank McGuinness's Dramaturgy of Difference and Irish Theatre*. New York: Peter Lang, 2011.
Jordan, Eamonn. *The Feast of Famine: The Plays of Frank McGuiness*. New York: Peter Lang, 1997.
Kiberd, Declan. "Frank McGuinness and the Sons of Ulster." *The Yearbook of English Studies* Vol. 35, Irish Writing since 1950 (2005): 279–97.

OURSELVES ALONE (1985) BY ANNE DEVLIN

Ourselves Alone explores the relationship between women and Irish republicanism in Northern Ireland's Catholic community during the "Troubles." The play "gives voice to women [and] shows women's involvement in and responses to a revolutionary situation and reveals the secrets of their participation in war."[1] It critiques the attitude of the Republican movement towards women, representing the female protagonists' struggles to escape the ideologies and mythologies upon which that movement is founded. Yet they are also bound to that ideology through their families and their lived experience and vacillate between their desire for self-fulfilment and their emotional and ideological attachment to their communities even as they are nurtured and comforted by their closeness to each other.

Ourselves Alone was first performed on 24 October 1985 at the Liverpool Playhouse Studio in a co-production with the Royal Court Theatre London. It was directed by Simon Curtis and the cast included Brid Brennan, Lise-Ann McLaughlin, Adrian Dunbar, and John Hewitt; interestingly, four of the smaller male roles are doubled as if to indicate that these men are largely interchangeable; despite coming from different sectarian communities their attitudes are very similar. The production played at the Royal Court in November 1985 and toured to the Dublin Theatre Festival in 1986. It was not widely reviewed, but it won the Susan Smith Blackburn Prize and the George Devine Award in 1986, and was performed at the Kreeger Theatre in Washington in 1987 and at the Tiffany Theatre in Los Angeles in 1989, as well as in Germany and the Netherlands. Yet Devlin's work has never been produced at the Abbey and *Ourselves Alone* has not to date been produced in Belfast.

The play is in two acts, structured into fifteen episodes. The action takes place in different locations in Belfast (with one scene in a Dublin hotel), in the early 1980s and in the aftermath of the Hunger Strikes when Republican prisoners in the H-Block in Long Kesh went on hunger strike to protest the removal of their political status by the British government. These are all interior spaces, and the play is realistic in its aesthetic. This is a feminist realism that aims to capture something of the lived experience of its protagonists. Although the action takes place over a number of months no passage of time is indicated in the text; the effect is to create a layering of different moments to build a picture of the women, their families, and their wider community. Scenes of violence are similarly layered one onto another, to create a portrait of a deeply divided society where the private domestic space is repeatedly torn asunder by ongoing warfare. The vivid phrase "an armed patriarchy" is used as a description of Northern Irish society by Eileen Evason in her study of domestic violence.[2] This is a space where the women and their children become pawns as two groups of armed men struggle for control of the state.

The title *Ourselves Alone* is a common mistranslation of *Sinn Féin*, the name of a left-wing political party which at the time the play was written was closely associated with the IRA (a more accurate translation would be "we, ourselves"). Although the title indicates the political allegiances of the women and their community, it is also suggestive of female solidarity, and the exclusion of men from the world the women create together. Though excluded, the men order this world; their actions determine the circumstances of the women's lives.

The three central characters are sisters Josie and Frieda and their brother Liam's wife Donna. Liam, Josie, and their father Malachy are all active members of the IRA, and Liam is in prison when the play begins. Josie lives with Donna to ensure that she remains faithful to Liam; ironically, this arrangement allows Josie to carry on a love affair with a married man. The younger daughter Frieda sings ballads in a republican club but cherishes the dream of singing her own songs one day. She is dating a young Protestant man, a left-wing activist who is opposed to the values of her family. Although Malachy's attitude towards his daughters and daughter-in-law is generally fond, he also clearly regards them as subject to his authority. He tells Josie that she must move back home when Liam is released from prison; he organises Frieda to care for his disabled sister, and when Josie becomes pregnant by an informer he extends his protection to her unborn child. This paternalism has a darker side, too: he beats Frieda when she publicly challenges him, in response to a taunt from his friend: "Have you no control over your daughter?"[3]

Amongst the scenes and intimations of violence are the sound of bin-lids indicating an army raid, and the women's dialogue about the soldiers destroying their homes and their possessions; Malachy beating Frieda; Frieda's boyfriend beating her when she challenges his political beliefs; Donna's troubled relationship with Liam; Josie's married lover repeatedly impregnating his wife so that she has ten children while still in her twenties; the portraits of the dead Hunger-Strikers on the walls of the club where Frieda sings, and the pervasive sense of threat that she describes there; a physical assault on her boyfriend; the closing images of the men's violence towards the women, who were playing naked in the sea. The women are acutely aware of threat and danger all about: Josie warns Frieda that her relationship with the Protestant man could "put all of us under suspicion" (22) and Donna warns her "You'll get your family a bad name" (22). Control of women's sexuality is essential for the honour of the family and the preservation of the group.

The women are shown as essential to the successful operation of the paramilitary movement. They perform the vital roles of keeping safe-houses, carrying messages, and hiding and moving arms. Yet despite their active engagement, they are explicitly depicted in the play as handmaidens, obedient daughters, submissive wives and political symbols, as illustrated by the horrifying story of Malachy's sister Cora. Frieda explains that when she was a young girl, Cora was terribly maimed while moving ammunition for Malachy. The explosives detonated prematurely and she was left blind, deaf, speechless, and without hands. Her sister has devoted her life to her care, and now that both are old Frieda is sent to care for them. Cora has been adopted as a symbol of the Republican movement: "They stick her out at the front of the parades every so often to show the women of Ireland what their patriotic duty should be," Frieda explains (98). Malachy continues his IRA career, marries, and has a family; meanwhile his sisters and daughters are expected to sacrifice their own lives and ambitions to care for Cora. In this scene, Donna and Josie speak the language of sacrifice for the sake of revolution and Irish freedom, but Frieda comments disparagingly that "when there's a tricolour over the City Hall, Donna will still be making coffee for Joe Conran, and Josie will still be keeping house for her daddy, because it doesn't matter a damn whether the British are here or not" (30). She challenges political ideological stances that prioritised the status of Northern Ireland as the main political question, with the liberation of women as secondary to the national goal.

It is tempting to read Frieda as the voice of the playwright, who has discussed her decision to leave Ireland in interview, and who is herself from a political family in Belfast.[4] Throughout the play, Frieda comments sardonically on Irish Republican attitudes to women and on her yearning to be free of the constraints of her community. Yet it is only when she has exhausted all other options that she decides to move away. Like Devlin, she chooses England rather than the Irish Republic, because she feels that she is "not that kind of Irish" (89); moments later, though, as the dawn breaks, she says "[…] it is Ireland I am leaving" (90). The need to leave Ireland will recur as a theme in *After Easter* (1994), Devlin's later play which again centres on three women.

Lisa Fitzpatrick

Notes

1 Elizabeth Doyle, "Women, War and Madness," *Fortnight* No. 334 (December 1994): 37.
2 Eileen Evason, *Hidden Violence* (Belfast: Farset Press, 1982), 73.
3 Anne Devlin, *Ourselves Alone* (London: Faber & Faber, 1986), 39. Subsequent references are entered in parentheses.
4 Anne Devlin, "About That: Irish Plays, Bill Morrison, Anne Devlin, Conor McPherson," in *State of Play I: Playwrights on Playwriting*, ed. David Edgar (London: Faber & Faber, 1999), 96.

Further Reading

Cerquoni, Enrica. "Women in Rooms: Landscapes of the Missing in Anne Devlin's *Ourselves Alone*." In Women in Irish Drama: A Century of Representation, edited by Melissa Sihra, 160–74. London: Palgrave Macmillan, 2007.
Kao, Wei H. "Awakening from the Troubles in Anne Devlin's *Ourselves Alone*." *Studies* Vol. 103, no. 410 (2014): 169–77.

Maloy, Kelli. "Disembodiment and the Re-membering of Female Identity in the Plays of Anne Devlin." *ANQ: A Quarterly Journal of Short Articles, Notes and Reviews* Vol. 25, no. 1 (2012): 19–23.

DOUBLE CROSS (1986) BY THOMAS KILROY

When the Field Day Theatre Company of Derry, Northern Ireland, premiered Thomas Kilroy's fifth stage play *Double Cross* on 13 February 1986, the sectarian "Troubles" were at their height, republicans and unionists were deeply entrenched in their positions, and political solutions to the conflict seemed impossible. Playwright Brian Friel and actor Stephen Rea had established Field Day in 1980 as a cultural space to investigate the intersection of language and identity, and to explore forms of discourse that might transcend the existing divides within the province. With *Double Cross*, Kilroy set out to write an anatomy of extreme nationalist ideology as madness, and he doubtless intended that the opposite and ultimately contradictory positions occupied by the play's central characters should resonate with the most extreme forms of sectarian nationalism on the island of Ireland. Set during the Second World War, however, the play functions more broadly to "undermine the black and white division of all wars, to subvert the righteousness of all political causes," and to expose the obscenity of all claims to absolute power or truth.[1]

Kilroy filtered his drama through the psyches of two historical figures: Brendan Bracken, Churchill's wartime Minister of Information, and William Joyce, the Nazi radio propagandist who announced himself in his broadcasts from Germany as "Lord Haw-Haw." *Double Cross* is, however, less a history play than a drama of ideas contrived to make a point about the perils of extremism. Both Bracken and Joyce are driven by self-hatred to deny their Irish origins and adopt ultra-English identities for themselves while allying themselves with opposite sides in the war. Bracken, who affects a British aristocratic manner, initially argues that the civilising qualities of Englishness are inherent in the English language that is being disseminated around the world under the aegis of the British Empire. At the mention of Gandhi, however, whose objective is to remove India from under British rule, his self-control crumbles: "these people," he fumes, knowing nothing of grace and cultivated living, would overrun the English with their "foul smells" and "obscene rituals."[2] Bracken uses his adopted English voice on the telephone to flatter, threaten, and cajole, but it eventually betrays him when, in a moment of extreme fear during the Blitz, he lapses into the strong Tipperary accent of his childhood. Joyce, born in the United States of Irish parents, raised in Galway, and claiming British citizenship, aspires to the eradication of imperfection in the human species. He, too, adopts an English accent – "backstreet Brixton", according to Bracken (22) – to persuade his listeners in Britain that England should join Nazi Germany in the "foundry of human progress" (79). In his final, incoherent broadcast, however, he rants drunkenly against "the American Jew-lover Churchill and his cronies," including "effete degenerates like Bracken" (79). Kilroy suggests that racism and antisemitism are the connection between Bracken's air of sophistication and Joyce's fascist brutalism. The picture of Sir Oswald Mosley, British Tory MP turned founder of the British Union of Fascists, is displayed throughout the play as an indicator of the commonalities between Empire and Reich.

The title *Double Cross* suggests doubling and betrayal, while the "cross" stands for the dark and debilitating ideological burden each man carries. Doubling is evident in the play's two-part structure. Part One, the "Bracken Play," is set in London, while Part Two, the "Joyce Play," takes place in Berlin. The two men never meet directly in the play, but each is aware of and haunted by the other: Bracken by Joyce's voice on the radio, Joyce by the image of Bracken on a video screen. To emphasise that the two figures are each other's equals as well as opposites, the script stipulates that both characters should be played by the same actor. Stephen Rea portrayed both men in the original Field Day production, to universal acclaim. His onstage transformation from Bracken into Joyce at the end of Part One was crucial in exposing the performative aspect of each man's identity as well as their similarities beneath the skin.

The scenes in which Bracken and Joyce interact with the women in their lives reveal the gap between their absolutist ideals and the inevitable messiness of their day-to-day existence. Bracken speaks to his lover Popsie of freedom as a removal of the self from "some tyrannical shadow, some dark father" (34), while Joyce insists that his marriage to Margaret should be "free" and without vulgar, middle-class inhibitions and restrictions (69). Bracken's fantasy of British nobility, pluck, and fair play is given comic erotic substance by Popsie's costumes: a boy scout uniform, a Highland Tartan, and a Florence Nightingale outfit. Yet through their sexual play, Bracken senses the impossibility of achieving his dream of perfection: he concludes that the aesthetic "composition" must remain a stand-in for "what might otherwise be beyond our reach" (32). Joyce's discovery of Margaret's affair with Erich – a German Anglophile dressed in "plus four tweeds" (66) and infatuated with the verse of

W. B. Yeats, whom he ironically believes to be English – unleashes a prolonged tirade in which Joyce alternates between needy insecurity and aggressive bullying. He, too, eventually concludes that freedom is "just beyond what is, it is the perfection of our desires and therefore cannot be achieved in the present dimension" (88). As Anthony Roche contends, "freedom" for each man amounts to a denial of history: "each character becomes not a free individual who has shed his Irish past, but someone who has traded in the role of historical victim for the mirror image of oppressor and placed all his faith in the symbols of the culturally dominant race."[3]

Joyce's mockery of Erich as a caricature of Englishness, a "ridiculous buffoon" (69), can only reflect back on his own faux identity, given that he is, in the words of the Actor-Narrator in *Double Cross*, "American but also Irish. He wanted to be English but had to settle on being German" (60), although, in a final irony, an English court eventually declared him British so that he could be hanged for treason. Bracken encourages the rumour that he is the illegitimate son of Winston Churchill who, he asserts, "was, always will be, a father to me" (25). His claim that both his actual father and his brother Peter have "the face of a condemned people" (89) goes to the heart of his self-hatred. Peter stands for all that his brother has suppressed, and Bracken fears he will one day appear on his doorstep to confront him with the evidence of his Irish past. When, at the end of the play, Bracken appears to Joyce on the video screen in his prison cell "as if behind bars" (88–89), both self-deniers fail to recognise the brother figure in each other. Kilroy revisited *Double Cross* ahead of its 2018 revival by the Abbey Theatre, in a co-production with Belfast's Lyric Theatre, and came to recognise that, as fraternal enemies, Bracken and Joyce embody the "ancient mythic shadow" of Cain and Abel.[4] That production noted the play's renewed relevance "in an era of heightened nationalism and 'fake news'."[5]

After the play's 1986 opening run in Derry's Guildhall, Field Day toured *Double Cross* through Northern Ireland, the Republic, and England. Reactions were very different in each location, with audiences not always willing to recognise aspects of themselves or their background in the play's themes and figures. *Double Cross* was well received, but generally criticised for being an undramatic, even static play. Kilroy himself, a "technically adventurous" playwright whose experimentation "is never a mere arid exercise in its own right,"[6] felt that he was continuing an innovative theatrical strand he had begun with *Talbot's Box* (1977). In that play, he had used expressionistic, overtly theatrical methods to explore society's responses to the ultimately ungraspable spiritual single-mindedness of the mystic Matt Talbot, including a huge box occupying most of the stage which served various metaphorical purposes. In *Double Cross*, too, Kilroy tried to create a dramatic environment that would invite an intellectual response to the imaginative action on stage. His subsequent play, *The Madame MacAdam Travelling Theatre*, produced and toured by Field Day in 1991, was a more light-hearted attempt to advocate the rejection of absolute certainty in favour of life-affirming conditionality. Also set during the Second World War, but featuring a female, maternal protagonist, *Madame MacAdam* was not a critical success, but its exploration of the dark side of patriarchal authority signalled what would become a dominant theme in important later plays like *The Secret Fall of Constance Wilde* (1997) and *Christ, Deliver Us!* (2010).

José Lanters

Notes

1 Thomas Kilroy, "Introduction," *Double Cross* (Loughcrew: Gallery Press, 1994), 11.
2 *Double Cross*, 44–45. Subsequent references are entered in parentheses.
3 Anthony Roche, *Contemporary Irish Drama*, second edition (London: Palgrave Macmillan, 2009), 146.
4 Thomas Kilroy, "Playing the Monster on Stage," *Irish University Review* Vol. 45, no. 1 (Spring–Summer 2015): 88.
5 See www.abbeytheatre.ie/whats-on/double-cross/ (14 February 2018).
6 Roche, 133.

Further Reading

Lanters, José. *The Theatre of Thomas Kilroy: No Absolutes*. Cork: Cork University Press, 2018.
Trotter, Mary. "'Double Crossing' Irish Borders: The Field Day Production of Tom Kilroy's 'Double Cross'." *New Hibernia Review* Vol. 1, no. 1 (Spring 1997): 31–43.

A HANDFUL OF STARS (1988) BY BILLY ROCHE

The first play in the award-winning *Wexford Trilogy*, by Wexford musician, Billy Roche, *A Handful of Stars*, which premiered at The Bush theatre, London in 1988, "is set in a scruffy pool hall [...] somewhere in Ireland."[1] The Boker Poker Club[2] is a man's world, tended by the club caretaker, Paddy, who maintains an inner sanctum with impressive furnishings and pristine billiard table and cues. This back room is for use by habitués, including Stapler, an over-the-hill amateur boxer, and Conway, "a big-mouthed know-all" (2). The outer room, site of the play's dramatic action, features a pool table, open to anyone with the price of a game, and a juke box. As the play begins, Jimmy Brady, a menacing force of nature, barges into Paddy's domain, and wrestles his sidekick, the ingénu, Tony, for the better cue. The first act unfolds over a period of some two weeks, and introduces Linda, "an attractive girl of seventeen or so," who works at the same factory as Conway, and Swan, "a wily detective" (2), both foils to Jimmy's violent excesses. Act II takes place a month later, and stages the events of one night – the eve of Tony's "shotgun wedding" – during which Jimmy rampages through the town with an actual shotgun, leaving a trail of wreckage behind him; the pool hall and his future in ruins as the play ends.

Class, and its intersection with masculinity under pressure, defines the social world of *A Handful of Stars*. Father/son relationships run like a seam through Roche's dramaturgy; Stapler and Jimmy are demonstrably flawed, and audiences learn that their shortcomings – selfishness, disloyalty, hurt done to mothers, wives and girlfriends – fatalistically repeat those of their own fathers. Stapler's father "jumped ship in South America or somewhere" (42) while Jimmy's da is driven from the family home by the protagonist's brother, to seek shelter in a homeless hostel. The plot turns on the egregious actions of this "tough, good-looking boy of seventeen or so" (2) who holds all authority, civic, social and paternal, in open contempt; Roche's deliberate re-working of Jim Stark, the titular anti-hero of *Rebel Without a Cause* (1955):

Stapler. Most of us wage war on the wrong people Jimmy. I do it meself all the time. But you beat the bun altogether you do.
Jimmy. How's that?
Stapler. You wage war on everybody.

(64)

Paddy and Stapler see Jimmy's father's shortcomings playing out in Jimmy's rage, and Jimmy is fully aware of his familial inheritance:

Linda. You'd rob your own Da? [...] (*shakes her head*) I can't ...
I mean I know your brother Dick real well and he's terrible nice.
Jimmy. Yeah well Richard follows me Ma. [...] If your Da was like mine you'd rob him too.

(36)

The social consequences of his paternity are all too clear to Jimmy, and generate acute awareness of double standards shaping broader society,

Jimmy. Like when I went looking for a job at your place. What did your man O'Brien ask me? What Brady are you then? [...] He wrote me off straight away. [...] I wouldn't mind only he was knockin' off stuff all over the place himself. They found the generator in his car, didn't they?

(37)

Stapler sees Jimmy's eruption in Act II as a response to the pressures of such irreconcilable contradictions:

Stapler. Well let's face it, if a young lad takes a good look around him what do he see? He sees a crowd of big shots and hob-nobbers grabbin' and takin' all before them. [...] Like your man down in the factory – O'Brien – knocking off stuff right, left and centre, caught red-handed too. What happened to him? Nothin'. Nothin' happened to him.

(51–2)

A Handful of Stars explores masculinities under pressure as Ireland's small-town manufacturing base contracted in the face of global circumstances, from the mid-1970s. Jimmy is infuriated by Conway's toadying to the factory owner and informing the foreman of his work-mates' peccadilloes to consolidate his job:

Jimmy. Yeh see that's the difference between me and Conway. He tiptoes around. I'm screamin'. Me and Stapler are screamin'. So if you want to join the livin' dead then go ahead and do it by all means Tony but don't expect me to wink at your grave-diggers.
(60)

Jimmy's rebellious worldview is a contest between two male types, zombies and playboys; Tony set to follow Conway in the former role, and Jimmy already eclipsing Stapler in the latter. Roche's drama-turgical approach is more complex, however, not least in staging moments of warmth and gentleness among the men, and between them and the women in their lives; all, except Linda, evoked in their absence. Contrary to Jimmy's schema, Stapler acts as a benevolent mentor to Tony, coaching him in playing pool, and chiding Jimmy for making the more self-effacing boy play with an inferior cue. As Stapler watches Tony play, "*his fondness for the boy show[s] in his smile*" (8).

In Linda's presence, in Act I, even Jimmy "*softens* [...] *She smiles at his tenderness*" (16). Later, in a moving monologue, Jimmy reveals to her the depth of his unhappy parents' capacity for love:

Jimmy. I once caught them kissin' yeh know. [...] I'm not coddin' you she looked absolutely ... radiant. (*Pause.*) Richard says he doesn't remember that happenin' at all. Me Ma don't either. Maybe it was just a whatdoyoucallit ... a mirage.

(37)

The poignancy of that memory – the emotional centre of Jimmy's psyche, and the play itself – is amplified in Paddy's account of the couple dancing in the Town Hall during their courtship: "And she'd be smilin' up into his face all the time. To look at her you'd swear she had just swallowed a handful of stars. Jaysus she was a lovely girl so she was" (50).

A Handful of Stars inaugurates Billy Roche's characteristic anti-phon between narrative and popular song, referencing Hollywood cinema and native loquaciousness, alike. When asked what had inspired his 1991 screenplay, *Trojan Eddie*, Roche said he had wanted to write something as identifiably Irish as a French film was unmis-takably French.[3] The canon of stage work he has produced since *A Handful of Stars* speaks to a similar ambition in relation to theatre, and his fictional Wexford; actors now learn Wexford accents, and grapple with the peculiarities of humour and expression particular to that town. Wexford has a social history quite at odds with the rest of Ireland; throughout most of the twentieth century, the town had a socialist ethos. Factor in Colm Tóibín's observation that "the Wexford Billy Roche was brought up in had all the characteristics of a metrop-olis and some of its energy,"[4] and Roche's dramatic world cannot be understood as congruent with versions of small-town Ireland so powerfully staged in, for instance, Tom Murphy's *On the Outside*, or Brian Friel's *Philadelphia, Here I Come!* Neither does Roche's approach to social class sit comfortably with O'Casey's fatalism towards a world of men, so caustically crystallised in the penultimate scene of *Juno and the Paycock*:

Mary. My poor little child that'll have no father!
Mrs Boyle. It'll have what's far betther – it'll have two mothers![5]

Roche's working-class men and boys have much more in common with the *dramatis personae* of James McKenna's *The Scattering* (1959), but with greater grit and purpose. As McKenna's young people depart on an emigrant ship to Holyhead, Ould Rock delivers a quietist elegy on the dockside, domesticating emigration and hopelessness as inevitable features of Dublin working-class life. By contrast, while the police search the town for Jimmy during his night of rampage, Paddy and Stapler act to save him from himself, and, in the face of threat and insult, Paddy stonewalls Swan when he comes looking for information.

Swan. You must have no respect for yourself Paddy.
Paddy. Ah sure, we can't all be Sergeant Majors.

(55)

Paddy names the moral chasm between these two men: Swan, a state functionary, whose self-worth resides in his role as enforcer; hence his vengeful demeanour – job and psyche are as one. Rooted in the social and familial relationships of his home town, Paddy, fully possessed of who he is, embodies and ennobles a compromised alternative, but an alternative nonetheless; Roche's abiding theme: the dignity of small lives.

Victor Merriman

Notes

1 Billy Roche, *The Wexford Trilogy: A Handful of Stars, Poor Beast in the Rain, Belfry* (London: Nick Hern Books, 2000), 2. Subsequent references are entered in parentheses.

2 *The Boker Poker Club* was the title under which the play was first performed, in a production by Patrick Sutton, at Wexford Arts Centre (1986). Cast from local actors, Gary Lydon played Jimmy Brady, and Billy Roche, Stapler.

3 *Trojan Eddie* Screenplay, Billy Roche; Director, Gillies Mackinnon (1991) Initial Films, for Channel 4.

4 Colm Tóibín, "The Talk of the Town: The Plays of Billy Roche," in *Druids, Dudes and Beauty Queens*, ed. Dermot Bolger (Dublin: New Island Books, 2000), 25.

5 Sean O'Casey, *Juno and the Paycock*, in *Sean O'Casey Collected Plays Vol. I* (London: Macmillan, 1984), 86.

Further Reading

Merriman, Victor. "Locked Out: Working-Class Lives in Irish Drama." In *A History of Irish Working-Class Writing*, edited by Michael Pierse, 318–31. Cambridge: Cambridge University Press, 2018.

Murray, Christopher. "Billy Roche's *Wexford Trilogy*: Setting, Place, Critique." In *Theatre Stuff: Essays on Contemporary Irish Theatre*, ed. Eamonn Jordan, 209–23. Dublin: Carysfort Press, 2000.

THE LAMENT FOR ARTHUR CLEARY (1989)
BY DERMOT BOLGER

The Lament for Arthur Cleary was staged at the Abbey's Peacock Theatre in 1989, as the winner of an Edinburgh Festival Fringe First Award, simultaneously announcing and problematising a moment emergent at the beginning of the 1990s. This was the occasion of an apparent willingness on the part of the Republic of Ireland at last to examine critically all aspects of the socio-cultural complex it had become. The defining event of that time is the election of Mary Robinson as President of Ireland. Public endorsement of Robinson's rhetoric of inclusion, elaborated in her careful handling of symbols, amounted to a political and cultural watershed. In the election of 1989, Mary Robinson defeated, against all the odds, the Fianna Fáil candidate Brian Lenihan, whose rhetoric provided a model for the smug Politician of Bolger's drama, "We know we cannot all live on this one island."[1] As a summary of the betrayals of neo-colonialism, Lenihan's phrase was remarkably efficient, a point not lost on Bolger, when he incorporated and elaborated on it in the Politician's speech in *The Lament for Arthur Cleary*:

> We know we cannot all live on this one island. But we are not ashamed. Young people are to Ireland what champagne is to France! Our finest crop, the cream of our youth, nurtured from birth, raised with tender love by our young state, brought to ripeness and then plucked! For export to your factories and offices. Fellow European ministers [...] we know you will not turn your backs on them. (6–7)

In Lenihan's remark, and Bolger's deft elaboration on it, the European ideal, attractive to the mass of Irish people for its evolved concept of citizenship, is reduced to the status of a waste disposal unit for surplus humanity.

Dermot Bolger was an established man of letters by the time his first play was staged, with well-received poetry collections and novels to his name, and a busy career as the founder of Raven Arts Press. *The Lament for Arthur Cleary* began life as a narrative poem of the same name,[2] Bolger's critical response to *Caoineadh Airt Uí Laoire* (1773), the lament of Eibhlín Dhubh ní Chonaill for her murdered husband Art Ó Laoire.[3] In Bolger's play, Arthur Cleary is at once fully present and tightly bound to the historical figure of Art Ó Laoire, and this doubleness enables him to play an important critical role. Rooted in a Gaelic past, he restores a sense of the participation of historical experience in contemporary narratives of identity. Commissioned, developed, and produced by Wet Paint Arts, the play is both an urban drama of intranational betrayal and of Ireland's complex relationships with Europe at the end of the 1980s.

The play favours montage over plot, making use of Epic strategies such as actors taking multiple roles, repetition of scenes, direct address to the audience, and heightened poetic language. David Byrne's approach as both dramaturg and director was sensitive to "the requirements, and the skills, of what I felt would be mainly a young audience, maybe not very patient with – or used to – large amounts of dialogue, but very adept at reading meaning from visual material."[4] Bolger's Arthur left Ireland in 1969/1970, for factory work in Germany, and on his return to Dublin begins a relationship with Kathy – fifteen years his junior – among the imploding social conditions of 1980s Dublin, "the heroin capital of Europe."[5] The narrative trajectory of *The Lament for Arthur Cleary* encompasses Arthur's return to Dublin, his meeting with Kathy, their courtship, life together, near break-up, and his grisly murder on the edges of the heroin economy. Wet Paint Arts' touring production tested the poem's fictional Dublin before audiences for whom dispossession, exile, and fruitless return were experiences first, and metaphors second.

Arthur's consoling image of "the streets of Dublin tattooed along the veins of my wrist" (61), fixed and immutable, sustained him while in Germany, but was uninformed by the changing circumstances of the actual city. On his return, the presence of so many familiar signs convey a sense of continuity, but his drama begins when personal myth collides, on actual streets, with the people Dubliners of his class had become during his absence:

Kathy. (*looking up at him with urgency in her voice*) [...] The pushers, they hate the way you look at them. Even the kids round here, Arthur, they haven't a clue who you are. I see them dismantling that bike with their eyes, breaking it down into needles and fixes. And now Deignan [the moneylender]. You remind him of things. His kind own this city now, Arthur. He'll want to own you as well.

(51)

Dramaturgically, the play punctuates and counterpoints a series of vividly realised narrative episodes with four border scenes depicting the harassment and disorientation of an Irishman positioned as an alien in the "common European home":

Frontier Guard. Passport please.
Arthur. (*turning*): Oh, sorry.
Frontier Guard. Ah Irish. Irish. Boom-boom, eh? (*He laughs*)
Arthur. Yeah. Boom-bleeding-boom.

(5)

As the dramatic action develops, these sinister checkpoint encounters become familiar, revealing their full significance in the final iteration:

Frontier Guard. So many trains run through here, day and night, in all directions, all times, coming and going.
Arthur. Who's on that one? Where's it going?
(*Looking down at platform*)
Frontier Guard. Europe ... The future ... Her children.
Arthur. Not mine.
Frontier Guard. (*smiles*) Life goes on, you pick the pieces up. Would you have had her put on black and spin out her life in mourning?

True to its source, Bolger's play gives voice to a woman's narrative: the lyrical expressions of her desolation at Arthur's death introduce the action, and are a key organising element of the drama. Arthur's murder is densely narrated in choric verse by Kathy, before it is played out in the temporal experience of the audience. Arthur's double presence exposes the failures, omissions, and exclusions of Independent Ireland, an urban heroin economy fully implicated in an official economy of commodity consumption, accelerating in range and quantity.

The Lament for Arthur Cleary is a radical text of late-twentieth-century Irish theatre, and an important site of negotiations around mutations in Irish identity. Dermot Bolger's appropriation and reworking of a canonical narrative of the Gaelic world in service of the concerns of contemporary Dublin sees an artist write back, not to empire, but to the canonised source of official nationalist iconography itself. As in his *In High Germany* (1990), Bolger is concerned to make visible the recalcitrance of Ireland's urban margins to the interests of a ruling class. By mapping a moment from the long narrative of colonial oppression onto the struggle for self-actualisation in 1980s Dublin, Bolger layers reality, not on to historical fact, but on to poetry and a mythic past, so clearly the repository of images mobilised to narrate to itself Ireland's improbable continuities.

Perhaps the most significant achievement of Wet Paint Arts' staging of *The Lament for Arthur Cleary* was registered at the level of cultural politics: the play included its audience. In pre-production and development, the company of five actors would hold open workshops and response sessions with people in areas to which it was intended to tour the finished play. In performance, the class whose experiences it stages, people who are also the play's primary point of address, claimed a place on the cultural map, and asserted a right to be considered as part of the public sphere. Wet Paint Arts' production and exhibition ethos complements the work of class-conscious companies such as Calypso Productions and the Passion Machine; critical artistic projects active during the 1980s and 1990s. It also anticipates the dramaturgical and production values of *The Ballymun Trilogy*, fruit of Bolger's formidable partnership with Ray Yeates at the *axis* arts centre, Ballymun (2004–2008).[6]

The past maintains a presence which shadows this contemporary drama, and yet Arthur Cleary is a truly new figure in Irish theatre, a marker of radical discontinuity between the historical circumstances of the 1980s, and the formal strategies of Irish theatre of the time.

Victor Merriman

Notes

1 Dermot Bolger, *The Lament for Arthur Cleary*, in *Dermot Bolger Plays 1* (London: Methuen, 2000), 6. Subsequent references are entered in parentheses.
2 Dermot Bolger, "The Lament for Arthur Cleary," in *Internal Exiles* (Dublin: Dolmen Press, 1986), 69–79.
3 Eibhlín Dhubh ní Chonaill, "Caoineadh Airt Uí Laoire," in *An Duanaire/ Poems of the Dispossessed*, ed. Thomas Kinsella and Seán Ó Tuama (Dublin: Dolmen Press, 1981), 200–19.
4 Author interview with David Byrne, 14 August 1994.
5 Fintan O'Toole "Introduction: On the Frontier," in *Plays 1*, 3.
6 Dermot Bolger, *The Ballymun Trilogy* (Dublin: New Island Books, 2010).

Further Reading

Mac Anna, Ferdia. "The Dublin Renaissance: An Essay on Modern Dublin and Dublin." *The Irish Review* No. 10, Dublin/Europe/Dublin (Spring 1991): 14–30.

Merriman, Victor. "Centring the Wanderer: Europe as Active Imaginary in Contemporary Irish Theatre." *Irish University Review* Vol. 27, no. 1 (Winter 1997): 166–87.

Merriman, Victor. "A Responsibility to Dream: Decolonising Independent Ireland." *Third Text* Vol. 19, Issue 5 (2005): 487–97.

DANCING AT LUGHNASA (1990) BY BRIAN FRIEL

Brian Friel's *Dancing at Lughnasa* (1990) is set in late summer 1936, the season of Lughnasa, named for the pagan Celtic deity Lugh. The play is framed by formal tableaux narrated by the adult Michael, who stands down stage in a pool of light, removed from the action by both time and space. He speaks directly to the audience, not only providing basic exposition but also telling of his awareness, even as a child, "of a widening breach between what seemed to be and what was, of things changing too quickly before my eyes, of becoming what they ought not to be."[1] The non-marital son of Chris, the adult Michael also speaks as his "imaginary" seven-year-old self. Michael's narration, Friel's description of the set, the family's diminished circumstances, and the centrality of dance all recall Tennessee Williams's *The Glass Menagerie* (1944), which Friel's daughter Judy directed for the Abbey's smaller Peacock Theatre in 1990.

In this, Friel's "most autobiographical" play,[2] the six Mundy siblings are finely characterised by age, temperament, dress, and demeanour. Kate, a forty-year-old teacher, the only one to work outside the home, is especially fearful of the family's precarious situation. Maggie, the housekeeper, is ebullient and optimistic, often joking, singing, and dancing while working. Agnes is the special protector of her "*simple*" (n.p.) sister Rose; they both earn pocket money knitting gloves. The youngest, Chris, is Michael's unmarried mother. The eldest of the six siblings, Jack, is a priest who has returned from his Ugandan leper mission to their native Ballybeg diminished in many ways. He "*looks frail and older than his fifty-three years*" (17), dresses inappropriately, and struggles with even common words. Despite living in "*lean circumstances*" (n.p.), the Mundys have acquired an erratic radio, christened "Marconi," that unpredictably brings music into their lives. While Michael constructs kites, his aunts lighten their never-ending domestic chores with chatter, song, and dance.

Kate arrives after a two-mile walk from town with groceries and news, including news of the annual Harvest Dance. Her sisters imagine a wonderful evening, but Kate will have none of it: "Do you want the whole countryside to be laughing at us? – women of our years? – mature women, *dancing*?" (13). Kate's mention of Bernie, who is visiting with her twin teenage daughters, triggers Maggie's plaintive recollection of a rollicking dance that she attended with Bernie twenty-two years ago. When Chris connects a new battery to Marconi, a blast of Irish ceili dance music inspires Maggie to streak flour through her hair and on her face and begin a wild dance: "*her features become animated by a look of defiance, of aggression; a crude mask of happiness* [...] *a white-faced frantic dervish*" (21). One by one her sisters join her, although Kate's dance is "*totally private*" (22). Friel's stage directions note: "*the movements seem caricatured; and the sound is too loud; and the beat is too fast; and the almost recognizable dance is made grotesque*" (21). In discussing *Philadelphia, Here I Come!* (1964), *Aristocrats* (1979), and *Faith Healer* (1979), Harry White describes the centrality of music to Friel's theatre: "music enters the text as a decisive agent in both the dramatic structure and emotional meaning of the drama."[3] Here music, as well as dance, is an expressive alternative to language.

Their dance marks a profound shift as an atmosphere of ease becomes one of unpleasant squabbling: Chris and Rose denounce the radio as "bloody useless" (23) and Agnes and Kate bicker. Their carping ends as abruptly as their dancing when they spot Michael's father, Gerry Evans, approaching. While Chris stares in amazement, her sisters scramble to make themselves and the home as presentable as possible.

It has been more than a year since Gerry last visited. When the unpredictable Marconi picks up the broadcast of "Dancing in the Dark," Gerry takes Chris in his arms and elegantly dances her around the garden while in the cottage her sisters provide a running commentary. Not for the first time, Gerry proposes to Chris, who, knowing his unreliability, again turns him down. Kate shares her deepest anxieties with Maggie: Chris will again fall into depression when Gerry leaves; her teaching post may not be renewed; "But what worries me most of all is Rose. If I died – if I lost my job – if this house were broken up – what would become of our Rosie?" (36).

Father Jack appears even more disoriented when he returns from a walk. He recalls his departure from the family when Chris was only a baby. He struggles to remember the word for "a sacred and mysterious" (39) event and finally lights on "Ceremony! That's the word!

How could I have forgotten that! The offering, the ritual, the dancing – a ceremony!" (40). Jack reminisces about his African mission and *"dances-shuffles"* (42) to the percussive rhythm he taps out with two sticks. Driving the first act to its conclusion, Michael's poignant narration reveals what will come: Kate will lose her job; the family will be broken up.

The second act, set three weeks later, begins with Maggie playfully dancing to 1934's "Play to Me, Gypsy." Jack, who is regaining his strength and language, describes Ugandan harvest festivals, "very special, really magnificent ceremonies" (47), that culminate with ritual community dancing. Rose and Agnes are off on the "annual ritual" (46) of picking bilberries for jam. Rituals, many of them such as the Harvest Dance or the "pagan" Lughnasa bonfires in the back hills, are unavailable to the family. In fact, all of the Mundys's many dances are transgressive; none is sanctioned by the community.

When Agnes returns alone, the sisters' near panic shows how vulnerable Rose is. Rose soon returns unharmed but has, in fact, met up with Danny Bradley, whose wife abandoned him and their children. Gerry reappears to report that he has joined the International Brigade to fight in Spain, a cause Kate has denounced as "godless Communism" (52).

The play's trajectory of loss and decline now carries a sense of inevitability: A knitting factory will leave Rose and Agnes without income and, not to burden the family, they will emigrate to abject poverty in London. Ballybeg will not honour Jack with a civic reception nor will he say Mass again. The nostalgia that suffuses Michael's final narration draws of the etymology of the word, which combines homecoming and pain. He concludes with an unreliable memory from his childhood that "owes nothing to fact": his family dancing to the "dream music that is both heard and imagined ... Dancing as if language no longer existed because words were no longer necessary" (71).

Directed by Patrick Mason, designed by Joe Vanek, and choreographed by Terry John Bates, *Dancing at Lughnasa* premiered at the Abbey Theatre on 24 April 1990, transferred to London's National Theatre in October of that year, and then to Broadway, where it ran for 421 performances. The most commercially successful of Friel's plays, it received superlative reviews and won multiple best play awards in London and New York. Mel Gussow noted that the Broadway production "received eight Tony nominations – the most a new play had ever received."[4]

The play engages the audience in a complex, nuanced relationship with the characters and stage action. As Richard Pine writes, "audiences witnessing *Dancing at Lughnasa* acknowledge the play's role as ritual."[5] But, as Nicholas Grene observes, "a production of *Dancing at Lughnasa* in London could be forced back towards nostalgic period-piece by the expectations of its audiences."[6] This was, in fact, the case in Pat O'Connor's 1998 film adaptation of the play.

Dancing at Lughnasa explores the harsh realities of economic isolationism and austerity, marriage practices, and emigration in a patriarchal Ireland whose 1937 Constitution judged that women should not "neglect [...] their duties in the home."[7] Despite Ireland's isolationism in the 1930s, international references abound: some are Jack's memories of Africa; many come from the music broadcast by the radio; others are familiar tales of emigration.

When it was revived at the Abbey by the original production team in 1999, *Dancing at Lughnasa* was seen in retrospective as a forerunner of *Riverdance* (1995) for its use of Irish dance. It remains among the most popular of Friel's plays.

Joan Fitzpatrick Dean

Notes

1 Brian Friel, *Dancing at Lughnasa* (London: Faber & Faber, 1990), 2. Subsequent references are entered in parentheses.
2 Anthony Roche, *Brian Friel: Theatre and Politics* (New York: Palgrave Macmillan, 2011), 169. Drawing on the Brian Friel Papers at the National Library of Ireland, Roche details Friel's selective inclusion of autobiographical elements.
3 Harry White, "Brian Friel, Thomas Murphy and Use of Music in Contemporary Irish Drama," *Modern Drama* Vol. 33, no. 4 (Winter 1990): 554.
4 Mel Gussow, "From Ballybeg to Broadway," *New York Times Magazine*, 29 September 1991, 30.
5 Richard Pine, *The Diviner: The Art of Brian Friel* (Dublin: University College Dublin Press, 1999), 268.
6 Nicholas Grene, *The Politics of Irish Drama: Plays in Context from Boucicault to Friel* (Cambridge: Cambridge University Press, 2004), 218.
7 See Melissa Sihra, ed., *Women in Irish Drama: A Century of Authorship and Representation* (Basingstoke: Palgrave, 2007), 1–22.

Further Reading

Dean, Joan FitzPatrick. *Dancing at Lughnasa*. Cork: Cork University Press, 2003.

Friel, Brian. *Brian Friel in Conversation*. Edited by Paul Delaney. Ann Arbor: University of Michigan Press, 2000.

Kiberd, Declan. "Dancing at Lughnasa." *The Irish Review* No. 27 (Summer 2001): 18–39.

DIGGING FOR FIRE (1991) BY DECLAN HUGHES

Digging for Fire premiered in 1991 at the Project Arts Centre in Dublin, where it met with immediate acclaim. A transfer to The Bush theatre in London soon followed, and the production is now seen as having established the national and international reputation of Rough Magic, the Dublin-based independent theatre company that Hughes co-founded with the director Lynne Parker in 1984.

Most of the action is set in the suburban Dublin home of Clare and Brendan, a young married couple who are hosting a reunion of their friends from university. That gathering is occasioned by the return to Ireland of two members of the group who had emigrated to New York: Danny is a writer who claims to have recently sold a story to the *New Yorker*, and Emily is a visual artist who, we soon learn, has been diagnosed with AIDS.

As the friends catch up with each other – and as they consume more alcohol – several tensions and secrets come to the surface. Another married couple, Breda and Steve, become the focal point for much of that negativity: Breda is resented by some of her friends because she works for an exploitative radio talk show, while her husband Steve's brazen (and frequent) infidelities are a source of both gossip and divided loyalties amongst the group. Also experiencing a growing sense of alienation from the others is Rory, a gay man whose lifestyle has diverged from that of his friends; it is important to note in this context that homosexuality would remain a criminal offence in Ireland until 1994, three years after the play premiered.

The drama's key relationship, however, is between Clare and Danny. They had been romantically involved while in college, and also had a brief affair after Clare's marriage to Brendan. As the drama moves into its final act, Clare resolves to leave her husband in order to be with Danny – but soon realises that she needs to be free of both men to fully realise her own potential. At the play's conclusion, Clare has decided to move to New York to begin a new life for herself. Danny has resolved to stay in Ireland, having admitted that his claims of being a successful writer in New York were false. And the other characters similarly must come to terms with the fact that several of their longest-held illusions have been shattered.

In many respects, *Digging for Fire* resembles several classic Irish plays. Its final scene presents Clare dancing alone, a moment of emotional intensity likely to remind audiences of the dance scene in Brian Friel's *Dancing at Lughnasa* (1990). Audiences may also be reminded of the conclusion of Friel's *Philadelphia, Here I Come!* (1964), which presents a young man on the eve of his departure from Ireland to America – but which (as is the case with Hughes's presentation of Clare) leaves uncertain the question of whether he will go through with his decision to emigrate. And with its presentation of a group of young people who grapple with emigration, loneliness, and alcohol abuse, the play evokes Tom Murphy's *Conversations on a Homecoming* (1985).

Hughes's play has, however, come to be seen as representing an important departure point for Irish drama. Unusually, it presented characters who resembled the Dublin audience-members who first saw it: cosmopolitan, middle-class, city-dwelling university graduates. Hughes's decision to present such characters was deliberate: as he later explained, "there was an active hostility to telling these stories [in the early 1990s], because they were about suburban, middle-class people. There seemed to be a sense that they had no right to be on stage."[1] The play's director Lynne Parker elaborated on that point, explaining how Rough Magic's ethos was based on a desire to show the internationalisation of Irish culture: "we felt very strongly that we were of a generation whose main influences were British and American television and American film as well, and that we were definitely being influenced by other cultures."[2] *Digging for Fire*, therefore, intended to show audiences the Ireland that Parker and Hughes actually lived in.

Those decisions give the play a topicality that many previous Irish dramas had tended to avoid. Early in the first act, for example, Breda observes that the "one good reason" to live in Ireland is that although "you can't get a divorce or an abortion … at least when you go to buy your paper in the morning, you don't have to run that nauseating gauntlet of porno wank mags" – accurately demonstrating the impact that Catholic ideology had on Ireland even in the early 1990s.[3] There is also an iconoclastic frankness about sex and sexuality, the Northern Ireland "Troubles," the international AIDS crisis, and the pernicious impact of class-based divisions in Irish society.

But perhaps the play is most notable for its integration of international culture. The original production included a lengthy debate about *American Psycho*, the controversial 1991 novel by Bret Easton Ellis (Hughes removed this sequence from the published script, reasoning that it had become outdated). The play derives its title from another 1991 release: *Bossanova*, the third album from the Boston alternative rock group Pixies ("Dig for Fire" is one of that album's most popular tracks). And it also features music from REM, Iggy and the Stooges, the Sex Pistols, Tom Waits, and, most memorably, New Order, whose song "True Faith" brings the action to a close.

Hughes would later explain that the play was a forceful attempt to change the Irish theatre. In his 2000 article, "Who the Hell Do We Think We Still Are?", he asked why Irish drama remained dominated by nostalgic versions of rural Ireland, suggesting that Irish playwrights had exhausted their store of images. "Even if we do it in an iconoclastic way, the iconography remains powerfully the same," Hughes complained: "half-door, pint bottle, sacred heart."[4] Frustrated by the large number of Irish plays set in pubs and country kitchens, he argued that Irish dramatists were ignoring the present because they were frightened of it: "We fear [that] the set of identities we have for ourselves won't add up any more. And foolishly, we think the fear is better avoided than faced."

In many of his subsequent plays, Hughes would develop the themes of *Digging for Fire*, while continuing to display that commitment to fearless confrontation of the present. His 2003 drama *Shiver* is in many ways a companion piece to the earlier work, presenting characters whose experience of the Celtic Tiger period has been overwhelmingly negative: they have acquired wealth but have also become materialistic, vulgar, casually racist, and complacent. His 2012 play *The Last Summer* explored the legacy of the Celtic Tiger after its collapse but, like *Digging for Fire*, also showed a preoccupation with the value of friendship, and with the ways in which adulthood forces a compromise with one's dreams.

Digging for Fire is also important for its impact on the development of Rough Magic. When the company was founded in 1984, it had initially staged Irish premieres of plays by British and American writers such as Caryl Churchill, Wallace Shawn, David Hare, and others. Under the influence of the international sensibility of those dramatists, Hughes shaped a new Irish play that was both rooted and cosmopolitan – something that had not been done much before in Ireland. The objective of creating plays that are focussed on Ireland but informed by the outside world has dominated the activities of Rough Magic since that time. The play has also had a strong impact on the practice of Irish playwriting. Three members of the original cast – Arthur Riordan, Gina Moxley, and Pom Boyd – would themselves go on to write successful plays, and Hughes's call for new ways of making Irish drama was resoundingly met by the emergence of exciting new companies in the early 2000s, among them ANU Productions, Brokentalkers, and THEATREclub.

The ongoing legacy of the play was evident in 2013, when it was revived by Rough Magic. Its director Matt Torney explained that it had "created a huge buzz, particularly among the younger generation," and argued that *Digging for Fire* still had the capacity to "talk to the present moment in order to start a dialogue about the future."[5]

Patrick Lonergan

Notes

1 Patrick Lonergan, *Irish Drama and Theatre Since 1950* (London: Bloomsbury, 2019), 95.
2 Lilian Chambers, Ger FitzGibbon and Eamonn Jordan, *Theatre Talk* (Dublin: Carysfort Press, 2001), 394.
3 Declan Hughes, *Digging for Fire*, in *Declan Hughes Plays 1* (London: Methuen Drama, 1998), 3.
4 Declan Hughes, "Who the Hell Do We Think We Still Are?" in *Theatre Stuff: Essays on Contemporary Irish Theatre*, ed. Eamonn Jordan (Dublin: Carysfort Press, 2000), 1.
5 Quoted in Patrick Lonergan "Digging around the Past," *Irish Times*, 22 April 2013. www.irishtimes.com/culture/stage/digging-around-in-the-past-for-a-glimpse-of-the-future-1.1365997. Accessed 12 December 2021.

Further Reading

Richards, Shaun. "'To Me, Here Is More Like There': Irish Drama and Criticism in the 'Collision Culture'." *Irish Studies Review* Vol. 15, no. 1 (2007): 1–15.

ECLIPSED (1992) BY PATRICIA BURKE BROGAN

Patricia Burke Brogan was a novice nun who served for a short period in a Magdalen laundry. These institutions were run by various orders of the Roman Catholic Church and while originally established to rehabilitate prostitutes, unmarried, pregnant women were also committed and required to work in the laundries. The babies were taken from the women and adopted out to Roman Catholic families, many of them in the United States. However, records show that some young women were committed simply because they were too pretty and the belief was that they would become promiscuous.

Burke Brogan's experience in the laundry never left her. She wrote a short story, "Sunflowers," which she adapted into a one-act play set in the fictitious Magdalen laundry of Killmacha. In her memoir she records that critic Fintan O'Toole said that the piece "shows great promise and that I should develop it into a full length play."[1] The full-length work premiered in 1992 at the Punchbag Theatre in Galway, later travelling to the Edinburgh Festival where it won a Fringe First Prize.

Eclipsed begins and ends in the present day of the play's production with a young woman, Rosa, in search of her birth mother who had worked in the laundry. The only member of the laundry left is the aged Nellie-Nora who shows Rosa a memento-filled basket left from years before. The scene then shifts back to 1963 as Sister Virginia, the white novice who is Burke Brogan's alter ego, is ringing the bell for morning prayer. As Sister Virginia exits, the stage becomes the Magdalen laundry and the women enter singing Elvis Presley's "Heartbreak Hotel." Each scene of the play is named; the first scene with the women is "Cathy's Birthday." The Magdalens, also known as penitents, are Cathy, Nellie-Nora, Mandy, and Brigit. In scene four, seventeen-year-old Juliet, raised in the adjoining orphanage, joins them. It is in this scene, we also meet the stern Victoria, Mother Superior of the order.

Each of the Magdalens has a story and as the women engage in the work of the laundry, their stories are heard. Nellie-Nora has been assaulted by her employer and he has committed her to the laundry. Brigit is desperate to escape to unite with her John-Joe who never knew she was pregnant (it is her child Rosa who is searching for her). Asthmatic Cathy has delivered twins who are in the next-door orphanage, and she longs to see them. The women surmise that Cathy may have been impregnated by a priest. Elvis-mad Mandy made love with her Richard on the seats of his shiny red car, but when she tells him of the baby, he abandons her. Nellie-Nora and Mandy's babies have been stillborn.

Sister Virginia has compassion for the women and she struggles to comfort them and pleads for more humane treatment from Mother Victoria. As she experiences the world in the laundry, she is filled with doubts about her vocation. These doubts mirror Burke Brogan's experience: she eventually left her order. In the "Credo" scene, Sister Virginia prays for help for herself and the Magdalens: "Mother of Jesus, do something about Cathy, Mandy, Nellie-Nora and the others … Help us! – Help me!"[2]

In Act II, scene 1 "Office 1" Sister Virginia defends the women to Mother Victoria. Cathy has tried to escape and been returned by the laundry truck drivers. Sister Virginia pleads for fresh air, vitamins, and sunshine for the women, but Mother Victoria responds that the women are dangerous and immoral. She says the women do not deserve her sympathy; they are fallen women, temptresses: "These women can't be trusted! They're weak, Sister! No control! They've broken the sixth and ninth Commandments!" (43).

Throughout the play, the women work, iron, mend, sort laundry, wash floors and yet they find small moments of escape, a birthday party for Cathy, reading tea leaves, and in one of the most poignant scenes, Brigit organises a mock wedding for Mandy with a dummy Elvis. Mandy is the penitent who has the most tenuous hold on reality and is severely mentally ill.

Brigit, clearly the ring-leader, pleads with Sister Virginia to give her the keys to let her escape to find her baby (Rosa). Ultimately, Cathy's second escape attempt ends with her death. Earlier Brigit has attacked Sister Virginia and in the penultimate scene of the play, Brigit stands before Sister Virginia who unclips the keys and hands them to her. Although the play is a tense drama, there are wonderful moments of humour and playfulness among the women as they try to distract themselves from the hardship of their day-to-day lives.

Burke Brogan's *Eclipsed* had a number of all-Ireland tours. There have also been productions on four continents from Australia to South America including numerous ones in the United States. The Irish Repertory Theatre in New York produced an acclaimed production in 1999. In 2013, Mephisto Theatre Company of Galway also produced a well-received production. The number of productions the play has received is remarkable considering that Burke Brogan acted as her own agent and denied rights to a company if she "didn't like the cut of them."[3]

Patricia Burke Brogan is an artist, a poet, a dramatist, and a memorist. Although she has written and had produced a number of plays, particularly *Stained Glass at Samhain* (2003) and *Requiem of Love: A Monologue for Stage* (2006), *Eclipsed* is her most important work. It is not often that a play changes history, but this is the case with *Eclipsed*. James Smith, a member of the survivor advocacy group Justice for the Magdalens, has credited Burke Brogan's play as bringing the plight of the Magdalens into the public consciousness:

More than any other contemporary representation, *Eclipsed* narrates a story that liberates these women from derisory discourses criminality and mental instability while manifesting the results of institutionalization on their daily lives and consciousness. The play's five penitent women, confined for a variety of reasons, belie the easy assumption that Magdalen women were invariably fallen. More significantly, *Eclipsed* dramatizes the strategies employed by these women to resist and survive their incarceration, to become active agents in their destiny.[4]

However, in her memoir, Burke Brogan recalls how she received hate mail and threatening phone calls, ultimately installing an alarm system in her home because of the anger directed at her and the play.

In a 2013 opinion piece for *The Irish Times* prior to the Irish State's public apology to the Magdalens, James Smith states that it was *Eclipsed* that provided the "narrative tropes with which to tell the story of the laundries and all the women confined therein." He writes that in her play, Burke Brogan "insisted that the whole story must emerge, that understanding would come only when all sides—the women, nuns, State, society and families—spoke their versions of our collective past."[5]

Eclipsed has been translated into numerous languages, telling a compelling story based on recent history which also gives directors and actresses a challenging vehicle. Over a decade before the film *The Magdalene Sisters* (2002) expressed similar concerns, Burke Brogan captured an important piece of women's history in a compelling drama which has continued to be studied and produced.

Charlotte Headrick

Notes

1 Patricia Burke Brogan, *Memoir with Grykes and Turloughs* (Galway: Wordsonthestreet, 2014), 117.
2 Patricia Burke Brogan, *Eclipsed* (Galway: Salmon Press, 1994), 30. Subsequent references are entered in parentheses.
3 Author conversations with Patricia Burke Brogan, Spring, 2013.
4 James Smith, *The Magdalen Laundries and the Nation's Architecture of Containment* (Notre Dame, Indiana: Notre Dame Press, 2014), 92–93.
5 James Smith, "Fair Compensation Must Follow Magdalene Apology," *The Irish Times*, 19 February 2013.

Further Reading

Finnegan, Frances. *Do Penance or Perish: Magdalen Asylums in Ireland.* Oxford: Oxford University Press, 2004.

Milotte, Mike. *Banished Babies: The Secret History of Ireland's Baby Export Business.* Dublin: New Island Books, 1997.

Smith, James. *Ireland's Magdalen Laundries and the Nation's Architecture of Containment.* Notre Dame, Indiana: University of Notre Dame Press, 2014.

THE STEWARD OF CHRISTENDOM (1995)
BY SEBASTIAN BARRY

The Steward of Christendom was first staged to great acclaim at The Royal Court Theatre, London in March 1995, an early entry in what would become the author's career-long undertaking to re-inscribe his family history in the forms of drama and prose fiction. The play, Barry's most successful work for theatre, is notable for the definitive portrayal in the title role of Thomas Dunne by the Abbey Theatre's Donal McCann who would die soon after this triumph.

When *Steward* appeared Barry's artistic experience and success was nearly exclusively a theatrical one, but his later reputation was as an award-winning novelist. Barry's *A Long Long Way* (2005) would later retrace the years before the setting of *The Steward of Christendom*, to tell the story of Thomas Dunne's son Willie who died in the First World War, and who first appeared as a ghost in this play. The earlier novel, *Annie Dunne* (2002), relates the story of Willie's sister as a middle-aged spinster decades later in County Wexford.

Thomas Dunne, and his story, can thus be seen as a fulcrum within Barry's oeuvre, and like so many others of Barry's characters, he does not slot easily into preconceived categories in Irish history. As a high-ranking Catholic member of the Dublin Metropolitan Police in the early years of the twentieth century, Dunne is in a distinct minority and remains loyal to the Crown during a turbulent time in Anglo-Irish relations. He has overseen police actions against striking workers during the infamous Dublin Lockout of 1913, and the handover of power from British to Irish authorities in Dublin Castle in 1922. His is an Irish story, but it is far from the main narrative of Irish history.

The two-act play is set a decade after Irish independence, and opens with Thomas, the erstwhile smartly uniformed authority figure and *pater familias*, lying on a bed in the county asylum, wearing only soiled long underwear and mouthing nonsense syllables – "Da Da, Ma Ma, Ba Ba, Ba Ba ... ."[1] He has, we learn, given his only suit of clothes to another inmate, an act of misplaced generosity, but one typical of his nature. Throughout the play a preoccupation with clothing as an indication of rank and respectability is a prominent motif. Thomas's initial babbling soon gives way to much more articulate, if at times, confused, speech. He reveals he is seventy-five years old and has been put in the asylum in County Wicklow, not far from where he grew up, because his behaviour had become erratic and at times violent. He then alternates between lucid conversations with the workers in the asylum and hallucinated memories of his childhood. Thomas relives the sporadic violence he experienced at the hands of his father, the steward of Humewood Estate, one of the largest demesnes in the country. Indeed the concept of stewardship is an overriding conceit within the play concerned as it is with duty and responsibility in both the public and familial spheres.

Playwright Barry's language is always highly lyrical, and many of Thomas's most poetic passages are those in which he recites fond memories of his wife, Cissy, whose death in childbirth left him with four children to rear. In his dementia he also confuses his intense love for his wife with his devotion to Queen Victoria, whom he served with pride. He identifies Victoria's reign with a sense of order – order in the realm, mirrored in the discipline of his working life and in his own well-run home. Thomas's addled mind also conjures his dead son Willie and engages him in lyrical dialogue.

As the ghost of Willie slowly fades, the set of the play changes, leaving the bare grimness of the institution, and revealing, in flashback, an earlier warm domestic scene as Chief Superintendent Dunne dons his uniform to go to Dublin Castle to witness Michael Collins take over the running of the country. Here Thomas's three daughters emerge, to a limited degree, as characters – plain, stern Maud, the eldest; dutiful Annie, a victim of polio; and frivolous Dolly, the youngest, on whom her father dotes. The girls iron their father's shirts, brush his uniform and shine his boots, taking pride in his position and appearance. Barry also seeds the future of the Dunne family in this scene, as it is revealed that Maud has a beau, a schoolteacher; that Annie will be unlikely to ever marry; and that Dolly is fearless and adventuresome. Although this emerging structure and detail begins to resemble a modern Irish version of *King Lear*, with a mad, deposed father figure and three daughters vying for his approval, *The Steward of Christendom* is much more a study of fathers and sons, and the poignancy of filial love with all its limitations and complexities. We learn that Thomas's father, disappointed by his son's school performance, consigned him to the police force. That Thomas accepted this imposed way of life and excelled at policing is much to his credit as a man. But Thomas holds himself in turn responsible for making a similar paternal decision that directed Willie into the British Army because he was not tall enough for the police force. Willie's death in battle, coupled with Thomas's enforced retirement, the changing political landscape of an emerging Ireland, and his loss of his dear Dolly to emigration, converge to explain the deterioration of his mental health.

The power of Sebastian Barry's work may seem thus to lie in the weaving of a good story, but his most compelling work is far less plot-driven than it is linguistically propelled. Barry's language is a nearly unique idiolect that can at times rise to a rhapsodic level. Thomas's descriptive paeans to both Queen Victoria and Michael Collins convey a surprisingly even-handed respect for opposing authority figures. His heart-breaking memory of his wife's death – "She died, as many persons do, at the death of candlelight, as the birds begin to sing" (129) – is, as a love poem, superseded only by the final speech of the play. Here Thomas recalls running away as a child, with his dog, because the dog had killed sheep; and he knew his father would be bound to shoot the animal to prevent additional marauding. Instead his gruff father was so relieved his boy was unharmed that he gave the dog an unexpected reprieve:

> And I would call that the mercy of fathers, when the love that lies in them deeply like the glittering face of a well is betrayed by an emergency, and the child sees at last that he is loved, loved, and needed and not to be lived without, and greatly.

> (133)

The Steward of Christendom was written and first performed at a crucial time in Irish literary and historical studies, and became part of the revisionist debate that informed its era. It addresses the multiple loyalties Irish people could subscribe to in the years leading up to the First World War. Many Irishmen, like Willie Dunne, went off in the British forces to fight a European war, and returned to find a country that had been transformed by the struggle for independence and that no longer valued their sacrifice. For many decades their service, their cultural and political loyalties, and to some extent their Irishness, were eclipsed. Theirs was a story that hadn't been told. Work such as Barry's set a marker in the debate which emerged decades later, and made a case for an acknowledgement of different forms of Irish heritage.

Because of Barry's choice to write his family's story against the predominant Irish historical narrative in this play, and in others of his works, he had to withstand some controversy; but as Roy Foster has observed, "personal preoccupations are transcended by his historical sense and Barry's evident commitment to understanding rather than judgement."[2]

Thomas Dunne is a man who has become an anachronism. His Victorian sense of duty and belief in a hierarchical social structure is out of tune with the post-First World War world. In Ireland, a new nation in an ancient land, his anachronistic position has rendered him a memorable and unlikely tragic hero.

Christina Hunt Mahony

Notes

1 Sebastian Barry, *The Only True History of Lizzie Finn, The Steward of Christendom, White Woman Street: Three Plays by Sebastian Barry* (London: Methuen Drama, 1995), 71.

2 Roy Foster, "'Something of us will remain': Sebastian Barry and Irish History," in *Out of History: Essays on the Writings of Sebastian Barry*, ed. Christina Hunt Mahony (Dublin: Carysfort Press, 2006), 184.

Further Reading

Grene, Nicholas. "Defining Performers and Performances." In *The Oxford Handbook of Modern Irish Theatre*, edited by Nicholas Grene and Chris Morash, 459–77. Oxford: Oxford University Press, 2016.

Mahony, Christina Hunt, ed. *Out of History: Essays on the Writings of Sebastian Barry*. Dublin: Carysfort Press, 2006.

Pine, Emilie. "Drama since the 1990s: Memory, Story, Exile." In *The Oxford Handbook of Modern Irish Theatre*, edited by Nicholas Grene and Chris Morash, 515–28. Oxford: Oxford University Press, 2016.

THE BEAUTY QUEEN OF LEENANE (1996) BY MARTIN MCDONAGH

Martin McDonagh is best known for writing and directing the award-winning films, *In Bruges* (2008) and *Three Billboards Outside of Ebbing, Missouri* (2017). However, it was *The Beauty Queen of Leenane*, a co-production between Druid Theatre Galway and London's Royal Court, that kick-started his career in Galway in February 1996. The following year not only were all three plays that formed the *Leenane Trilogy* produced in Galway and London – the others are *A Skull in Connemara* and *The Lonesome West* – but the National Theatre, London, also staged *The Cripple of Inishmaan*, first in the Cottesloe Theatre (now the Dorfman Theatre) and later in the larger Lyttleton space. A previously unheralded playwright with four significant productions in one calendar year is pretty unique.

Initial critical responses to *Beauty Queen* were divided and divisive; some acclaimed the originality, non-conventionality, and subversiveness of the writing, others saw it as generically derivative and too reliant on stereotypes, while others reflexively dismissed the work, not disguising their visceral disapproval, outrage, and sometimes disgust.

Born on 26 March 1970 in London to Irish parents who had emigrated in the 1950s to find employment, McDonagh did not follow the more traditional career route into theatre by studying theatre or literature at university or attending an acting school. Instead, as an early school-leaver, McDonagh was self-taught, relying in part on experiencing and absorbing the wide range of film and other expressions of popular culture/media to which he had access, and on extensive literary readings, some suggested by his older brother, the writer/ director, John Michael. By his early 20s, prior to the premiere of *Beauty Queen*, McDonagh had established affiliations with an array of London theatres, including the Bush, Finborough, and National Theatre, in addition to achieving some small but significant successes writing radio plays. The alleged rejection of an estimated twenty-two radio scripts by the BBC left him not only frustrated and somewhat hard-nosed, but he saw such a rebuff as being linked to his working-class background.

The advice to most playwrights is to write about what you know. So, with *Beauty Queen*, what was a young, cosmopolitan male doing writing about the dysfunctional relationship between an elderly woman, Mag, and her forty-year-old, unpartnered daughter, Maureen, two characters locked in patterns of toxic connection, dependency, resentment, and fear, set in Leenane, County Galway? In interviews, McDonagh has said that he situated his early work in the West of Ireland, not because it was a place affiliated with his parents, not because it was the location familiar to him thanks to annual holidays there, and not because of a need to unpack a second-generation diasporic sensibility. He did so to evade the influences of writers like Harold Pinter, David Mamet, and Joe Orton, playwrights variously associated with predominantly male, urban, and contemporary contexts, where violence and comedy intermingled in sometimes controversial ways, and where the language and subtext bore some of the burden of intimidation. In *Beauty Queen*, the language spoken is not simply a quaint Hiberno-English, and McDonagh's West of Ireland simultaneously embraces but also contests some of the more traditional pastoral sensibilities and romanticisations associated with marginalisation, otherworldliness, and affinities with native, religious, or pagan beliefs.

Beauty Queen's cottage setting is a quaint, frugal, if not quite an impoverished space, marked as much by gender as class; the traditional iconography such as the crucifix on the wall, the images of Robert and John F. Kennedy, and a "touristy looking embroidered tea-towel hanging" with the inscription, "May you be half an hour in Heaven afore the Devil knows you're Dead,"[1] bear an ironic intention to destabilise the sentiments connected with the conservative values associated with the pastoral tropes of Irish drama. Through the mother–daughter relationship McDonagh filters actions, dilemmas, and outcomes that not only challenge audience expectations but also percolate the grotesque, uncanny, and performative. If few plays have single, pure forms, and most rely on a mingling of compatible or incompatible genres, *Beauty Queen*'s form is especially intricate, making it difficult for critics, commentators, and audiences to self-orientate in terms of genre convention and expectation.

If the work seems to veer towards naturalism or realism it is troubled, as Fintan O'Toole pointed out, by its evocation of melodrama and fairy tale, and the infiltration of a dramaturgy more associated with Le Théâtre du Grand-Guignol in ways that neither fulfil generic expectations nor anticipate character outcomes.[2] Who is the play's protagonist/antagonist, victim/perpetrator, what behaviours are rewarded or punished, or where is the moral point of view? Genre complications place particular demands not only on any production's *mise-en-scène*, but especially on the acting choices made. McDonagh's approach is to destabilise concepts of freedom, choice, and agency and uncouple characterisation from the notionally real.

The play's opening exchange between Mag and Maureen has them both expressing limited social observations, frustrations, fears, and annoyances. Mag is relatively incapacitated and relentlessly demanding, treating Maureen like a "skivvy" (5). A feeling of being endlessly on call to meet her mother's whims gives rise to Maureen's discontent. If macabre comments in relation to Mag's death are expressed by Maureen in early exchanges, what is notable is how the dialogue moves from the sinister to the incidental. Later, Maureen's initial anger in response to Mag's not disclosing an invitation to a party seems to abate when she offers to drive them both to Westport to buy a new black dress.

The audience cannot then easily establish character motive, intent, or place the dynamic between mother and daughter. What transpires between them is almost a game that is tense and offensive, yet less toxic because of their sense of familiarity. Earlier in Scene One, Maureen's discontent had turned to something else, when unfinished tea and porridge are taken from Mag and dumped; as distinctions between frustration and annoyance, threatening behaviour and elder abuse are fragile. Mag has done her best to deny Maureen maturation and expresses an ongoing disdain for Maureen's needs for connection, pleasure, and intimacy. After Pato stays overnight in Maureen's bed, Mag is determined to destroy any budding connection between them by announcing that Maureen force-fed and tortured her and, more-over, had spent time in a mental institution in England. Pato returns to London, but writes to Maureen inviting her to emigrate with him to Boston, as he is increasingly frustrated with migrant life in London – the loneliness, isolation, and dangers on building sites.

The contents of Pato's letter, along with the fact that Mag intercepted and burned it, is disclosed by her under torture with hot chip oil, Maureen then leaving her mother writhing on the floor as she goes to join Pato's farewell party for his departure to America. When she returns Mag slumps forwards in her rocking chair and falls to the floor in a moment reminiscent of Grand-Guignol's sensation scene, "*a red chunk of skull hangs from a string of skin at the side of her head,* Maureen *looks down at her, somewhat bored*" (51); she has cracked her mother's head open with the poker. Then, a month later, Maureen packs a case, and readies herself to leave after Mag's burial, supposedly to join Pato; an inquest having delayed the funeral. However, it is Pato's brother, Ray, who counters Maureen's grasp on reality; there could not have been a meeting of the lovers in a train station as Maureen has said, as Pato left by taxi. Maureen's prior actions can then only be accounted for if she is in a psychotic state, even if she remains insightful enough to have prepared a version of events that satisfy the police. However, if local law enforcement fails to investigate Mag's death adequately, the play's genre sets out its own punishment.

Maureen's fairy tale or melodramatic-style comeuppance is that she is denied escape, punished by solitary confinement, and entombed within her homeplace; "The exact fecking image of your mother" (60) as Ray observes. Additionally, Pato is already engaged to someone else. The suitcase that Maureen dusts down and caresses will not be going anywhere, and the case is symbolic of the Irish diasporic consciousness more broadly. As Maureen begins to mimic the mindset, forgetfulness, ticks, and behaviours of Mag, such a transformation serves as an additional punishment for her murderous action.

In balancing gore, terror, sensation, horror, madness, and injustice with a playfulness that is carefree as it is sinister, the play's multilayered register complicates if not disavows the basic realist or naturalist conventions with which it initially flirts. The dramaturgical sensibility is one where character motivation is suspect and not clearcut, where distinctions between victim and perpetrator, agency and passivity, courage and fatalism collapse, as sanity is perilous, rationality overrated, and justice precarious.

Eamonn Jordan

Notes

1 Martin McDonagh, *The Beauty Queen of Leenane*, in *Martin McDonagh Plays 1* (London: Methuen, 1999), 1. Subsequent references are entered in parentheses.
2 Fintan O'Toole, "Introduction," in *Plays 1*, xi–xii.

Further Reading

Chambers, Lillian and Eamonn Jordan, eds. *The Theatre of Martin McDonagh: A World of Savage Stories*. Dublin: Carysfort Press, 2006.
Jordan, Eamonn. *Justice in the Plays of Martin McDonagh*. Basingstoke: Palgrave, 2019.
Lonergan, Patrick. *The Theatre and Films of Martin McDonagh*. London: Methuen/Bloomsbury, 2012.

THE WEIR (1997) BY CONOR MCPHERSON

Place and space are pivotal to Conor McPherson's award-winning play, *The Weir*. Set in a rural Irish pub vaguely located in Northwest Leitrim or Sligo, the play's title also identifies a nearby dam built in the early 1950s by the Electricity Supply Board. *The Weir* is not the first Irish play to be set in a pub. Renowned precursors include John Millington Synge's *The Playboy of the Western World* (1907) and Tom Murphy's *Conversations on a Homecoming* (1986), plays which likewise feature storytelling, and characters attempting to escape their pasts. As a social location the pub is, moreover, a crucial feature of the Irish cultural imaginary, enmeshed in a web of meanings. Historically the preserve of male sociality, it is a communal space that has become increasingly romanticised as a site of authentic Irish customs and commodified as an experience to be consumed not only in Ireland but around the globe. McPherson's stage directions detail traditional furniture and décor with realistic precision, intimating the pub's connectedness with its milieu – "*[t]he bar is part of a house, and the house is part of a farm*"[1] – and as Eamonn Jordan has noted, signalling a pastoral authenticity that is both performed and problematised by the play.[2]

The Weir is a masterpiece of social portraiture and meandering storytelling. It presents interactions among five characters, four local men, Brendan the owner of the establishment, Jack a mechanic, Jim an odd-job man, Finbar a hotelier and businessman, and, the newly arrived Dubliner, Valerie. Physical action is minimal, there are no grand or violent gestures. With the exception of pouring drinks or the occasional trip to the lavatory, the characters remain in a static arrangement around the bar and fireplace. Jack is first to arrive and, in the absence of Brendan, carefully serves himself and places his money in the till – a telling gesture of familiarity and trust. Brendan enters with fuel for the fire, and they chat about the broken Guinness tap, the direction of the wind, Brendan's sisters who want him to sell part of the farm, Jack's trip to Carrick earlier in the day and his betting win on the horses. The idle banter comes to revolve around the news that a long-vacant nearby house owned by Finbar has just been let to a new tenant. Jim's arrival brings some small additions to the conversation, not least details of Finbar's efforts to show the Dublin woman the area, that are greeted with contempt from Jack and, to a lesser extent, Brendan. Jack, in particular, seems to resent Finbar's business success and is sceptical of his motives for shepherding Valerie to the pub. When Finbar enters with Valerie, these tensions simmer beneath the humorous exchanges among the men.

It's no accident that the titular weir, documented in the photos on the wall of the pub, is only mentioned when "the history of the place" (27) is presented to an outside eye. While the weir's literal function is to "generat[e] power for the area and for Carrick" (27), McPherson is conscious of the figurative resonances of this structure. He notes "[o]n one side it is quite calm, and on the other side water is being squeezed through. Metaphorically the play is about a breakthrough. Lots under the surface is coming out. It's resonant of two worlds, the supernatural and our ordinary world past and present."[3]

Valerie's presence prompts a series of reactions and stories that are released in the course of the evening. Somewhat ironically, the men are not well informed about local history, rather what is shared is a sequence of tales each of which hinges on an experience of the supernatural. Jack begins with an anecdote about a fairy road that supposedly leads through the house now occupied by Valerie. He delivers it with a jokey self-consciousness of its conventional folk form – "And there's no dark like a winter night in the country […] Am I setting the scene for you?" (31) he teases. Not to be outdone by Jack, Finbar then tells a tale of a neighbour's experience with a Ouija board. The terror of that night leads him to give up smoking and move from his isolated family place to the town. Finbar's story ends on a less assured note, "Yous all think I'm a loolah now" (40) he says. After replenishing their drinks and chatting about Finbar's hotel for a while, Jim shares a story of a gravedigging job he took while he was ill with the flu. Jim and his friend go to a parish in the neighbouring glen and work all day in the rain, fuelled on poitín. Shortly after the deceased is laid out in the church attended by a meagre group of mourners, a stranger approaches Jim and insists that they have prepared the wrong grave. The man leads Jim to the grave of a young girl, and then returns to the church. Later, Jim hears that the deceased had a reputation as a paedophile, hence the lack of local gravediggers, and is convinced that it was the ghost of this man who spoke to him that day. This story chills the joviality in the room. "Jaysus, Jim," protests Finbar, "That's a terrible story, to be telling" (48). Jack dismisses it as an alcohol-induced hallucination, but Valerie, who has suddenly paled, seems less convinced.

While Valerie is in the lavatory, the grievances between Jack and Finbar erupt. Some critical words are exchanged, the quarrel subsides, and they resolve to "tell a few jokes when she comes back" (52). Instead, Valerie tells her story. It is personal and painful in a way the men's narratives have not been. She recounts how her young daughter drowned in a swimming accident. Months later, still traumatised by grief, she answers the phone and is convinced her daughter is on the other end of the line, begging to be rescued. This precipitates a nervous breakdown and her decision to move to the country. The men are, unsurprisingly, stunned by this revelation. They respond with protective sympathy, hastening to explain away the supernatural aspects of their own tales, blaming illness, eccentricity, and alcohol. Nevertheless, a residue of something painfully unresolved and uncanny hangs in the air. The play ebbs to a close with a simple poignant narrative, told by Jack of how he fumbled his chance to marry someone he loved and was unobtrusively comforted by a barman in a pub in Dublin on the day of her wedding.

The Weir opened at the Royal Court Theatre London on 4 July 1997, later transferring to a West End run at the Duke of York's Theatre in 1998 and to the Walter Kerr Theatre on Broadway in 1999. On the way it gathered the Laurence Olivier Award for Best New Play and many rave reviews. Charles Spencer of the *Daily Telegraph* described it as "an unmistakable modern classic, with its roots deeply embedded in the great tradition of Irish drama."[4] It was the first of McPherson's plays to break with solo or ensemble monologue formats, however much of the drama is still constructed around telling and listening. Notably, at the time the play was first presented Ireland's Celtic Tiger economic boom was transforming Irish life, making places like the one presented on stage seem even more circumscribed by nostalgia. So, the disjunction between the world on stage and the locations where the play was first performed could hardly have been more pronounced. *The Weir* knowingly offers a gratifyingly traditional Irish scene, but beneath the familiar surface flows a more ambivalent undertow. Jack, Jim, and Brendan are emblematic of a receding existence, receding not only due to age, but also due to isolation and a reluctance to change. What the future might hold for them, or for Valerie, is far from reassuring. The slow accumulation of interleaved narratives is indeed powered by the supernatural, but the persistent sub-motifs of loneliness, failure, emotional vulnerability, mutual dependence, and alcoholism are as much a part of this environment as the pub fireside stories and are at the heart of what makes McPherson's quiet drama so potent.

Clare Wallace

Notes

1   Conor McPherson, *The Weir and Other Plays* (New York: Theatre Communications Group, 1999), 7. Subsequent references are entered in parentheses.

2   Eamonn Jordan, "Pastoral Exhibits: Narrating Authenticities in Conor McPherson's *The Weir.*" *Irish University Review* Vol. 34, no. 2 (Autumn–Winter 2004): 351.

3   Mel Gussow, "From Dublin to Broadway, Spinning Tales of Irish Wool." *New York Times*, 1 April 1999, section E, 1.

4   Charles Spencer, "Unmistakable Modern Classic," *Daily Telegraph*, 10 March 1999, 17.

Further Reading

Cummings, Scott T. "Homo Fabulator: The Narrative Imperative in Conor McPherson's Plays." In *Theatre Stuff: Critical Essays on Contemporary Irish Theatre*, edited by Eamonn Jordan, 303–12. Dublin: Carysfort Press, 2000.

Grene, Nicholas. "Ireland in Two Minds: Martin McDonagh and Conor McPherson." *The Yearbook of English Studies* Vol. 35, Irish Writing since 1950 (2005): 298–311.

Kerrane, Kevin. "The Structural Elegance of Conor McPherson's *The Weir*." *New Hibernia Review* Vol. 10, no. 4 (Winter 2006): 105–21.

Wallace, Clare. "A Micronarrative Imperative—Conor McPherson's Monologue Dramas." *Irish Studies Review* Vol. 14, no. 1 (2006): 1–10.

Wood, Gerald C. *Conor McPherson: Imagining Mischief*. Dublin: Liffey, 2003.

BY THE BOG OF CATS (1998) BY MARINA CARR

By the Bog of Cats premiered at the Abbey Theatre on 7 October 1998 and won *The Irish Times* Awards for Best New Play and Best Actress for Olwen Fouéré who played the role of Hester Swane. It has been produced in countries as diverse as Iceland, Estonia, and China as well as at California's San Jose Repertory Theatre in 2001 with Holly Hunter, who reprised her role in London's West End in 2004, as well receiving an Abbey Theatre revival in 2015 with Susan Lynch. Set in the Offaly Midlands, *By the Bog of Cats* is a three-act play which presents a matriarchal lineage of exile and empowerment through three generations of Traveller women from Big Josie Swane to her daughter Hester and granddaughter Josie. Big Josie has been missing for over thirty years and Hester is now being forced to leave the Bog of Cats where, like Beckett's tramps, she has been "waitin' a lifetime for some wan to return [...]."[1] The play opens at dawn on "*A bleak white landscape of ice and snow*" as Hester is seen dragging the corpse of a dead swan, "auld Black Wing" (13). The action unfolds over the course of one day where it is revealed that Hester has been abandoned by her lover Carthage Kilbride who plans to marry Caroline, the daughter of local big farmer Xavier Cassidy. As Hester digs a grave for Black Wing she is watched by a "Ghost Fancier" who announces: "I'm ghoulin' for a woman be the name of Hester Swane." Foreshadowing Hester's death, the Ghost Fancier realises that he has gotten his times mixed up and exits hastily: "I'm too previous. I mistook this hour for dusk. A thousand apologies" (14). In Act II Carthage marries Caroline and when he tries to force Hester to leave the Bog of Cats she burns down his house and livestock in retaliation. Knowing that her mother will now never return, Hester kills herself and her child in the final tragic moments of the play.

By the Bog of Cats is a loose re-working of Euripides's *Medea* in which the action is transposed to a contemporary Irish rural location. Carr infuses her story with a regional flavour of Midlands dialect and landscape in which to explore themes of familial kinship, bigotry, patriarchal power, and womanhood. The Abbey Theatre did not publicise the play as a Greek adaptation and it took audiences and critics a while to realise that it was inspired by *Medea*. In the play Hester Swane and Big Josie are outcasts who, like Euripides's "foreign witch," challenge Classical Greek and Irish feminine ideals of domesticity, motherhood, and social propriety. Carr also challenges Greek dramatic form by presenting fantastic beings, eternal spaces, and death on-stage. Set on the bog in bleak midwinter Carr blends realism with a supernatural atmosphere where the Otherworld is given equal credence to the everyday.

As a feminist re-working of a Classical play, Carr transforms Euripides's Medea from a vengeful child-killer to a mother who kills her child in a desperate act of love. At the end of the play Carthage wants to take seven-year-old Josie from Hester in order to ostensibly offer her a better life. Hopeless and alone, Hester decides to kill herself but is discovered by young Josie who begs her not to abandon her. In that split second Hester decides to kill Josie as well as herself: "Alright, alright! Shhh! (*Picks her up*) It's alright, I'll take ya with me, I won't lave ya as I was, waitin' a lifetime for someone to return, because they don't Josie, they don't" (78). While the moment that Hester slits her daughter's throat on-stage is deeply shocking, Fouéré, for whom Carr wrote the part, emphasises the way in which Carr transforms the original Euripidean motivation:

> It has nothing to do with revenge. It has to do with love. [...] When Josie doesn't want to be left alone, she begs her mother, pleading, "Take me with you", and it is in order to comfort her that Hester kills her. It is the loving nature of that gesture from Hester, and something about that "Take me with you" that I find extraordinarily touching [...].

Carr places Hester's suicide and infanticide within a macro-context of women's anger against social oppression and Fouéré argues that "Articulating that kind of rage is a huge part of Marina's work. I don't know if any other writer in Ireland has confronted it with the same authenticity. At times I feel that she is actually articulating the female rage of the nation."[2] On the same stage twenty-three years later, Carr developed her themes of fearless femininity in the one-woman Abbey Theatre production *iGirl* (2021), written for, and performed by, Olwen Fouéré. Echoing *By the Bog of Cats, iGirl* charts epic realms of personal and mythic womanhood through Carr's and Fouéré's unique artistic relationship.

Hester Swane's marginalised status within her community echoes women's historical exclusion from the main stages of Irish theatre. Prior to *By the Bog of Cats* there had not been a play by a woman on the main-stage of the Abbey in a decade – since Jean Binnie's *Colours – Jane Barry Esq.* As an Irish Traveller, Hester is an outsider who holds up a lens to the moral shortcomings of the local community; "As for me tinker's blood, I'm proud of it, gives me an edge over all of yees, allows me to see yees for the inbred, underbred, bog brained shower yees are" (35). Carr points out, "I chose to make [Hester] a Traveller because Travellers are our national outsiders."[3] Fouéré observes that, "*By the Bog of Cats* is a deeply political play about the outsider. Carthage is not just marrying another woman; he's entering this land-grabbing gombeen society. So Hester's rage is also a cultural rage, of a colonised culture which is being driven out and where her sexuality and creativity are being suppressed."[4] Hester's battle for recognition, and her reclamation of the bog as a site of origins, mirrors the historic lack of place for women in Irish theatre. "The truth is you want to eradicate me, make out I never existed," she cries and tenaciously claims her territory on the bog, "I was born on the Bog of Cats, same as all of yees, though ya'd never think it the way yees shun me" (56).

Big Josie Swane, who never appears, weighs heavily upon the action as when Hester was seven years old she walked away across the Bog of Cats and never returned. Hester's attempts to reconnect the arterial severing of her maternal origins mirrors the rupture of Irish women's histories in theatre; "Tell me about my mother for what I remember doesn't add up" (21). Missing for over three decades Big Josie is a spectre of womanhood on the Irish stage whose disappearance has been unexplained and simply accepted.

By the Bog of Cats is central to Carr's Midlands plays in which women bravely attempt to shape their own destinies amidst deep trauma and unresolved confrontations with oppressive forces of racism, bigotry, class conflict, murder, and sexual violence. Carthage's mother Mrs. Kilbride's bigotry towards women and Travellers is a constant thread, as is Xavier Cassidy's implied abuse of his daughter

Caroline and murder of his wife Olive. Opposed to them the enigmatic Catwoman is central to the matriarchal lineage of wise-women which forms the spine of the play, her blindness giving her a clarity of perspective which is lacking in the moral myopia of the local Settled community.

Landscape and nature are central to the meaning of the play and as Carr says of all of her work, "I find a particular metaphor or image and start chasing it down [and] that becomes plot as much as anything else."[5] As a symbolic through-line of the play, the bog expresses a fecund doubleness that is both mundane and supernatural. It is synonymous with female agency where the ungovernable terrain is a psychic recess of Hester's character as much as a physical location. The visceral muck and radical otherness that characterises the bog is a metaphor for Carr's theatre as a whole, where "we are as much not of this world, as we are of it."[6]

Melissa Sihra

Notes

1 Marina Carr, *By the Bog of Cats* (Loughcrew: The Gallery Press, 1998), 78. Subsequent references are entered in parentheses.
2 Olwen Fouéré, "Journeys in Performance," in *The Theatre of Marina Carr: "...before rules was made"*, ed. Cathy Leeney and Anna McMullan (Dublin: Carysfort Press, 2008), 162, 169.
3 Eileen Battersby, "Marina of the Midlands (Part 2)," *The Irish Times*, 4 May 2000.
4 Fouéré, 169–70.
5 Adrienne Leavy, "An Interview with Marina Carr; Introduced by Melissa Sihra," *Reading Ireland: The Little Magazine* 1:4 (2016): 24.
6 "Marina Carr in Conversation with Melissa Sihra," in *Theatre Talk: Voices of Irish Theatre Practitioners*, ed. Lillian Chambers, Ger FitzGibbon, and Eamonn Jordan (Dublin: Carysfort Press, 2008), 57.

Further Reading

Russell, Richard. "Talking with Ghosts of Irish Playwrights Past: Marina Carr's *By the Bog of Cats*." *Comparative Drama* Vol. 40, no. 2 (Summer 2006): 149–68.

Sihra, Melissa. *Marina Carr: Pastures of the Unknown*. London: Palgrave Macmillan, 2018.

Wallace, Clare. "Tragic Destiny and Abjection in Marina Carr's *The Mai, Portia Coughlan* and *By the Bog of Cats*," *Irish University Review* Vol. 31, no. 2 (Autumn–Winter 2001): 431–49.

THE WALWORTH FARCE (2006) BY ENDA WALSH

Enda Walsh's two-act drama *The Walworth Farce* was commissioned by the Druid Theatre New Writing Program and premiered in Galway in March 2006. Described by Walsh as "a Druid-type play that is going to be done in the rhythm of farce,"[1] it has subsequently been produced worldwide, including a 2015 revival, staged by Landmark Productions in Dublin, that featured Brendan, Domhnall, and Brian Gleeson with Leona Allen as Hayley. Reviews have cited the innovative mashup of styles in the play, with *The Guardian*'s Lyn Gardner describing its formal experiments as if "The Waltons had been rewritten by Joe Orton with an added dash of Beckett's despair, Genet's love of dressing-up and ritual, and recipes for poisoned chicken."[2] *The New York Times* said it was "directed with unfaltering brazenness by Mikel Murfi in a style that walks the line between madcap and stark, raving mad."[3] The *Irish Times* heralded the 2015 production as the play's "induction into the canon, an impossible and inescapable performance of identity and fantasy, the real story, perhaps, of who we are."[4]

In the play, an Irish immigrant named Dinny directs his adult sons, Sean and Blake, in a recurring theatrical performance that recounts the history of the family's exodus from Cork to their ratty council flat on the Walworth Road, South London. This raucous play-within-a-play, whose *"performance style resembles The Three Stooges,"*[5] stages a fictional account of Dinny's final action-packed hours in Ireland roughly two decades prior. To realise this production, the sons portray themselves as children; they also don costumes to perform supporting roles assigned by their father, with Blake taking on the female roles and Sean the male ones. Dinny plays an idealised version of himself, a brain surgeon whose family members die after eating a poisoned chicken and who leaves Ireland to build a new life. In reality, as Sean reveals late in the play, Dinny actually fled Cork after murdering his brother and sister-in-law.

The family's fictional world is completely sealed off from the realities of the outside world, and Dinny's repetitive narrative has come to supplant actual experience, senses, and memories. As Blake laments, "This story we play is everything ... I say his words and all I can see is the word" (22). However, Sean is allowed to leave the flat to fetch goods, which serve as props, from the local Tesco supermarket. At the close of the first act a Tesco cashier named Hayley arrives at their door with a bag of groceries Sean had mistakenly left behind and interrupts the men's routine. In the second act, with Hayley in attendance, the farce resumes. First confused and then briefly entertained by their performance, Hayley soon becomes disturbed by what she witnesses and unsuccessfully attempts to escape. Dinny endeavours to incorporate Hayley into the narrative, adjusting the performance so that this young Black English woman assumes the role of his wife Maureen. But Hayley's unsettling presence leads to chaos: the farcical narrative is exposed as a lie; Blake murders Dinny after extracting a promise from Hayley that she will watch over Sean in the outside world; Sean murders Blake after mistakenly assuming he intended to harm Hayley. A terrified Hayley finally escapes, and the play closes with Sean alone in the flat quickly and silently recapitulating the entire performance by and to himself. The play ends as Sean dons Hayley's coat and purse, picks up the plastic Tesco bag, and blackens his face, preparing to take her role "*as we watch him silently lose himself in a new story*" (85).

Though pulsing with broad humour, *The Walworth Farce* reveals through its outlandish depiction of violence and depravity the disturbing manifestations of personal and collective trauma. The Irish characters in this play find themselves incapable of distinguishing between fantasy and reality, and they are ensnared in a set of repetitive beliefs, histories, and behaviours. The play can be read as a critique of disabling emigrant nostalgia, a theme underscored by the soundtrack that accompanies the farce, which includes recurring tunes such as "A Nation Once Again" and "An Irish Lullaby" blasting from a tape recorder. It also offers a telling assessment of contemporary Irish culture. Hannah Greenstreet has read the play, which foregrounds the legacy of childhood trauma that malforms Sean and Blake, as a response to the late twentieth-century exposure of the widespread sexual abuse of Irish children,[6] while Patrick Lonergan has identified it as one of several contemporary Irish plays in which national identity is defensively asserted though violence and racism directed towards non-white individuals.[7] Further, as Charlotte McIvor notes, Hayley's presence in the play evokes the changing contours of Irish migration, both inward and outward, that have defined the post-Celtic Tiger years.[8]

The Walworth Farce offers a striking account of suffering and oppression that span across class, gender, nationality, generation, and race, among other identity categories. This comes to the fore at the play's conclusion, when Sean blackens his face to prepare for his role as Hayley. In a charged moment from the second act, the play also demands a heightened attention to the intersections of race and gender when Dinny, having cast Hayley as Maureen, "*takes his moisturiser and whitens* Hayley's face" (79). In a historical moment of racial reckoning, a play written by a white Irish man that employs blackface is appropriately contentious. For some, this might mean deliberately not staging or teaching the play. For others, it might mean using the play to interrogate the legacies of blackface performance in its global as well as Irish contexts. James Joyce, for example, references the Christy Minstrels in "The Dead" and Eugene Stratton in *Ulysses*, and as Vincent Cheng has argued, draws attention to an early twentieth-century Irish culture in which "the only available experience of 'blackness' is the essentialized otherness of a stereotyped construction" drawn largely from stage tradition.[9] In an American context, critics such as Eric Lott have explored how blackface minstrelsy both embodied and disrupted the racist tendencies of largely white, male, working-class audiences, seeking to establish the privilege of white immigrant populations like the Irish, even as it exposed the tensions latent in that identification.[10] Such perspectives provide a valuable, even necessary, complement to readings of Walsh's play.

The Walworth Farce not only examines personal and national histories, but also puts on view a select history of drama – not least through its evocation of farce. Set in contemporary London, the play with its admixture of calamity and humour resembles the rural tragicomedies of the early Abbey Theatre by playwrights such as Augusta Gregory and J. M. Synge. Such formal synergies across works written roughly a century apart underscore the play's theme that the past powerfully influences the present. It also has expressionist elements intended to heighten emotion and meaning; these appear in the distorted use of sound and the characters' repetitive phrases and gestures, as well as in Dinny and Blake's nightmarish perceptions of the London beyond their door. Critics have noted other affinities, both formal and thematic, including with the plays of David Mamet and the bare dystopian dramas of Samuel Beckett. An engagement with global media culture, through references to television shows like *Ready, Steady, Cook* or popular songs like "I'm a Survivor" by Destiny's Child, provide one harbinger of Walsh's subsequent commitments to multimedia performance as seen in later, more abstract stage productions including *Lazarus* (2015, written with David Bowie) and *Arlington* (2016).

Paige Reynolds

Notes

1 Quoted in Eamonn Jordan, "'Stuff from back home': Enda Walsh's *The Walworth Farce*," *Ilha do Desterro* 58 (2010): 333.
2 Lyn Gardner, "The Walworth Farce," *The Guardian*, 6 August 2007. www.theguardian.com/stage/2007/aug/06/theatre.edinburghfestival20079. Accessed 17 November 20021.
3 Ben Brantley, "Another Day, Another Play, for Rotten Old Dad," *The New York Times*, 19 April 2008. www.nytimes.com/2008/04/19/theater/reviews/19walw.html. Accessed 17 November 2021.
4 Peter Crawley, "Gleeson Family Values Put to the Test in this Fantastical Farce," *Irish Times*, 15 January 2015. www.irishtimes.com/culture/stage/gleeson-family-values-put-to-the-test-in-this-fantastical-farce-1.2067075. Accessed 17 November 2021.
5 Enda Walsh, *The Walworth Farce*, in *Enda Walsh Plays: Two* (London: Nick Hern Books, 2014), 7. Subsequent references are entered in parentheses.
6 Hannah Greenstreet, "Narrative Dysfunction in *The Walworth Farce* by Edna Walsh and *On Raftery's Hill* by Marina Carr," *Studies in Theatre and Performance* 38:1 (2017): 1–13.
7 Patrick Lonergan, *Irish Drama and Theatre Since 1950* (London: Bloomsbury, 2019), 171–80.
8 Charlotte McIvor, Review of *The Walworth Farce*, *Theatre Journal* 62:3 (2010): 462–4.
9 Vincent Cheng, *Joyce, Race, and Empire* (Cambridge: Cambridge University Press, 1995), 175.
10 Eric Lott, *Love & Theft: Blackface Minstrelsy and the American Working Class* (Oxford: Oxford University Press, 2013).

Further Reading

Caulfield, Mary P. and Ian R. Walsh, eds. *The Theatre of Enda Walsh*. Dublin: Carysfort, 2015.
Jordan, Eamonn. *Dissident Dramaturgies: Contemporary Irish Theatre*. Dublin: Irish Academic Press, 2010.
Lonergan, Patrick. "'The Lost and the Lonely': Crisis in Three Plays by Enda Walsh." *Études Irlandaises* 40:2 (2015): 137–54.
Pilný, Ondřej. "The Grotesque in the Plays of Enda Walsh." *Irish Studies Review* Vol. 21, no. 2 (2013): 217–25.
Reynolds, Paige. "Contemporary Irish Drama and Media." In *Irish Literature in Transition, Vol. 6, 1980-2020*, edited by Eric Falci and Paige Reynolds, 81–95. Cambridge: Cambridge University Press, 2020.

TERMINUS (2007) BY MARK O'ROWE

Terminus is a visceral play that has left most of its early audiences enthralled, shocked, and at the same time bewildered. First staged on the Abbey Theatre's Peacock stage in Dublin in June 2007, it consists of interlocking monologues in which three unnamed speakers recount their lives beset by violence. A, a woman in her forties, is a former teacher working as a counsellor on a crisis hotline, having taken the job by way of atonement for wilfully destroying her daughter's relationship. She describes her attempt to save a pregnant ex-pupil of hers, Helen, from her monstrous friend Celine who has come to dominate Helen's life; A ends up brutally murdering Celine as the latter is about to impale Helen's unborn baby, only to learn that Helen actually wanted the child to die, since it had been diagnosed with an incurable debilitating disease. B is a young woman living a frustrated single life, whose best friend tricks her into an adrenaline-fuelled sexual adventure in which B ends up falling to her death from the arm of a crane, only to be caught mid-air and whisked away by a flying demon with a body made of worms. C, a man in his thirties, has bartered his soul to the devil for the gift of singing in order to conquer his shyness in women's company. However, Satan deceived him, since he has become a divine singer in private only, and in front of people is possessed by crippling stage fright. As a result, C has turned into a serial killer, savagely murdering women in particular as a form of revenge for his fate. Gradually, the connections between the three speakers are revealed: B's depressive existence is the result of her mother – speaker A – having had an affair with her fiancée. The demon who (temporarily) saves her in her fall and becomes her lover is actually the soul of C, now come to reclaim him. Shortly after A has freed her former pupil from the grip of Celine, Helen jumps under C's truck and as she is dying, gives birth to a baby girl who is revealed to be a reincarnation of A's daughter.

In employing the monologue form, O'Rowe not only followed up on his previous works, the award-winning *Howie the Rookie* (1999) and the much less successful *Crestfall* (2003), but also continued a strand of Anglophone theatre that had become increasingly prominent since the mid-1990s, with a lineage to be traced in terms of Irish drama from Brian Friel's *Faith Healer* (1979) and *Molly Sweeney* (1994) to the work of O'Rowe's contemporaries, particularly Conor McPherson. What *Terminus* shares with McPherson's monologue plays is its focus on broken individuals, their unfulfilled desires, frustrated love relationships, and the alienation they experience amidst the buzz and pressures of a prosperous city. The affinity appears the closest with McPherson's *Port Authority* (2001), a play that is also set against the backdrop of Celtic Tiger era Dublin. However, McPherson's lyrical, nostalgic play outlines the city in a comprehensive way, both in social and geographical terms, while *Terminus*, as much as it reflects the current construction boom with tall cranes erecting yet another shopping centre or office block, uses Dublin essentially as a setting for an action movie or a ghastly thriller in which it could be easily replaced by any contemporary city. The Dublin of *Terminus* is teeming with swishing knife blades and martial arts feats, it is a location of spectacular car chases, brutal assaults on public transport, sexual attacks and sadistic disembowelments. O'Rowe's imagery clearly reflects his avid interest in this type of cinema: "heart in mouth and knuckles white on the wheel, I peel ahead in a fever, totally juiced, toward Heuston Station, where another collision sends a taxi crashing off the bridge and into the Liffey, the driver still steering as if he can prevent his descent – a splash – he can't."[1]

The ubiquity of graphic violence merits a resuscitation of the term "neo-Jacobean," used in the late 1990s to describe some of the early works of British "in-yer-face theatre" such as Sarah Kane's *Blasted* (1995), highlighting the controversial viscerality which they shared with the Jacobean tragedies of John Webster and Thomas Middleton, and their predecessors such as Shakespeare's *Titus Andronicus* or Christopher Marlowe's *Massacre at Paris*. Aestheticised brutality and carnage indeed comes across as a principal characteristic of *Terminus*, and has been typical of much of O'Rowe's earlier work. However, unlike most of "in-yer-face theatre" or Jacobean tragedy, O'Rowe's play prominently involves supernatural elements and mythical creatures. *Terminus* not only features a Faustian pact with the devil and gives a major role in the plot to a demon, but it also includes a version of the epic *katabasis* in which the demon carrying the woman B is chased by seven angels into the underworld. This is an empty cavernous space where a battle between the demon and the angels ensues, and where the young woman eventually drowns in a river, to be soon reborn as a child presented to her own mother. The demon in turn locates C, his "other half" (46), prizes him out of a speeding Mercedes and on top of the arm of a crane, effects the final revenge for C's murderous deeds. Notwithstanding their ancient origin, the motifs are simultaneously reminiscent of a computer game, a fantasy novel or film[2] and their incongruity, together with the terror involved in watching a profoundly alienated version of a familiar world, make *Terminus* a prime example of the contemporary grotesque.[3]

What is at least as remarkable as the seamless amalgam of disparate motifs and references is the peculiar aestheticidsation of language, which is reminiscent of rap. The basic rhythm of the speeches is iambic and ostentatiously features rhyme. The rhyming is perfect at times but almost as frequently descends into unabashed half-rhymes, while irregularities in the metre abound. The effect of rhyming, enhanced as it is with improvised patterns of assonance, alliteration and consonance, is often that of comedy, or alternately, shock: "the wheels just turn of their own volition: we're out of control, then there's a collision. A pole. And, one second he's there, the next: thin air. He wasn't wearing his seat belt, see, and so was catapulted through the windscreen. This has-been, or once-was, so-called because he's no more" (31). O'Rowe's use of language bespeaks an exuberant sense of mischief and a propensity for excess, but this near-parody of verse drama also strongly enhances the sense of a casual swagger that audiences have known from numerous "gangland" films since the early 1990s, including contemporaneous Irish features such as *Intermission* (2003), scripted by O'Rowe himself. Similarly to this cinematic genre – and its stage equivalents, such as the dark comedies of Martin McDonagh – *Terminus* is much concerned with justice, which is chiefly retributive, and the question of adequacy looms large: it may be true that Satan played foul on C but is becoming a sadistic murderer of innocents an appropriate answer? Or, given the multiple references to the transcendental, what to think of a universe in which B's tribulations are compensated by the provision of a demonic lover and eventual rebirth as a terminally ill child?[4]

The title may indicate that *Terminus* is a play about our final destination. But this remains likewise ambivalent: A is awaiting an extended prison sentence for murdering Celine; B transcends death in a sad instance of metempsychosis; and C receives his final punishment from his soul, being hanged by his entrails from a crane. In his dying moment, C flawlessly sings a pop song to an awed audience on the ground, engraving the sublime moment deep in his memory, since he has "heard tell that even the Devil remembered Heaven after he fell" (49). While a fine production of *Terminus* is bound to provide a tantalising theatrical experience, its emphasis on the "power" and "splendour" of transgression (48) makes the charge of glorifying violence – repeatedly raised against O'Rowe's work by critics – rather difficult to contest.

Ondřej Pilný

Notes

1 Mark O'Rowe, *Terminus* (London: Nick Hern, 2007), 45. Subsequent references are entered in parentheses.
2 See also Chris Morash and Shaun Richards, *Mapping Irish Theatre: Theories of Space and Place* (Cambridge: Cambridge University Press, 2013), 120–1.
3 For further details, see Ondřej Pilný, "Wild Justice: Mark O'Rowe," in *The Grotesque in Contemporary Anglophone Drama* (London: Palgrave, 2016), 69, 72–6.
4 See Pilný, 69–70, 75.

Further Reading

Haughton, Miriam. "Performing Power: Violence as Fantasy and Spectacle in Mark O'Rowe's *Made in China* and *Terminus*." *New Theatre Quarterly* 27, no. 2 (2011): 153–66.
Keating, Sara, and Emma Creedon, eds. *Sullied Magnificence: The Theatre of Mark O'Rowe*. Dublin: Carysfort Press, 2015.

THE PLAYBOY OF THE WESTERN WORLD (2007) BY BISI ADIGUN AND RODDY DOYLE

Adigun and Doyle's adaptation of *The Playboy of the Western World* first appeared at the Abbey Theatre in September 2007, marking the centenary year of the premiere of the original J. M. Synge play. It proved popular with audiences and would go on to receive extensive scholarly attention – but a legal dispute between Adigun on the one hand, and Doyle and the Abbey Theatre on the other, has overshadowed that success.

The plot of the adaptation closely tracks Synge's original in which a stranger arrives at a remote pub, claiming to have killed his father; he becomes the subject of the competing attentions of two women, Pegeen and the Widow Quin, and is celebrated by the local community – until his supposedly dead father reappears, bringing about a violent denouement.

In the 2007 version, the stranger is not Christy Mahon but Christopher Malomo, a refugee from Nigeria; the shebeen is not in rural Mayo but in contemporary west Dublin; and Christopher does not "kill" his father with a loy but with a pestle used for grinding yams. The language spoken by the characters is not a poeticised version of rural Irish speech but a heightened version of the working-class Dublin vernacular that Doyle had perfected in his many novels and screenplays. There is also a deliberate coarsening of the language. Synge's play, for example, concludes with Pegeen's famous lament,

"Oh my grief, I've lost him surely. I've lost the only Playboy of the Western World."[1] In this version, Pegeen's final words are "fuck off."[2]

The impact of such changes is to highlight important features of the growing multiculturalism of Irish society. Nicholas Grene has observed that:

> On the whole, Irish drama has continued to look to social margins for its setting, whether the western country districts or the working-class inner city. It is thus typically other people that a largely middle class urban audience watches in an Irish play, other people who speak differently – more colloquially, more comically, more poetically.[3]

Grene's statement is relevant to both versions of *The Playboy*: Synge's is set in the west of Ireland and the Adigun/Doyle version in a working-class community in Dublin, and both use a colloquial form of speech. Intriguingly, however, the characters on stage who most resemble the audience in the Adigun/Doyle version are the two Nigerians, Christopher and his father. Both are middle-class, highly educated, and well spoken. This simple shift in dynamic alters Irish audiences' understanding of who the outsiders in this play (and thus in Irish society) might be.

Adigun first encountered Synge as a university drama student in Nigeria in the late 1980s, but did not see a production of *Playboy* until he visited Dublin in 1998. After he had settled in Ireland, he read the play again:

> [I]t occurred to me that Synge's Christy is the archetypal "asylum seeker." It is exactly what Christy Mahon does in Synge's master-piece that asylum seekers must do to be allowed stay in Ireland. Like Christy, an asylum seeker must have a story to back up his/ her refuge application. It does not matter whether to story is true or not, but it must be compellingly convincing.[4]

For these reasons, Adigun began to think seriously about a new version of the play, telling the journalist Rachel Andrews in 2003 that he could imagine a black actor playing Pegeen in a new produc-tion – while in a 2004 article for *Irish Theatre Magazine*, he stated that he looked forward to the day when he might see a Nigerian actor playing Christy on the Abbey stage.[5] In early 2006, Adigun finally decided to approach Doyle to see if he would co-write the play, and the two quickly set to work together, completing a first draft in June of that year, and submitting the final version to the Abbey Theatre in October 2006.

Doyle was the ideal collaborator for such a venture, having already shown a strong interest in giving voice to Irish immigrants, as shown by his contribution of short stories about immigration to *Metro Eireann* magazine.[6] These soon developed into a play called *Guess Who's Coming for the Dinner* (the title borrowed from the 1967 Stanley Kramer film), a 2001 drama that explores the impact upon a Dublin family when a young Nigerian asylum seeker visits them (Adigun had participated in a workshopped reading of that play but was not part of the full production). Doyle had also supported Adigun's 2003 launch of Arambe productions, a theatre company that aimed to stage African plays in Dublin. The combination of the two writers thus seemed like a good example of interculturalism in practice. But while the play was success-fully revived at the Abbey in 2008, it gave rise to a legal action by Adigun, who alleged that the theatre had made alterations to the script without his consent, and had not paid royalties that were due from the original run.

That case was settled in 2013. Doyle defended himself against any accusation of responsibility for changes to the play and transferred its authorship and licensing fully to Adigun. Doyle has continued to work with the Abbey but Adigun's work has not been presented there since – and Arambe productions is no longer in operation. As Charlotte McIvor noted, the adaptation of Synge's play became "the paradigmatic example" of an "emergent intercultural Irish theatre" but, because of the collapse of the relationship between Doyle and Adigun, it also represented "the climax" of that form of interculturalism.[7]

The Adigun/Doyle *Playboy* was in dialogue with other important productions of Synge's work. These included Garry Hynes's *DruidSynge* project (2005), a staging of all of Synge's plays in a single day. Also significant was Pan Pan Theatre Company's 2006 adaptation of *The Playboy*, which relocated the action from the Mayo shebeen to a contemporary Beijing "whoredressers" (a hairdresser's that doubles as a brothel). In its Dublin production, the dialogue was performed in Mandarin, but there were also projected surtitles that did not translate the script directly but displayed Synge's original text – creating a contrast between the action onstage and audiences' knowledge of the original. This contrast between the new version and the old made clear how Pan Pan were rewriting Synge's play for the present. Because of the success of such work, the Adigun/Doyle

Playboy was able to presuppose a high level of awareness of Synge's work in its audience.

Other associations can be made. Christopher Murray has shown how the Adigun/Doyle *Playboy* must be seen as a development of the work of the Dublin-based theatre collective The Passion Machine, which had been founded in 1984 to stage new Irish plays that reflected the realities of contemporary Dublin life – often focusing on working-class communities in the city's sprawling suburbs. Their work included several plays by Paul Mercier, as well as Doyle's own *Brownbread* (1987) and *War* (1989).[8]

Adigun would continue to work on intercultural Irish performances after his relationship with the Abbey Theatre had concluded. In 2009, working with a youth theatre in Waterford, he wrote and directed *The Playboy of the Sunny South East*, a light-hearted relocation of Synge's play to contemporary Ireland. And in 2013, he presented an adaptation of Jimmy Murphy's *The Kings of the Kilburn High Road* – a play about Irish immigrants to London – which now became *The Paddies of Parnell Street*, which is about a group of Nigerian emigrants to Dublin. But of particular significance is the fact that the success of the adaptation of *Playboy* created space for new voices, particularly those of people who had recently emigrated to Ireland – including the establishment of theatre companies such as Polish Theatre Ireland and autobiographical or semi-autobiographical works such as Mirjana Rendulic's *Broken Promise Land* (2013).

Patrick Lonergan

Notes

1   J. M. Synge, *The Playboy of the Western World*, in *Collected Works IV: Plays II*, ed. Ann Saddlemyer (Gerrards Cross: Colin Smythe, 1982), 112.

2   I am grateful to Bisi Adigun for supplying an original copy of the script, from which this quotation is taken.

3   Nicholas Grene, *The Politics of Irish Drama* (Cambridge: Cambridge University Press, 1999), 264.

4   Bisi Adigun, "Re-Writing Synge's *Playboy*," in *Synge and His Influences*, ed. Patrick Lonergan (Dublin: Carysfort Press, 2011), 261.

5   Rachel Andrews, "All the World's a Stage," *Sunday Tribune*, September 2003; Bisi Adigun, "In Living Colour," *Irish Theatre Magazine* Vol. 4, no. 19 (Summer 2004): 31.

6   See Maureen T. Reddy, "Reading and Writing Race in Ireland: Roddy Doyle and *Metro Eireann*," *Irish University Review* Vol. 35, no. 2 (Autumn–Winter 2005): 374–88.

7   Charlotte McIvor, *Migration and Performance in Contemporary Ireland* (Basingstoke: Palgrave, 2016), 72.
8   Christopher Murray, "Beyond the Passion Machine: The Adigun-Doyle *Playboy* and Multiculturalism," in *Irish Theatre: Local and Global Perspectives*, ed. Nicholas Grene and Patrick Lonergan (Dublin: Carysfort Press, 2010), 105–20.

Further Reading

King, Jason. "Contemporary Irish Theatre, the New *Playboy* Controversy, and the Economic Crisis." *Irish Studies Review* Vol. 24, no. 1 (2016): 67–78.
Leeney, Cathy. "Being Intercultural in Irish Theatre and Performance." In *The Palgrave Handbook of Contemporary Irish Theatre and Performance*, edited by Eamonn Jordan and Eric Weitz, 527–45. London: Palgrave Macmillan, 2018.
McIvor, Charlotte. "*Playboy of the Western World* and Old/New Interculturalisms." In *Migration and Performance in Contemporary Ireland*, 39–83. London: Palgrave Macmillan, 2016.

I ♥ ALICE ♥ I (2010) BY AMY CONROY

In the final moments of *I ♥ Alice ♥ I*, Alice Kinsella, having, with her partner Alice Slattery, recounted the story of their lives together, and their decision to "come out of the closet" as a lesbian couple, says to the audience gathered in the theatre:

> We were here all along. Somebody has to do this, to stand up and be seen. We can't, in good conscience, always leave it to others. So here we are, warts and all. We have lived, lived well; we have loved, loved well. Alice will you dance?[1]

The couple, who had been uncomfortable with public displays of affection, kiss and dance to *Endless Love*, by Diana Ross and Lionel Ritchie, and at the song's conclusion, turn again to the audience and say together: "We will be seen" (219). This is where one might expect this piece of autobiographical, documentary theatre to end. But it doesn't. This moment of revelation is reversed by the play's actual ending, when, in a *coup de théâtre* the two actors playing Alice Kinsella and Alice Slattery, Amy Conroy and Clare Barrett, slowly take off their wigs to reveal themselves as actors and what the audience has just witnessed as a fiction, saying together, "They will be seen" (219).

Originally staged in 2010 as part of the Dublin Fringe Festival, written by Conroy and produced by her company, HotForTheatre, *I ♥ Alice ♥ I* invokes the techniques and conventions of documentary and autobiographical performance. Its central conceit is that a year earlier, in a moment of slight abandon, Alice Kinsella kissed Alice Slattery in an aisle of the Crumlin Shopping Centre's Tesco. This kiss was witnessed by an unnamed actor and writer, who approaches Alice Kinsella to ask if the couple would work with her to create a performance about their relationship. The performance that audiences see is meant to be the culmination of the work done during that year, charting not only the Alices' lives together but their change in consciousness, their decision to make the play, to come out and, in two years' time, on their thirtieth anniversary, to be married.

As a methodology for performance, documentary theatre has a long and complex history, but had enjoyed a resurgence in the United States and the United Kingdom in the 1990s and 2000s. In the Irish context, documentary theatre of various kinds by a variety of companies and artists also enjoyed currency in the 2000s.[2] Generally speaking, documentary theatre is often politically engaged, and its performance, according to Janelle Reinelt, "evoke[s] a public sphere where a gathered group might investigate and consider the meaning of individual experience in the context of state or societal responsibilities and norms."[3] In the case of Conroy's play, the immediate political context is the civil partnerships and civil marriage debate in Ireland. In the early 2000s, civil partnership had been advocated by Senator David Norris and others, and in July 2010 the Civil Partnership Act was passed into law. However, it did not grant gays and lesbians full equality with their heterosexual counterparts, nor did it guarantee them the same protections afforded by civil marriage.

The first steps towards civil marriage for gays and lesbians in Ireland were taken in 2004, when Katherine Zappone, then a lecturer in Trinity College Dublin, and her wife, the late Ann Louise Gilligan, then a theologian teaching at Saint Patrick's College, sought to have their marriage, which had been performed in Canada in 2003, recognised by Irish Revenue. Their case successfully litigated all the way to the High Court, where, in December 2006, Ms Justice Elizabeth Dunne denied their claim, and found in favour of the State. In 2008, the KAL Advocacy Initiative, the support group named after the initials of the couple's first names, developed into Marriage Equality, which built upon the recognition and support that Zappone and Gilligan had garnered across the country. One of the key strategies was to focus on gay and lesbian couples and to stress the negative impacts that being excluded from civil marriage had on their lives and their families. By highlighting personal stories, Marriage Equality hoped to "shift this debate from a political and legal one to a real-life issue."[4]

Zappone and Gilligan are, arguably, the real-life corollary of the Alices: a committed lesbian couple who want to make their more than two-decade-old relationship official in Ireland through civil marriage rather than civil partnership. However, in comparison to Zappone and Gilligan, and many of the other public faces of the Marriage Equality campaign, the two Alices are invisible. They were not "out" and they had never been politically active: "We don't fly the rainbow flag; we never publicly danced or kissed ... well, not until that day in Tesco's. We seem to blend" (196). The most striking thing about these charming but ordinary women is their love of one another, which the play represents by having them share the trials and tribulations they've have faced and overcame as a couple – an infidelity, a cancer diagnosis, and their own individual differences and eccentricities – as well as the mundane pleasures – birthdays, family parties, and trips abroad. As Eamonn Jordan suggests, while the

> broader contexts for the play [...] are social justice, human rights, civil partnerships, and marriage equality. There is something extraordinary in the ordinariness of their day-to-day living, and something vital and purposeful in the normalcy of their differences, conflicts, mutual likes and dislikes, shared and unshared passions.[5]

The play is a remarkable portrait of a "normal," loving couple, purposeful in showing how they are the same in almost every way as many of their heterosexual counterparts, barring they are not legally recognised as a couple by their society.

In its autobiographical and documentary style, *I ♥ Alice ♥ I* resonates with the strategy of Ireland's Marriage Equality campaign, and in its original and touring productions, it intervened into the debates on civil partnership and same-sex marriage in Ireland. But precisely because the play *is* fiction, and not based on the lives of real people, it can also suggest other, broader interpretations, while, in Conroy's words, it "poke[s] [...] at the form and structure of documentary theatre" and represents older queer women, who "are really under represented on stage and screen."[6] The play's fiction resonates with Benedict Anderson's contention that nations are "imagined communities" in part because "the members of even the smallest nation will never know most of their fellow-members [...] yet in the minds of each lives the image of their communion."[7] *I ♥ Alice ♥ I*'s fiction allows its audiences not only to "see" the Alices but also the actors who played them. In doing so, it invites us to imagine other such lives, those whose stories are not told, not staged, but who can, even must, be imagined as we collectively create an Ireland that "cherish[es] all the children of the nation equally."[8] In its fiction, the play can make a metaphor of the Alices' change in consciousness, one that echoes the same shift undergone in Ireland over the course of the twenty-eight years of their relationship, a time that saw homosexuality legalised (1993) and which would see gay men and lesbians legal right to civil marriage affirmed, by overwhelming majority, in an historic referendum in May 2015.

J. Paul Halferty

Notes

1   Amy Conroy. *I ♥ Alice ♥ I*, in *This is Just This. It Isn't Real. It's Money: The Oberon Anthology of Contemporary Irish Plays*, ed. Thomas Conway (London: Oberon Books, 2012), 219. Subsequent references are entered in parentheses.
2   See Beatriz Kopschitz Bastos and Shaun Richards, "Introduction," in *Contemporary Irish Documentary Theatre* (London: Bloomsbury, 2020), 1–6.
3   Janelle Reinelt, "The Promise of Documentary," ed. Alison Forsyth and Chris Megson, (London: Palgrave Macmillan, 2011), 11.
4   Sonja Tiernan, *The History of Marriage Equality in Ireland: A Social Revolution Begins* (Manchester: Manchester University Press, 2020), 39.
5   Eamonn Jordan, "Suburban Sensibilities in Contemporary Plays Set in Dublin," in *Imagining Irish Suburbia in Literature and Culture*, ed. Eoghan Smith and Simon Workman (London: Palgrave Macmillan, 2019), 172.
6   See www.contemporaryirishwriting.ie/books/i-heart-alice-heart-i. Accessed 25 October 2021.
7   Benedict Anderson, *Imagined Communities: Reflections on the Origin and Spread of Nationalism* (London: Verso, 1991), 6.
8   See www.gov.ie/en/publication/bfa965-proclamation-of-independence/. Accessed 22 November 2021.

Further Reading

Murphy, Oonagh. "Making Space: Female-Authored Queer Performance in Irish Theatre." In *That Was Us: Contemporary Irish Theatre and Performance*, edited by Fintan Walsh, 63–76. London: Oberon Books, 2013.

O'Connell, Brenda. "'We are here, we were here all along': Queer Invisibility and Performing Age in Amy Conroy's *I ♥ Alice ♥ I.*" In *The Golden Thread: Irish Women Playwrights, Volume 2 (1716–2016)*, edited by David Clare, Fiona McDonagh, and Justine Nakase, 147–56. Liverpool: Liverpool University Press, 2021.

Walsh, Fintan. *Queer Performance and Contemporary Ireland: Dissent and Disorientation*. Basingstoke: Palgrave Macmillan, 2016.

Yates, Samuel. "'We Will Be Seen': Documenting Queer Womanhood in Amy Conroy's *I ♥ Alice ♥ I.*" In *Radical Contemporary Theatre Practices by Women in Ireland*, edited by Miriam Haughton and Mária Kurdi, 89–104. Dublin: Carysfort Press, 2015.

NO ESCAPE (2010) BY MARY RAFTERY

Mary Raftery's *No Escape* is a piece of documentary theatre, the script for which is derived verbatim from selected passages of the Report from Judge Sean Ryan's Commission to Inquire into Child Abuse – commonly referred to as "The Ryan Report." The project was initiated by the Literary Director of the Abbey Theatre, Aideen Howard, who saw it as the National Theatre's duty to respond to this Report. This play is notable as, until its premiere on the Abbey's Peacock Stage in April 2010, there were few examples of Irish-produced documentary theatre. The formal approach taken with *No Escape* can be linked to the prevalence of verbatim theatre in the UK during the 1990s and 2000s; most especially, the tribunal plays of the Tricycle Theatre, London, under the directorship of Nicholas Kent. Indeed, *Bloody Sunday: Scenes from the Saville Enquiry* (2005), co-directed by Kent and Charlotte Westenra and edited by journalist Richard Norton-Taylor, was brought to the Abbey in October 2005 after its world premiere in London. Howard, mirroring the journalist-as-editor model of the Tricycle, asked Raftery – a journalist who was key in exposing institutional clerical abuse in Ireland – to create a script from the 2,500-page Ryan Report. The scope of the project was limited by the practical parameters of a live performance: the resulting production was only ninety minutes in length, accounting perhaps for the demanding nature of the material for audiences. Within such constraints, it was Raftery's brief to identify "that which was absolutely non-omissible" from the report.[1] This necessitated and enabled the privileging of certain voices over others; in the show's redressed hierarchy, the historically silenced voice of the victim holds more credit than the voice of the Church.

In spite of the formal and structural similarities between Kent's tribunal plays and what was being attempted by the Abbey and

Raftery with *No Escape*, Howard was uneasy with attaching certain designations to their production:

> I struggled to call it a verbatim piece because what does that say about 2,500 pages? Are we giving an impression that this is conclusive? So, we settled on documentary theatre. And I walked around the building, all day, every day, telling people not to call it a play, ever![2]

The insistence on never referring to the show as a "play" ("from a publicity standpoint") speaks to a certain degree of self-consciousness surrounding the piece. It seems Howard was aware of how the entertainment connotations attached to the word "play" might give an impression that this solemn material was being taken lightly. Furthermore, and in spite of Raftery's editorial guidance, Howard's concern that the production might be perceived as being conclusive speaks to a certain transcendental quality that *No Escape* was beginning to take on. This was not just a piece of theatre; it was also a commemoration.

The scenographic choices of the Tricycle tribunal plays were known for their minimalism and restraint; the set design of *No Escape* is somewhat more semiotically rich relative to those realist sets. Cardboard boxes containing the pages of the Report pile up at the edges of a set that is surrounded by panes of Perspex. Facts and figures are written on the panes in marker, representing a "window" into the contents of the Report: these contents, previously only available to the public in text, are now embodied. The panes – aided by Paul Keoghan's lighting design – also create a mirroring surface, as the witnesses reflect on their lives, past and present. The overall aesthetic of *No Escape* is not of a condensed re-enactment but a staging of the essence of the Ryan Report.

No Escape presents a series of juxtapositions of the Ryan Report's findings (with the character of Sean Ryan acting as narrator), witness statements, and scenes from public hearings where members of the religious orders give evidence as to their appraisal of how these schools were run. The Abbey production is divided into seven parts: a prologue and six acts, each exploring a particular theme or finding of the Report. The prologue – in direct address to the audience – contextualises the findings of the Report by interspersing witness statements recalling the horrific nature of their experiences in these schools, while narration from Judge Sean Ryan outlines the background of the Commission's establishment. This reflects the overall rhythm of the show. For example, Act II focuses on the punishment methods used at these schools: official Department of Education punishment regulations are juxtaposed with actual punishment practices, as outlined by the findings of the Report and witness statements:

Department of Education. The Manager must … remember that the more closely the School is modelled on a principle of judicious family government the more salutary will be its discipline, and the fewer occasions will arise for resort to punishment.[3]

The supposed irregularity of punishment is immediately contradicted, as Sean Ryan lists twenty-nine different weapons that were reportedly used on children. The following witness account is then delivered:

Witness (male) 1. *You could hear the screams all over the whole building at night it was so quiet. Up to 4 Brothers would come and take a boy out of bed on some pretext and give him a hammering […] They were like a pack of hunting animals.*

(22)

This pattern establishes how the show attempts to peel away the layers of language and reveal the truth of what witnesses experienced in industrial schools. Department guidelines are factually contradicted in Sean Ryan's legalese, before the more human and authentic voices of witnesses are presented. The voices of Ryan and the witnesses dissent against the Department of Education guidelines: a shift in the hierarchy of truths that are being presented.

The show occasionally breaks from passages of direct address, as Raftery augments the Ryan Report with material from Transcripts of Public Hearings (Commission to Inquire into Child Abuse, 2006). These are presented as a dialogue, but interrupted by harrowing witness statements. As the majority of the testimony in the Report is given by victims, these scenes allow the religious orders' perspective to be represented – damning them through their own evidence. For example, Act III intersperses the questioning of Sr Helena O'Donoghue – representing the Sisters of Mercy at Goldenbridge – with witness statements outlining the brutal punishment methods used at that school:

Sr O'Donnoghue. We accept that children were beaten in terms of corporal punishment. We do not accept that it was excessive or excessively harsh.

Witness (Female) 5. *I can remember praying every night that I wouldn't wet the bed because I knew the next morning I would be severely beaten, reprimanded and I remember feeling very cold and standing naked and just the shame, the absolute shame of it.*

(28)

These temporal and textual shifts suggest a hybrid approach to the standard practices of documentary theatre: *No Escape* combines recreations of public hearings with excerpts from the Report in the form of direct address. This approach de-emphasises the temporal structure of the archive it is adapting and the appearance of direct re-enactment in order to, as Howard herself puts it, "privilege voices over character."[4] The final statement of the show is emblematic of this:

Witness (male) 13. *They all said "that couldn't have happened" but they can't say that to 5000 of us when we all have a similar story to tell.*
Lights Out.

(44)

Instead of ending the performance with the conclusions of Judge Sean Ryan, Raftery has provided space for the witnesses' voices to have the last word. In so doing, Raftery creates a narrative structure within the overall archive of the Ryan Report that correctively privileges historically marginalised voices.

Howard has noted that the decision to approach Raftery in order to respond to the Ryan Report was, in part, due to the fact that the artists she had been collaborating with and commissioning during her tenure were not "desperately interested in tackling that subject."[5] It is notable that, since this production, there has been a proliferation of theatrical engagement with Ireland's history of institutional and clerical abuse: from Brokentalkers' *The Blue Boy* and *Laundry* by ANU (both 2011), to the more recent *Pasolini's Salo: Redubbed* (2019) by Dylan Tighe and *Home: Part One* (2020) by the Abbey Theatre. Furthermore, these are all characterised by their various use of documentary theatre methods. While there had been Irish examples of the documentary form, *No Escape* represents the first major Irish production in this genre; one which has since become a mainstay in contemporary Irish theatre.

Luke Lamont

Notes

1 Aideen Howard, "Ways of Representing the Past: Documentary Theatre in Ireland and Brazil" by UCD Humanities Institute. *Soundcloud*. Podcast Audio. 25 November 2014. https://soundcloud.com/ucd-humanities/repre senting-the-past-documentary-theatre-ireland-brazil? in=ucd-humanities/ sets/irish-memory-studies-network. Accessed 29 March 2021.
2 Author interview with Aideen Howard, 2 February 2017.
3 Mary Raftery, *No Escape*, in *Contemporary Irish Documentary Theatre*, ed. Beatriz Kopschitz Bastos and Shaun Richards (London: Bloomsbury, 2020), 22. Subsequent references are entered in parentheses.
4 Author interview.
5 Ibid.

Further Reading

Lamont, Luke. "Staging a Response: No Escape and the Rise of Documentary Theatre in Ireland." In *The Palgrave Handbook of Contemporary Irish Theatre and Performance*, edited by Eamonn Jordan and Eric Weitz, 777–82. London: Palgrave Macmillan, 2018.
McCormack, Sheila. "*The Darkest Corner*: Documenting Institutional Abuse and its Consequences at the Abbey Theatre." *Irish Studies Review* Vol. 20, no. 2 (2012): 179–91.

LAUNDRY (2011) BY ANU PRODUCTIONS

The smell of carbolic soap is intensely pungent. It was the first thing to greet the spectators, if not engulf them, who experienced *Laundry*, directed by Louise Lowe and produced by ANU Productions as part of the Ulster Bank Dublin Theatre Festival 2011. *Laundry* was performed in the disused St. Mary Magdalen Convent on Lower Seán McDermott Street (formerly Gloucester Street), the last Magdalen laundry to close its doors in 1996. It played for over two hundred performances and won the *Irish Times* Best Production award. *Laundry* was the second in ANU's "Monto Cycle," four site-specific immersive productions which explored the history of "The Monto," the area around former Montgomery Street in inner-city North Dublin; others in the cycle being *World's End* (2010), *The Boys of Foley Street* (2012), and *Vardo* (2014).

The soap was used in large quantities so that the smell escaped the heavy doors and framed each performance space throughout the building. It defined the space and the experience. Water filtered through the sound design, trickling along as background noise, reminding the audience that they were in a punitive place of work;

an active Magdalen laundry. The movement of water, the cleaning of bodies and clothes, and the related steam and smells all merged to heighten the already tense environment captured through the traditional convent architecture, such as the large stained-glass windows, tiled floors, and heavy doors. The smell of carbolic soap in this quantity and space was deeply discomforting. It assailed the senses and immersed both audiences and performers. This sense of punishment via the senses was intentional. Women were sent to Magdalen laundries in Ireland as a punishment; for pregnancy outside of marriage, for suspected sexual activities, and for not aligning with the hegemonic Catholic, nationalist, and patriarchal ideologies of respectable womanhood, often as a result of economic disadvantage or other conditions rendering them vulnerable.[1] They were to clean society's filth, and in so doing, attempt to make amends for their fallen souls, though these women were exploited and victimised by those very institutions and ideologies proclaiming morality. The laundries implemented "The Rule of Silence"[2] to prevent friendships and community emerging among the women, and so this staging choice by ANU – silent of women's voices but deafening of their torment – was deeply resonant. Dialogue or narrative could not capture a history designed to be unheard and unseen.

Theatre scholarship does not focus much on smells in performance analysis but in *Laundry*, the smell was constant. It was planned, managed, and directed; it operated as an overarching scenographic and dramaturgical thread that connected the past with the present, each scene, each performer, and each audience member regardless of overlapping entrances and exits, audience interactions and interpretations. The cleaning was of cloth and soul, all deemed sufficiently dirty to warrant oversight by religious institutions behind high walls and locked doors who managed accounts with the support of the modern Irish state.

The smell that met each audience member on entry into the building marked the beginning of the performance. One cannot refer to Act 1 or Scene 1 as there is no play text and it would be misleading to recount the experience through traditional dramatic analytic structures. No suspension of disbelief was required; each encounter in the performance spaces was based on testimonial and archival accounts specific to that particular laundry. Audience members entered the building in groups of three at a time and were then separated, experiencing scenes individually. In the scenes audiences encountered women and the relatives implicated in their incarceration. The final scene involved a taxi journey to experience work in a neighbouring modern launderette. Experience of individual scenes could then alter depending on the nature of decisions to participate, such as answering questions or responding to provocations posed by performers. However, each audience member's journey was designed to experience all of the encounters, though in a different order.

Sensory experience framed the unfolding of the performance. Smell was followed by sight, an eerie dimly lit former convent building, lying vacant, with dust and memories all that adorn it. The building still possessed a few material remnants, including toothbrushes and an old bath; the remaining evidence of those lives incarcerated, and nearly forgotten, for most of the twentieth century. One scene focused on the old bath brought soap and water together as performer Laura Murray exited the bath and started wrapping herself in cloth, clearly vulnerable and suffering, asking for assistance from the solitary audience member. Through all the scenes audiences had to confront directly this deliberately forgotten history, to decide how to respond to appeals from the inmates for help, to demands for escape.

Stolen lives, denial of human rights, families separated, and female bodies and their children hidden; it was this politics that enabled the performativity of the modern Irish republic. We will never fully know these histories as too many have died without access to public space and discourse, thus the few remnants become all the more symbolic as a result. Mairéad Ní Ghráda's *An Triail* (1964) and Patricia Burke Brogan's *Eclipsed* (1994) had staged similar territory decades previous to *Laundry*, receiving both critical acclaim and cultural dissent in varying degrees. However, these plays were always framed by play texts and their performances in theatre buildings, ensuring some sense of distance from the difficult history they staged.

Since *Laundry*, marginalised histories appear to be clamouring their way into present-day politics. The McAleese report into the Magdalen laundries (2013) conducted under pressure from the United Nations Committee Against Torture, remains contested. The Decade of Centenaries (2013–2023) commemorative events have observed a rich questioning of Ireland's complex canonical and lesser-known histories. 2013 also saw the release of feature film *Philomena* which centres on a Mother and Baby Institution, attracting global acclaim and starring Judy Dench for which she received an Oscar nomination. International outrage at the findings of historian Catherine Corless regarding the mass burial site at the former Mother and Baby Institution in Tuam emerged in 2014. The recent Mother and Baby

Homes Commission of Investigation in Ireland, which remains in heated debate by communities of survivors, scholars, and politicians, published its findings in 2021. The Northern Irish research report into Mother and Baby Homes and Magdalen laundries in Northern Ireland was published in 2021, leading to calls for a public enquiry.

Laundry produced a shadowed part of Irish history, but also spoke to modern western structures of social management and control more widely. In *Discipline and Punish* Michel Foucault considers the major shift in how hegemonic power is expressed and executed since the emergence of modernity. While historically, the tortured body of the condemned was once centralised in public space so communities could witness their pain and the consequences of crime, modern society now expresses crime and punishment through judicial and carceral systems that operate behind closed doors. The obvious change in this dynamic is the removal of physical torture as punishment by the state and/or crown. However equally significant is the removal of the punishment from visible and centralised public space, and therefore, consciousness. As Foucault suggests:

> Punishment, then, will tend to become the most hidden part of the penal process. This has several consequences: it leaves the domain of more or less everyday perception and enters that of abstract consciousness [...] As a result, justice no longer takes public responsibility for the violence that is bound up with its practice.[3]

Large institutional buildings successfully managed this politics of visibility and thus power, keeping society out and women in. What followed was a practice of power and punishment that could continue without any significant intervention, resulting in Irish society as the most institutionalised in the world throughout the twentieth century. Who held and continues to hold the keys to these buildings, and indeed archival records, requires further scrutiny. Will any individual or organisation ever be prosecuted for these crimes?

Laundry paid tribute to the women we did not know of, could not see, and had not remembered. These women constitute our matrilineal heritage and conditions for kinship today. If patriarchal history has not written of these women, then feminist performance and scholarship must bypass the assumed power of canonicity and stage both the human body and the crimes that disposed of them.

Miriam Haughton

Notes

1 Miriam Haughton, Mary McAuliffe, and Emilie Pine, eds, *Legacies of the Magdalen Laundries: Commemoration, Gender and the Postcolonial Carceral State* (Manchester: Manchester University Press, 2021), 1–29.
2 Miriam Haughton, "From Laundries to Labour Camps: Staging Ireland's 'Rule of Silence' in Anu Productions' *Laundry*," *Modern Drama* Vol. 57, no. 1 (2014): 65–93.
3 Michel Foucault, *Discipline and Punish: The Birth of the Prison*, trans. Alan Sheridan (London: Penguin, 1998), 9.

Further Reading

McGettrick, Claire, Katharine O'Donnell, Maeve O'Rourke, James M. Smith, and Mari Steed. *Ireland and the Magdalene Laundries: A Campaign for Justice*. London: Bloomsbury, 2021.

Singleton, Brian. *ANU Productions: The Monto Cycle*. London: Palgrave Pivot, 2006.

Smith, Jim. *Ireland's Magdalen Laundries and the Nation's Architecture of Containment*. Manchester: Manchester University Press, 2008.

QUIETLY (2012) BY OWEN MCCAFFERTY

Quietly opened on the Abbey Theatre's Peacock stage in November 2012, going on to win an award for new writing at the Edinburgh Festival Fringe in 2013. The following year saw the production play at London's Soho Theatre and Belfast's Lyric Theatre followed by a transfer to New York's Repertory Theatre in 2016. However, it originated as a commission from the National Theatre, London. As McCafferty explained:

> It was originally a bigger play, with a bigger cast. But the more I worked on the notes and thought about it, I came to realise that the reconciliation element was what was the most important and significant thing [...] Gradually, the play became smaller and smaller, more closely focused, more condensed. At the end of the day, it was not a play for the National, it would not have worked on any of its stages. So I sent it to the Abbey.[1]

The resulting "condensed" play, with an unbroken running time of seventy-five minutes and a focus on three characters in one set, carries an emotional charge which evokes the intensity of classic naturalism where the principle *"faire grand"* meant that the events should be of major, even life-changing, significance. The pub set, created in all its authentic minutiae by Alyson Cummins, suggests the classic location of Irish dramas such as *Conversations on a Homecoming* (1985) and *The Weir* (1997) where men meet to drink and swap stories about the past. However, this pub is on Belfast's Ormeau Road, the site of sectarian violence during the "Troubles." The basis of the play was the bombing in 1974 of the Catholic-owned Rose and Crown pub on the Lower Ormeau Road by two teenage members of the Ulster Volunteer Force which destroyed the pub and killed a total of six people. The historic resonances of this massacre are amplified by the fact that the play's set was modelled on that of the original Rose and Crown. In *Quietly* the "Troubles" are nominally over and the play takes place over a decade after the Good Friday Agreement of 1998 which moved to end the violence and initiate a Peace Process intended to lead to reconciliation and the removal of sectarian conflict. However, the play suggests that the process of peace is long and fraught and even forty years after the act of violence which is the play's subject, its ripples still scar and mar lives. As McCafferty commented, "It felt like that was the aspect that was so difficult to escape from, the idea of people confronting that possibility years later. Dramatically, the aftermath is more important. The pain doesn't end with the event."[2]

The play is set in "*A bar in Belfast, 2009. Northern Ireland are playing Poland in a World Cup qualifier on a big screen TV.*"[3] The opening minutes are occupied with banter about the match between Robert, the Polish barman, and Jimmy, a pub regular, until the latter's line, "there's a man comin in later on to see me – he wants to talk with me – there might be a bit a trouble with him" (196), intimates a potential for violence underscored when Jimmy head-butts Ian within seconds of his entrance. This is followed by a verbal tirade directed at Ian although the cause of Jimmy's anger is at first only hinted at in his line "there was flesh stuck to the wall across the road – where you were standin – difficult to scrape off – because it's flesh an you don't want to scrape it off" (206). As their conversation develops it transpires that Ian has sought the meeting because "on the third of july nineteen-seventy four" (211) when they were both sixteen (they are now fifty-two), he was a member of the Ulster Volunteer Force and, shouting "fuckin fenian bastards" (218), hurled a bomb into the pub, killing Jimmy's father and five other men. Now, Ian has come to say "i'm sorry for what happened" (220).

The anguish of Jimmy's life after the event – delivered at mono-logue length – dominates the conversation, punctuated by his dis-ruption of Ian's story – "don't tell me any more [...] it doesn't help" (226). But when Ian finally says "i'm trying to do the right thing,"

Jimmy declares "i know – when twenty thousand of you marched by the top of our street I screamed at the top of my voice – fuckin orange bastards – fuckin orange bastards – I was sixteen as well – I know what world you lived in" (229). Then "*Ian stands up and offers Jimmy his hand. Jimmy stands. They shake hands.*" But any sense of easy celebration in this moment is punctured by Jimmy's next line: "don't ever come back here" (229).

Robert, the barman, is what Jimmy ironically calls "our truth and reconciliation committee" (210), silently observing what takes place between him, on-stage, and the audience in the auditorium; both witnesses of the uneasy path to, if not peace, then at least understanding. But as the play's title suggests, this can only truly take place at a low-key personal level. Indeed, as Connal Parr says, "Owen McCafferty's thesis is simple: Northern Ireland's politicians have failed, utterly failed, to deal with the past. This does not, however, prevent individuals from pursuing their own odysseys of truth and reconciliation. They are going about it quietly."[4] But this is not a play with easy answers. Not only is the resolution between Jimmy and Ian tentative but Robert's presence suggests the potential for another cycle of violence as outside the pub kids beat on the shutters and shout "fuckin polish bastard […] go back to where you come from." The play closes as "*Robert gets a baseball bat from behind the bar and stands waiting. Lights fade to dark*" (233). As McCafferty commented the year after the play was produced: "If we're honest with ourselves […] I would have thought that the next big subject to come out of here would be encroaching racism. I hinted at it at the end of *Quietly.*"[5]

Critics were unanimous in praise of the power of the play, especially the performance of Patrick O'Kane as Jimmy: "with the drawn features of an insomniac, he looks like a man whose past is burning from inside."[6] And there was a general consensus that "it feels utterly truthful."[7] The most telling critique of the play is that of Emilie Pine who, after acknowledging the play's "psychologically nuanced" writing, added:

> But I have another, almost as strong reaction to this play too – that it is yet another narrative of men and violence and the north, that stages forgiveness and closure in an unconvincing handshake. Except for plays like Tinderbox's "True North" series, Christina Reid's *Tea in a China Cup* and Anne Devlin's *Ourselves Alone*, the Troubles is consistently framed as a male-dominated narrative.

In its anticipation of the interventions of #WakingTheFeminists in 2016, her conclusion that this was "the issue that remains to be reconciled, and that is just as important as the reconciliation of men from opposing sides, is the glaring absence of women in too many narratives of the Troubles" has a particular force.[8]

McCafferty has suggested that *Quietly* is the last of a line of his plays concerned with the "ripple effect" of an act of violence, starting with *Mojo MickeyBo* (1998), with *Quietly* culminating with what Patrick O'Kane termed "the potential for healing – and that's where it leaves us."[9] And while analysis has focused on the Northern Irish context, McCafferty has been at pains to emphasise *Quietly*'s broader reach: "I may set plays in Belfast, but in my head I am not writing specifically about here. My job is to open things up and try to convey the bigger picture, the universal stories."[10] Indeed, as the *New York Times* reviewer said of the American production: "It is difficult to imagine a piece of theater more perfectly suited to our jittery, antagonistic American moment than 'Quietly,' Owen McCafferty's rage-filled, wounded, mournful play about terrorism, civil war and the damage that remains after the hatred cools."[11]

Shaun Richards

Notes

1 Jane Coyle, "Owen McCafferty Brings *Quietly* to the Lyric," *Culture Northern Ireland*, 3 April 2014. www.culturenorthernireland.org/features/performing-arts/owen-mccafferty-brings-quietly-lyric. Accessed 15 December 2021.

2 Ibid.

3 Owen McCafferty, *Quietly*, in *Owen McCafferty Plays 2* (London: Faber & Faber, 2016), 191. Subsequent references are entered in parentheses.

4 Connal Parr, "Review of *Quietly*," *Culture Northern Ireland*, 10 April 2014. www.culturenorthernireland.org/reviews/performing-arts/quietly-0. Accessed 15 December 2021.

5 Ryan Crown, "Collecting Owen McCafferty," *Culture Northern Ireland*, 11 November 2013. www.culturenorthernireland.org/features/literature/collecting-owen-mccafferty. Accessed 15 December 2021.

6 Helen Meany, "Quietly – Review," *The Guardian*, 28 November 2012. www.theguardian.com/stage/2012/nov/28/quietly-review. Accessed 15 December 2021.

7 Lyn Gardner, "*Quietly* – Edinburgh Festival 2012 Review," *The Guardian*, 8 August 2013. www.theguardian.com/stage/2013/aug/08/quietly-edinburgh-festival-2013-review. Accessed 15 December 2021.

8 Emilie Pine, "Review of *Quietly*," *Irish Theatre Magazine*, 23 November 2012. http://itmarchive.ie/web/Reviews/Current/Quietly.aspx.html. Accessed 15 December 2021.

9 *"Quietly* – Owen McCafferty and Patrick O'Kane Interviewed by Marie Louise Muir," BBC Arts Extra, 13 November 2012. https://sou ndcloud.com/abbeytheatre/owen-mccafferty-and-patrick. Accessed 15 December 2021.

10 Coyle.

11 Laura Collins-Hughes, "Review: *Quietly* Rivetingly Revisits the Troubles in Belfast," *New York Times*, 28 July 2016. www.nytimes.com/ 2016/07/29/theater/review-quietly-rivetingly-revisits-the-troubles-in-belfast.html. Accessed 15 December 2021.

Further Reading

Parr, Connal. "Something Happening Quietly: Owen McCafferty's Theatre of Truth and Reconciliation." *Irish University Review* Vol. 47, Special Supplementary Issue (Autumn/Winter 2017): 531–48.

Phelan, Mark. "From Troubles to Post-Conflict Theatre in Northern Ireland." In *The Oxford Handbook of Modern Irish Theatre*, edited by Nicholas Grene and Chris Morash, 372–88. Cambridge: Cambridge University Press, 2016.

Privas-Bréauté, Virginie. "A Quiet 'Rehearsal for the Revolution': *Quietly* (2012) by Owen McCafferty." HAL Open Science (2014). https:// halshs.archives-ouvertes.fr/halshs-01342488/document. Accessed 15 December 2021.

BROKEN PROMISE LAND (2013)
BY MIRJANA RENDULIC

Mirjana Rendulic's semi-autobiographical one-woman play *Broken Promise Land* premiered at Dublin's Theatre Upstairs in 2013, directed by Aoife Spillane-Hinks, dramaturged by Gavin Kostick, and produced by Stones Throw Theatre and Matthew Smyth. Rendulic would subsequently take the play on a limited national tour and perform it in London. The play was also adapted as a radio play for RTÉ in 2014.[1]

Rendulic describes herself as "living abroad half of my life and the other half in Croatia," but identifying herself now as "the inbetweener who grew up twice, but [...] very much an Irish artist."[2] At the time of *Broken Promise Land*'s premiere, Rendulic described the play as "about lap dancing and the immigrant experience, but it's also about a girl growing up. She's not a tragic martyr, she's just a girl with a mission."[3] She also unequivocally claimed it as an Irish play: "The way it's expressed. I've lived here. I've studied here. It's the way an Irish person would say something, even if it's in an accent."[4]

Drawing on Rendulic's own experiences working as a lap dancer to fund her studies in Ireland, *Broken Promise Land* tells the story of Tea (birth name Stefica) who is born in Zagreb, Croatia and comes of age during the Yugoslav wars of the 1990s and early 2000s. These experiences form only a small section in the play with Rendulic focusing on Tea's childhood poverty and lack of opportunity for educational or other advancement as most formative of her eventual path. The language in the play is direct and matter-of-fact, with Rendulic directly addressing the audience conversationally throughout, and the story being told entirely through Tea's perspective rather than mediated by the voices of other characters.

At twenty-one Tea finds herself with a permanent job in the shopping centre in her village and is told by her mum it is a "great opportunity" but she disagrees:

> It was like being in school again, but without books. And our tasks were a bit more repetitive. Sliding, Scanning, Typing, Bagging ... Sliding, Scanning, Typing, Bagging ... Sliding, Scanning, Typing, Bagging ... I thought that life is meant to be full of excitement, big things, and possibilities, but what I mostly heard were stories of disappointment and helplessness.[5]

Dreaming instead of a future "in sunny California, sitting under a tree at Berkeley University and reading literature," Tea decides to pursue an advert inviting her to work as a dancer in Italy – a risk that brings her first to Italy, then Japan, and finally Ireland (327). Each stopover brings risk and near-misses – having her client expose himself to her in her first dance in a private room at the club, hearing about a roommate's rape by her former boss in the industry, conflict with other girls at a club where she works, and most traumatically, paying a trafficker six thousand dollars to "get over the Mexican border to work in the USA" with a "passport and a job in a top club" (336). Despite this disappointment, she is given one more direct shot at the United States dream in the play when she meets an "American Sugar Daddy. J.F. Kennedy lookalike" (339) who first agrees to sponsor her student visa, and then to marry her when they are told that she is not eligible as "I don't have enough ties to my own country. No house, no husband, no baby" (340).

It is in fact the very moment that she considers whether or not to take this step with this American Sugar Daddy that frames the entire play. We hear Tea repeat the play's opening lines at the moment of decision that closes the play: "I can live in New York. I can live in his house, drive his car ... go to university" (340). Ultimately, she decides to go back to Croatia and apply for a student visa to Ireland, declaring "No more hiding. No more Tea. Stefica is starting now" (340). Through this reversal, "Rendulic's play challenges the reduction of sex workers to the function of their job, and portrays her time in the sector as only one aspect of her history, and not its determining feature."[6] As Eva Urban too observes, "This defiant portrayal of a woman's life remaining whole in the face of great adversity is in fact a critique of a concept of trauma that habitually insists on the inevitability of brokenness after trauma."[7]

Indeed, throughout, *Broken Promise Land*'s "narrative arc and (autobiographical) characterization runs counter to most media and theatrical depictions of the sex industry in Ireland and beyond," even provocatively so.[8] In the original production, the play was set in Tea's bedroom with Rendulic dressed in an everyday casual dress and jean jacket, a conscious decision not to "present Stefica as a curiosity or sex object," with her "physical movements and gestures" in performance "decisively small and non-sexualised"[9] even when re-enacting moments from her dancing career. But while working in Japan, Tea declares of herself and her co-workers:

> We are emancipated young women. We are our own bosses. We decide what we are. And if one day, we can decide to become someone else, we can do that too, by changing our name, our hair colour, our lips, our cheeks or our nationality.
>
> (333)

However, the play is ultimately more nuanced than Tea's confident declaration. Soon after this pronouncement, she finds herself on the move again not by choice, but by the necessity of an expired visa and as she gains more experience in the industry, she sees how quickly she loses clients' interest when she is no longer "new": "I am not even exotic anymore" (339).

Crucially, Rendulic's performance as a fictionalised version of herself in the play's original production added another set of layers to the work's unique perspective on the experiences, motivations, and (artistic) desires of female migrants recently arrived in Ireland. Her own double-jobbing in the performance (as playwright and performer) tracked with the trend towards one-person plays (both fictional and semi-/autobiographical) in Irish independent theatre at the time by playwright/performers also including Stefanie Preissner, Pat Kinevane, and Sonya Kelly. But it also gestures towards Rendulic's own multi-faceted approach to making a living in the Irish theatre industry as a migrant theatre-maker as she continues to work as not only an actor and writer for theatre, film, and television but also as a drama facilitator.

While this is typical of many independent artists in Ireland today, Rendulic and other theatre artists of minority ethnic and/or migrant backgrounds continue to face additional challenges relative to their peers. As Cathy Leeney notes, "The non-Irish or Traveller performer experiences incomprehension and miscomprehension of their training, experience and potential to perform a variety of roles," with "accented speech" (which *Broken Promise Land* embraces and celebrates) regularly being cited as a "definitive barrier to many agents and directors."[10] However, Rendulic's unique dramatic voice and onstage persona have brought nuanced representations of migrant female experiences in Ireland to the stage, in the process redefining and living out in performative time what an Irish play looks and sounds like today as told from her perspective.

Charlotte McIvor

Notes

1 RTÉ Drama on One, "*Broken Promise Land* by Mirjana Rendulic," 19 February 2014, www.rte.ie/radio/dramaonone/647620-genres-society-brokenpromiseland. Accessed 18 October 2021.

2 Centre for Creative Practices, "Mirjana Rendulic: CFCP New Voices of Ireland Series 8," https://cfcp.ie/nvoi8/nvoi8-rendulic-muotto/nvoi8-artist-rendulic/. Accessed 18 October 2021.

3 Caomhan Keane, "New Play Captures Life as a Lap Dancer in Celtic Tiger Ireland," *Irish Examiner*, 11 March 2013, www.irishexaminer.com/lifestyle/arid-20225019.html. Accessed 18 October 2021.

4 Centre for Creative Practices, "Mirjana Rendulic."

5 Mirjana Rendulic, *Broken Promise Land*, in *Staging Intercultural Ireland: Plays and Practitioner Perspectives*, ed. Charlotte McIvor and Matthew Spangler (Cork: Cork University Press, 2014), 327. Subsequent references are entered in parentheses.

6 Charlotte McIvor, *Migration and Performance in Contemporary Ireland: Towards a New Interculturalism* (London: Palgrave Macmillan, 2016), 170.

7 Eva Urban, "Intercultural Arrivals and Encounters with Trauma in Contemporary Irish Drama," in *The Palgrave Handbook of Contemporary Irish Theatre and Performance*, ed. Eamonn Jordan and Eric Weitz (London: Palgrave Macmillan, 2018), 565.

8 Charlotte McIvor, "Introduction to *Broken Promise Land*," in *Staging Intercultural Ireland: Plays and Practitioner Perspectives*, 320.
9 Ibid., 321.
10 Cathy Leeney, "Being Intercultural in Irish Theatre and Performance," in *The Palgrave Handbook of Contemporary Irish Theatre and Performance*, ed. Eamonn Jordan and Eric Weitz (London: Palgrave Macmillan, 2018), 541.

Further Reading

King, Jason. "Interculturalism and Irish Theatre: The Portrayal of Immigrants on the Irish Stage." *The Irish Review* 33 (2005): 23–39.

McIvor, Charlotte. "When Social Policy Meets Performance Practice: Interculturalism, the European Union and the 'Migratory and Refugee Crisis'." *Theatre Research International* 44.3 (2019): 230–47.

McIvor, Charlotte. "Staging the 'New Irish': Interculturalism and the Future of the Post-Celtic Tiger Irish Theatre." *Modern Drama* 54.3 (2011): 310–32.

Nakase, Justine. "'Recognise My Face': Phil Lynott, Scalar Interculturalism and the Nested Figure." In *Interculturalism and Performance Now: New Directions*, edited by Charlotte McIvor and Jason King, 257–80. London: Palgrave Macmillan, 2019.

Salis, Loredana. *Stage Migrants: Representations of the Migrant Other in Modern Irish Drama*. Newcastle upon Tyne: Cambridge Scholars Publishing, 2010.

SPINNING (2014) BY DEIRDRE KINAHAN

Award-winning playwright Deirdre Kinahan's *Spinning* had its debut in the Smock Alley Theatre as part of the Dublin Theatre Festival in 2014. It was produced by Fishamble: The New Play Company directed by Jim Culleton and harvested appreciative reviews, especially for its contemporary relevance. *The Irish Times* noting "the unspeakable cases of parental homicide that have shocked the country are one of the play's unspoken themes."[1] Since then *Spinning* has made its way to the United States and other countries where its productions have been successful with audiences and critics alike. This popularity is earned by the exploration of themes appealing to general interest: how to live on with unfading memories of a guilty act committed in the past and how to forgive the person who has caused one irretrievable loss even though inadvertently? The context to these weighty questions is the precarious situation of partnerships, divorce, and parent–child relations in Ireland on the cusp of the final phase of the economic boom and its sudden collapse in 2008.

Spinning opens on the male protagonist, Conor, staring at the water near the pier of a seaside village. Sarah, the other protagonist, works in the café close by and the action unfolds through their meeting and talking with each other. Both are in their forties; their dialogue centres on the traumatic incident that happened some years previously when Conor drove his car into the sea with his own six-year-old and Susan's sixteen-year-old daughter, Annie, sitting in it. The outcome was tragic: Annie drowned but Conor and his daughter, Kate, survived thanks to the quick rescue work of the police. In the present Conor, just after his term in prison for causing Annie's death and apparently tortured by remorse and self-hate, harbours thoughts of suicide at the site of the tragedy. Recognising him, the devastated Susan is full of rage against the killer of her child while eager to find answers to her burning questions about the circumstances in which Annie got into Conor's car before its fatal plunge into the sea.

The protagonists' heated exchange in the present is frequently interrupted by scenes of private conversations Conor and Susan recall alternately, which took place in the years leading up to the tragedy. These flashbacks are acted out with great vividness; as Kinahan says in her "Author's Note" to the play, "the past insists on being played."[2] With three acting areas on stage representing three distinct periods of time, present and past run side by side, disclosing both protagonists' relations with Annie and, in the case of Conor, the decline of his marriage to Jen which ended in divorce and left him a weekend father. Presented non-chronologically, the recollected scenes are literally spinning through the protagonists' consciousness and become revelatory for them.

Conor's memories date back to a scene in which he met Jen, his former girlfriend, after arriving home from a long stay abroad. Their dialogue is replete with passion, yet shows some then insignificant-looking differences. In the later scenes these small signs and the unease they cause multiply as evidence that bodily desire in itself cannot be a stable basis for marital happiness. At the height of the Celtic Tiger boom which provides the background for Conor and Jen's marriage, the "experience of accelerated modernization had produced a variety of cultural and social collisions between different and often incompatible forms of life, collisions between 'traditional' and 'modern'."[3] The couple's views on family life and gender roles in *Spinning* also appear to be widely apart. Conor, Patrick Lonergan contends, "is attempting to fill a role of husband/father that no longer corresponds to the realities of his society and relationships."[4]

While Conor believes in traditional norms and the unquestionable familial dominance of the husband, Jen represents a woman who has independent goals in life, exemplified by resuming work after the birth of their daughter. A scene proves crucial in making plain the failure of their marriage; Jen's refusal to have sex with Conor elicited a characteristically patriarchal reaction from him:

Conor. I LOVE you.
> And I WANT you all the time. But I don't think I like this ... change.
> ...

Jen. *She goes to leave. He grabs her arm quite violently. She stops, shocked.*
> Let go. ... You can't touch me this way.

> (42)

Recalling the scene, Conor is confronted with his conventionally male-centred attitude to marriage as probably the main reason for Jen's decision to divorce him.

In the year *Spinning* premiered, David Quinn revealed the disadvantages that many Irishmen suffer in divorce:

> New research based on over 1,000 judicial separation and divorce cases that appeared before the Circuit Courts over the last four years had confirmed that women almost always get custody of the children, they get to live in the family home, and the father has to pay maintenance which can sometimes push him below the poverty line.[5]

Conor's situation bears a strong resemblance to the grievances Quinn sums up: Jen is granted custody of Kate, and Conor has to move out of the home he worked so hard for. Adding to his humiliation is the impact of the post-boom financial crisis on the business he runs with his brothers. As he doted on Kate, Conor could not tolerate the arrangement of seeing her only on weekends and brought the little girl to the seaside village where the play is set, instead of driving her back to Jen when "his time" was over. Accidentally, here he met Susan's daughter, Annie, who became attracted to him, a man about the age of her never-known father and lonely like herself. The scenes Conor remembers about his talks with Annie clearly show that he was not sexually interested in the girl. A teenager abandoned by her boyfriend, Annie felt herself useful and needed by Conor and acted as babysitter for Kate.

After a while the police started to watch then encircle the house rented by Conor, who thought that committing suicide with his daughter by driving into sea was the only way to keep Kate and escape the misery of his dispossession. In preparations for the fatal journey Annie helped him and insisted on getting into the car. Through his conjured-up memories Conor realises that while cherishing his irrational plan he completely forgot about Annie's safety.

Susan raised Annie without a father, who had disappeared before she discovered her pregnancy. She recalls scenes of a special love between her and Annie but also one in which she frustrated the girl by rejecting the idea of searching for her father:

Annie. I'm sure we could find him!

   ...

Susan. For God's sake, Annie. He's probably married now with two
   kids ... he won't want to know about us.

              (35–6)

Reliving this conversation allows Susan to understand that her discouraging behaviour could be the explanation for the fact that Annie never told her about meeting Conor. Susan is also tormented by the memory of a rushed and irrelevant conversation at home on the morning of the tragedy, which was the last time she spoke to her daughter. Sensing her distress, Conor tells about his final memories of Annie in a way to give some comfort to the bereft mother:

Conor. Mam ... she called Mam ... Mammy.

   ...

You were with her as we hit the water.

   ...

Susan *sees* **Annie** *now. She reaches out her hand to her. She whispers.*
Susan. *Annie.*
Annie *smiles at* **Susan**.
   Thank you.
   Thank you Conor Bourke.

              (86)

Helping Susan with a white lie to gain peace Conor manages to shed his self-absorbed inertia while Susan is able to advise him that by committing suicide on the spot of the tragedy he would only hurt Jen and Kate again. Recognising each other's needs has proven essential for the two protagonists' transformation: now Susan can think of moving on, while Conor leaves the place, giving up thoughts of suicide. Hanging in the air there remains though the question of how Kate will fare without a father since Conor's ex-wife refuses to look beyond the surface of his deed and does not allow him to see the little girl any more who, thus, might become another Annie, unsure of herself and choosing the wrong company.

The dramaturgy is unique in that the protagonists are audience for each other's enacted memories, which inspires a feeling of their togetherness added to self-scrutiny. In this innovative self-reflexivity *Spinning* is analogous to theatre itself where playing and viewing interact, potentially helping all participants achieve transformation and renewal.

Mária Kurdi

Notes

1 Mick Heaney, "Review – Spinning," *The Irish Times*, 4 October 2014. www.irishtimes.com/culture/stage/review-spinning-1.1952533. Accessed 10 September 2021.

2 Deirdre Kinahan, *Spinning* (Dublin: Fishamble, 2014), 2. Subsequent references are entered in parentheses.

3 Carmen Kuhling and Kiaran Keohane, *Cosmopolitan Ireland: Globalisation and Quality of Life* (London: Pluto Press, 2007), 12.

4 Patrick Lonergan, *Irish Drama and Theatre since 1950* (London: Methuen, 2019), 200.

5 David Quinn, "Terrible Bias that Men Suffer in Divorces Badly Needs Rectifying," *Independent.ie*, 21 March 2014.

Further Reading

Fitzpatrick, Lisa and Mária Kurdi, eds. *"I Love Craft. I Love the Word": The Theatre of Deirdre Kinahan*. New York: Peter Lang, 2022.

Kurdi, Mária. "A Talk with Irish Playwright Deirdre Kinahan." *FOCUS: Papers in English Literary and Cultural Studies* XI (2018): 125–36.

INDEX

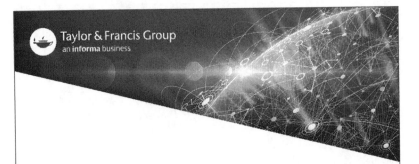